Leadership and
Management in the
Early Years

Leadership and Management in the Early Years

From Principles to Practice

Caroline A. Jones and Linda Pound

Open University Press

Open University Press
McGraw-Hill Education
McGraw-Hill House
Shoppenhangers Road
Maidenhead
Berkshire
England
SL6 2QL

email: enquiries@openup.co.uk
world wide web: www.openup.co.uk

and Two Penn Plaza, New York, NY 10121–2289, USA

First published 2008
Copyright © Caroline Jones & Linda Pound 2008

A catalogue record of this book is available from the British Library

ISBN–13: 9780335222469 (pb)   9780335222452 (hb)
ISBN–10: 0335222463 (pb)   0335222455 (hb)

Library of Congress Cataloguing-in-Publication Data
CIP data applied for

Typeset by YHT Ltd, London
Printed in the UK by Bell and Bain Ltd, Glasgow

The *McGraw·Hill* Companies

Contents

Acknowledgements

We would both like to thank Fiona Richman of Open University Press, the commissioning editor of this book, for her patience, advice and support. Caroline would like to express appreciation to all those colleagues who have contributed ideas, particularly Beth Casey for reading and commenting on the earlier drafts. Caroline is indebted to all the staff at Pathways Childcare Centres for providing case studies. Additional thanks to all the parents, practitioners and children whose experiences have been used in this book. Most importantly, she thanks her baby grandson Corley, whose smile inspired her to start and to persevere in the writing of this book.

Linda wishes to thank all those practitioners whose commitment and enthusiasm has taught her so much about the privilege and responsibility of working with young children. She owes Chris more than she can say for his unstinting support but the biggest acknowledgement goes to all the young children in her life (especially Isabel, Florence, Charlie, Zac, Lucy and Renée) who have helped her to maintain the vision.

1 Introduction: leadership, principles and practice

> Leadership must be visionary. Leaders must hold some idea of the future, the distant horizon and full game plan and they need the capacity to maintain personal and team momentum on the journey towards securing the desired goal. They must also show rich human qualities such as an allegiance to a mission, curiosity, daring, a sense of adventure and strong interpersonal skills, including fair and sensitive management of those who work with them. They must be able to motivate themselves and others, demonstrate a commitment to what they espouse, release the talents and energies of others, have strength of character, yet remain flexible in attitude and be willing to learn new techniques and new skills.
>
> (McCall and Lawlor 2000: 87)

There is no doubt that working in early years settings is becoming increasingly complex and demanding in terms of the knowledge, skills and attitudes required by practitioners and leaders. As a consequence, leaders and managers play a significant role in enabling other practitioners to develop the necessary capabilities in a climate of significant change and developments. Early childhood leaders are in the unenviable position of needing to develop high levels of expertise in order to empower and influence others to enhance the quality of provision, while at the same time meeting a number of legal requirements. This book stems from a personal commitment to respond to the growing pressures on early childhood practitioners as well as a growing national and international interest in early childhood leadership. This chapter introduces some of the key issues in practice and summarizes the underlying principles which underpin the rest of the book. It concludes with an overview of the chapters that follow.

The drive for graduate leaders and the introduction of Early Years Professional Status (EYPS) signifies an increasing emphasis on leadership as a factor in influencing quality in early years settings. However, there has been very little formal training or support for existing, aspiring, new or inexperienced early childhood leaders. There are many questions which remain unresolved both in theory, policy and practice. What does leadership involve and who can be a leader? Is there a difference between leadership and management? What makes leadership and management effective? It is important to acknowledge that there are no simple answers, no universal remedies. As the quote at the beginning of this chapter shows, leadership, whether individual or collective, is more than the application of a set of professional skills. Rather we view leadership and management as a people-orientated, problem-solving, culturally influenced process of reflection and concerted efforts by individual practitioners working together with parents and others to improve outcomes for children.

In practice, leadership and management in early years provision is a varied and fragmented, complex and often hectic process enacted in a context of rapid and unprecedented change. Recent years have seen significant developments in early years in terms of the curriculum and national standards for childcare, notably the *Curriculum Guidance for the Foundation Stage* (QCA/DfES 2000), the *Birth to Three Matters* (DfES 2002a) framework and the *National Standards for Under Eights Daycare and Childminding* (DfES 2001a). The Early Years Foundation Stage (EYFS) (DfES 2007) *Statutory Framework* and guidance to be implemented from September 2008 replaces these three documents while drawing together their principles, pedagogy, standards and approach. Keeping up to date with and managing changes heralded by legislation – for example, the Children Act 2004 and the Childcare Act 2006 – is a key issue for leaders and managers in all early years provision.

Furthermore, a central issue in this book is one of accountability to children and families, to communities, to colleagues and to ourselves. At the front-line level, self-evaluation has been placed at the heart of best practice. Monitoring and evaluation of the quality of leadership and management is also high on the national agenda. We believe that this is because the quality of leadership and management is paramount in determining the extent to which a setting meets young children's individual needs. Although good 'quality' provision is a slippery concept, the Office for Standards in Education (Ofsted) clearly links overall judgements on practice with the effectiveness (or otherwise) of leadership and management. The following extracts from Ofsted inspection reports illustrate the point.

> Children's care was not sufficiently supported during the inspection due to a failure to maintain appropriate adult child ratios within the baby and toddler room. Neither the nursery owner or manager was present during the course of the inspection and there were inadequate contingency arrangements in place to effectively cover staff absences and ensure that sufficient staff were available at all times.

This resulted in individual children's needs not being met ... children's health is being placed at risk by a failure to ensure that rooms within the nursery are maintained at appropriate temperatures.

(Ofsted 2006)

By contrast the next extract shows that where leadership and management were judged to be 'outstanding', children were making good progress in learning, and their individual needs were being met.

The leadership and management is outstanding. All managers and staff are passionate about their work, continually striving to make improvements. A yearly action plan, linked to the self-assessment record monitors the progress made in terms of the service provided and the delivery of the Foundation Stage curriculum. Recruitment, vetting and induction procedures are thorough and ensure that staff are of high quality and are well qualified. Ongoing training and appraisals for staff support children's development and learning. Management and staff are enthusiastic, dedicated and work very well together as a strong and supportive staff team. They are totally committed to providing a high level of care and education for the children and are constantly looking at and implementing ways to move the setting forward. The managers are hands-on, working with the children at different times throughout the day and acting as positive role models for both children and staff. They are involved in the planning for the Foundation Stage and work closely with staff in the delivery of the curriculum and also to evaluate activities. This ensures that all areas of learning are successfully delivered which ensures that children make very good progress in all areas of learning. Overall the setting meets the needs of the range of children for whom it provides.

(Ofsted 2007)

In the setting described above the managers demonstrate the importance of personal qualities such as passion, dedication and enthusiasm. They draw attention to the impact of staff appraisal and development, monitoring, self-evaluating and action planning. By working closely with and acting as role models for staff they have been able to developing a strong, motivated and committed team. In essence they have created a culture of reflection and commitment to improve. By culture we mean the climate or ethos of a setting, which stems from the central values, attitudes and beliefs, explicit and implicit, which it holds and attempts to reflect on a day-to-day basis. It is this culture or way things are done which provides the basis of the organization and decision-making, the principles of the setting which steer it in one direction or another.

Similarly, this book is based on a number of key principles:

- some aspects of leadership are particular to work with young children and their families but we can learn from other areas;
- everyone involved in early years care and education needs to develop their professional knowledge and skills and adopt a leadership and management approach;
- professional knowledge, skills and attitudes can be learnt and need to be developed throughout our working lives;
- reflection helps practitioners, including leaders, to become better practitioners and leaders;
- working knowledge of leadership styles and characteristics can support reflection on our roles;
- leadership is only effective if it develops the leadership of others by supporting a team or group in meeting their declared aims or vision;
- leadership is about influencing others to improve and enhance children's care, learning and development;
- leadership is ultimately distributed, shared and dispersed in early childhood settings.

In the chapters that follow we aim to:

- provoke reflection and discussion of approaches to leadership and management in early years settings;
- challenge some of the ideas associated with leadership in early years settings by providing a range of theoretical and practical perspectives on key issues;
- reduce isolation and build the confidence of early years practitioners in themselves as part of a community of leaders and managers;
- provide guidance on the roles, responsibilities and tasks facing leaders in a climate of ever-increasing pressure.

The rest of this book explores early years leadership and management, in principle and in practice. We recognize, of course, that early years provision is located in a diversity of contexts. It would be impossible to represent the many different types of setting in every chapter; instead we draw on a range of generic themes, using case studies from which we hope you will make connections with your own practice.

Chapter 2 provides the backdrop for the chapters that follow. It looks at why the concept of leadership in early years settings has become increasingly important and suggests that it has unique characteristics as compared to other types of educational leadership. It defines how we, the authors, interpret the concepts of leadership and management and why consideration of these concepts is essential in striving to develop good quality early years provision in a variety of contexts. It introduces the notion of 'inclusive leadership' or distributed leadership which starts from the premise that in early years settings leadership and management are the concern of all practitioners and not the exclusive remit of the person 'in charge'. However, this does not imply that formal leadership structures are redundant. Instead there is an important relationship between the vertical and lateral structures in early years settings. Chapter 2 highlights key leadership styles and identifies some of the characteristics of effective leaders. It outlines the key challenges facing early childhood leaders which form the thread of the chapters that follow.

It would be naïve to assume that all practitioners are automatically dedicated, able and committed to working smoothly together on a day-to-day basis. Chapter 3 concentrates on one of the most important aspects of leadership in the context of early years settings: the role of the leader in the development of people, and the process of building and leading a team. It emphasizes the importance of communicating with and motivating staff to promote a sense of being valued. The chapter looks at the nature of teams in early years settings, the influence of the designated leader on teamwork, and the concomitant impact of teamwork on the quality of the provision. We discuss the importance of promoting shared goals while simultaneously meeting the needs of individual practitioners through continued professional development (CPD). We consider the management of change and conflict, and suggest that a collegial culture can be developed in early years settings which in turn should be regarded as nurturing and learning communities.

Chapter 4 builds on the themes raised in the previous chapters. It considers the complex and changing tasks, roles and responsibilities which leaders and other early years practitioners assume and the relationship between them. It discusses the idea of a 'leaderful' community (Raelin 2003). The chapter concludes by highlighting the responsibilities which a team leader has both *to* and *for* the team in terms of self-development and reflection.

Chapter 5 highlights the role of the leader in working with the team to develop and implement essential, desirable, written and unwritten policies. The chapter sets out the legal requirements relating to welfare which are given force by the regulations under Section 39 (1) of the Childcare Act 2006. We examine the purposes of developing policies and analyse a framework for developing written policies. The chapter uses extracts from policies to emphasize the links between philosophy, principles, policy, procedures and practice.

In Chapters 6 and 7 the focus shifts to the role of leaders and managers in supporting staff in planning, providing and evaluating the curriculum as a prerequisite to effective support for children's care, learning and development. Chapter 6 explores views of the curriculum from birth to 5. It highlights the importance of evaluation and the assessment of children's learning and development in an inclusive environment. Chapter 7 focuses on the leadership role in meeting the learning and development requirements incorporated in the statutory framework for the EYFS. It examines a number of approaches to planning, assessment and evaluation.

The Children Act 2004 and other initiatives including the Common Assessment Framework (CAF) mean that many early years practitioners will in the future find themselves working within multi-agency contexts requiring high-level skills and knowledge. Chapter 8 illustrates the importance of partnership with 'outside' agencies in relation to all children, not only those described as having special educational needs (SEN). It evaluates the impact of information sharing and inter-agency working on the role of individual practitioners.

A text on leadership and management would not be complete without the inclusion of a chapter concerning working with parents and listening to children. Chapter 9 unpicks the role of the leader in promoting partnership with parents and children. It considers the barriers to effective relationships, linking the impact of positive relationships to bridging the gap between home and the early years setting.

Chapter 10 centres on leadership and self-evaluation as tools for promoting quality and in preparing for your Ofsted inspection. It looks in detail at the purposes, conduct and outcomes of inspections. It offers suggestions as to how leaders and managers can best prepare themselves and their staff by maintaining quality on a day-to-day basis. The chapter concludes that rather than being seen as a threat, inspections should be seen as a valuable tool in the process of evaluating practice.

The concluding chapter looks at remaining tensions and future possibilities of leadership in this sector. It provides a summary of the key points presented in the book and concludes that effective leadership and management are of central importance to improved outcomes and services for young children and their families. In summary, this book is based on the authors' central belief that every early years practitioner is a leader and can contribute towards improved outcomes for children. We hope that reading this book will help you come to see yourself as a leader and to develop the leadership of others you work with in this sector.

2 Leadership, management and reflective practice

> Leadership emanates out of vision that is based in philosophy, values and beliefs, which in turn guides policy, day-to-day operation and innovation. It is manifested through strategic planning that grows out of reflection. Management is distinguished by active involvement in pedagogy, positive relationships, effective communication and high expectations for increasing professionalism.
>
> (Solly 2003 cited in Rodd 2006: 21)

Introduction

Although the concepts of leadership and management have taken centre stage in the early years sector there is little agreement about what the terms mean. This chapter explores a number of views on leadership and management. It concludes that in practice they are inextricably linked, albeit that each may have different emphases. Hence, the terms 'leadership' and 'management' are used together or interchangeably throughout this book. We elaborate on the idea of collective, distributed or 'inclusive leadership', moving beyond the idea of leadership as being the exclusive preserve of one named or designated person. We present leadership and management as a reflective process, involving practitioners, parents, children, other agencies and communities. In the latter part of the chapter, we look at links between personal qualities, effective leadership strategies and leadership styles, highlighting some of the challenges facing leaders and managers.

Defining leadership and management

The notion of leadership has recently been at the forefront of the debate on quality in early years settings. This may be partly due to the fact that in school contexts effective leadership has been shown to result in improved outcomes for children. Literature on leadership in the context of early years settings is limited but work on primary educational leadership can, to some extent, help to formulate ideas and develop understandings of leadership in early childhood. Coles and Southworth (2005), for example, suggest that good leadership is crucial to a school's success, determining whether a school struggles with divisions between pupils and staff or whether it is a place where everyone works collaboratively towards shared goals and high academic achievement. Bush and Coleman (2000) note that schools and colleges are more likely to be effective if they are well managed. They point out that research on school effectiveness in a number of countries shows a correlation between good management and the quality of schools, including the educational outcomes of the students. Logically, if we can identify and foster the qualities of effective leadership in early years settings this will impact on outcomes for children. However, this is difficult without any shared understanding of what is meant by the term 'leadership' and how it relates to 'management' in an early years context.

The traditional tendency has been to view management as something more tangible and visible than leadership, possibly of secondary importance and more associated with the day-to-day running of a setting or the organizing of processes and structures. Over 20 years ago, Hersey (cited in Isles-Buck and Newstead 2003: 2) attempted to draw a distinction between the two terms stating that management is 'working with and through others to accomplish organisational goals' whereas leadership is 'any attempt to influence the behaviour of another individual of group'. Schön (cited in Bush and Coleman 2000:19) supports the view that leadership and management are different, suggesting that leadership is more symbolic in nature:

> Leadership and management are not synonymous terms. One can be a leader without being a manager. One can, for example, fulfil many of the symbolic, inspirational, educational and normative functions of a leader and thus represent what an organization stands for without carrying any of the formal burdens of management. Conversely, one can manage without leading. An individual can monitor and control organizational activities, make decisions, and allocate resources without fulfilling the symbolic, normative, inspirational, or educational functions of leadership.
>
> (Schön cited in Bush and Coleman 2000: 19)

The DfES (2002b: 3), in a booklet entitled *Developing Management Skills*, echoes this view, identifying management as about the tasks of the present including planning, organizing, co-ordinating and controlling, and leadership as concerned with vision and influencing the future:

Leaders, therefore, tend to have a longer-range perspective, a vision of the future, a picture of what their organisation will look like in, say, three or five years time. A vision may sound rather grand, but formulating your vision of the future is a vitally important first step in the planning process ... So a strong vision, allied to an optimistic, can-do attitude on the part of the leader can inspire other people onto greater things.

(DfES 2002b: 3)

If you think about your own context you may find that leadership and management are interwoven and take place simultaneously. We would agree with Isles-Buck and Newstead (2003) who view leadership as *part* of management. They suggest there is a 'doing' part of management including filling in forms, managing finance and managing resources, and a 'more vital' part of management, that of leadership for which there is little support. In most early years settings these aspects are likely to operate together. While there may be different emphases when using the term 'leadership' as opposed to 'management' and certain characteristics have been identified in those with a tendency to assume a leadership role, we argue that constantly maintaining that leadership is 'x' and management is 'y' is unhelpful and perpetuates confusion, especially in the early years sector. It disguises the reality of practice and encourages the view that leadership may be the exclusive domain of one person but not another. The case study below illustrates how leadership and management may be indistinguishable in practice.

CASE STUDY

Teddies is a small chain of five day nurseries. The limited company has two directors who assume both leadership and management responsibilities but these are at a strategic rather than a day-to-day level. Although they retain some management responsibilities, such as managing financial affairs, at the same time the emphasis is on 'leadership' as they strive for constant improvement, monitor and evaluate practice, conduct staff appraisals and support the settings by regular visits and meetings with the individual nursery managers. They focus on quality and implementing the company philosophy in practice. The individual setting managers, on the other hand, are seen more as managers than leaders. They are responsible for the day-to-day management of the provision at a practical level. They plan and implement the curriculum, manage registers, oversee invoices and order resources. However, at the same time they assume a leadership role in that they lead staff meetings, work with other professionals, evaluate practice, build, lead and motivate their team.

Reflection point

Think about your own setting. How are leadership and management linked in practice? How are members of staff involved in leadership and management? Where is the emphasis in your own role?

We take the view that leadership is concerned with providing a culture in which each individual child's learning and development will flourish and at the same time each individual adult working in the setting will also have opportunities to learn and develop through a process of reflecting on their own practice.

Inclusive leadership and management

Although a setting may well have a designated 'manager' or 'officer in charge', 'registered person' or 'boss', leadership in early years settings should not only involve a 'leader' and 'followers'. Rather, the identified person in charge should be viewed as a 'leader of leaders', who allows others to develop leadership qualities and skills, a point discussed further in the next chapter. This creates a broader concept of leadership in early years settings as a collective responsibility, inclusive of the skills and personal attributes of all practitioners. In a culture of 'inclusive leadership', each individual is encouraged to see themselves as a potential leader and manager. The extent to which they are given the opportunity to develop and apply these skills may vary depending on their role within the setting. The move away from the idea that leadership is the exclusive preserve of one person to a process of sharing professional knowledge, skills and personalities, combining and reflecting, striving for continuous improvement, suggests that the actions of every member in the early years team impact on the quality of the provision.

As a childminder or a nanny, you might be taking a lead in a discussion with a parent about his or her child's sleeping patterns. In a group setting, someone else might be chairing a staff meeting but another practitioner may display leadership qualities by sharing suggestions about changing an aspect of practice. Inclusive or distributed leadership leads to teams that have been described as 'leaderful' (Raelin 2003). Whalley (2005) describes effective contexts for children as 'leaderful' – indicating that there is room for everyone to take on leadership roles. This can be illustrated if, as practitioners, you think about yourself as a leader.

Reflection point

By looking at the attributes of leaders and identifying them within yourself you can see that the idea of everyone taking on a leadership role is achievable. What knowledge, skills and personal qualities do you possess? What attitudes do you show which can enable you to take on a leadership role?

A closer look at the personal characteristics, professional knowledge and skills associated with effective leaders develops this idea further.

Characteristics of early childhood leaders

Not many practitioners possess all the personal qualities, characteristics and skills shown in Table 2.1, as well as having the required professional knowledge. However, most early years practitioners possess some leadership and management skills.

Reflection point

Use Table 2.1 as a starting point to assess yourself as a leader. Write a pen portrait of yourself as leader from another person's perspective or simply identify your own leadership skills and characteristics.

Jane, who works in a preschool, analysed herself as a potential manager noting that:

> I think I would make a good manager because I am very patient and a good listener. However, I am not very good a time management and also I tend to bury my head in the sand if a conflict or difficult issues occurs. I can see other people's points of view and have a calm personality. I am very keen to learn and enjoy going on courses. One challenge for me, though, would be that I am afraid of not being liked and worry about what people think of me. Making decisions is hard as I like to please everyone and it's not always possible. I think I am a good communicator and also I can lead by example. I am developing the ability to reflect on and improve my practice.

This ability to reflect, evaluate and respond is of paramount importance in leadership and management. If leaders are to be learners they need to engage in reflective practice.

Table 2.1 Summary of characteristics, skills and attitudes of leaders

Rodd (2006)	Edgington (2004)	Goleman, Boyatzis and McKee (2002)	DfES (2002b)	McCall and Lawlor (2000)
Kind, warm and friendly	Loyalty to the team	Achiever, seeks performance improvement	Leader as learner	Being people conscious
Visionary	Provide vision and communicate it	Show empathy and listen	Communicator and listener	Effective communicator
Goal-orientated	Set goals and objectives	Influencer and inspirer	Motivator	Decision-maker
Mentor, guide, empowering	Facilitate and encourage the development of individuals	Catalyst of change	Inspirer	
Nurturing, sympathetic	Consistent and sense of fairness		Claim and live strong values	Value-rooted
Self-aware	Ability to earn respect by example	Accurate self-assessment	Trust and respect people	Honest appraiser of self
Professional, professionally confident		Self-confidence	Role model Risk-taker	Being ethical
Effective communicator	Develop a team culture	Teamwork and collaboration, optimist		Team builder and sustainer, optimist
Assertive and proactive	Monitor and communicate achievements	Developing others	Coach and developer of others	Being conscious of circumstances

Reflective practice and leadership

Reflective practice is widely identified as supporting learning and development. In the training and CPD of health, education and social care practitioners, reflection is commonly identified as a means of improving the way in which things are done, dealing with issues and learning from experience. The National Professional Qualification for Integrated Centre Leadership (NPQICL) – a qualification developed for the leaders of integrated centres – requires participants to maintain a reflective journal throughout the course. The rationale behind this requirement is that writing ideas, thoughts or feelings down on paper enables you to look at them and learn from them. Over time, strategies for dealing with issues or solutions for solving problems emerge from the reflective process. For busy practitioners, and particularly for busy leaders, there is a danger that without taking time to reflect, the same problems go on repeating themselves. All too often managers can hear themselves complaining that events keep recurring or that particular people always do something or other that is unhelpful or annoying. Without taking what is often a small amount of time to find ways of changing these habits, large amounts of energy and time can be wasted.

Thinking about or reflecting on practice has been described as having three levels (Schön cited in Furlong 2000: 22). First, practitioners may act on the level of 'knowing-in-action'. If you are a driver, for example, you will be familiar with situations where your driving is entirely unconscious. In work with children this often occurs in situations where there is a strong routine, perhaps when reading a story or serving meals: you can do these things almost automatically. At this level thought is implicit and practitioners do not find it easy to articulate their ideas because it is such a familiar pattern of behaviour. Second, practitioners may move to a level of 'reflection-in-action', usually when something goes wrong. As a driver, this happens when something untoward or unusual occurs and you immediately switch into a conscious mode of thought. A further example of this might be a situation where you are working with a group and some children become restless. We can often 'think on our feet', changing what we are doing, drawing more consciously on a range of familiar (and sometimes untried) strategies. The third level is 'reflection-on-action'. This tends to 'take place after the event, when we try to articulate, to ourselves or others, some of the processes that were going on in our actions' (Furlong 2000: 22). Here, you may switch into reflecting-on-action or thinking about whether you could have behaved or responded differently. As a driver, you may try to replay something that was a near-miss or where you became anxious about the actions of other drivers. As a practitioner you may replay an incident with a parent where things went wrong or were not resolved satisfactorily.

What is vital to the process of reflection is that you find ways to learn from it. Educators or practitioners can learn from experience when they:

- make connections between small details and the bigger picture;
- take a new or different perspective, seeing things in a new light;
- make an effort to see the world as others see it in order to understand their point of view;
- recognise the impact of feelings and emotions on what others say, think and do;
- postpone judgement and go on asking questions.

Eide and Winger (2005: 83) underline this view when they suggest that researchers (or those learning from their investigations) need to bring to their work 'insight ... knowledge about children and ... the ability to be a humble interpreter reflecting upon the children's statements'. They also write of the importance of 'being a spokesperson for the children', 'and constantly wishing to improve'.

The work of Vivian Gussin Paley offers many positive examples of reflective practice. The extract below from Paley (1990: 15–6) highlights the ways in which you may be unaware of your own prejudices or biases; how looking and listening carefully and sharing perceptions with colleagues can help you to clarify your thinking; and the importance of being aware of the extent to which you may see things differently from others.

A graduate student named Fritz helped me to begin to listen to the children. He wondered about the accuracy of a teacher's perceptions and, among other things, he proved to me that a boy named Charles was not a villain disguised as a five-year-old.

'Charles, you're grabbing all the sand!' I cry, rushing to defend his classmate.

'He don't mind. I need it.'

'But that pile is in front of Tommy. You didn't ask him.'

'He knows that's where the castle hasta be.'

Charles is the biggest troublemaker, I complained, but Fritz's charts revealed otherwise. Charles, in fact, was a leader in non-aggressive play 80 per cent of the time. Apparently, I was the troublemaker: 75 per cent of my comments to Charles were negative.

None of this surprised Fritz, who measured and charted each day the amount of time I believed Charles was misbehaving and the reality of the case. Fritz was accustomed to such large variances, but I was distraught. Pitying me, Fritz offered charts with which to improve my behaviour, the goal being an 85 per cent positive response. Obediently, I kept an eye on the clock, said good things to Charles, and checked off the daily columns.

The chart-keeping lasted only a week but was not without value. As with nearly all the research I encounter, it made me observe the scene more closely. Listening to Charles in order to compliment him, I heard the reasons for his classmates' esteem. He provided them with an unending supply of characters and plots.

'Hey, Tom, y'wanna play castle? This is a drawbridge.'

'I got the key for it.'

'You can't. There wasn't no keys invented yet. This is the only place keys can go. Okay, put it there. It's a fighting space-ship. It can kill someone by its power. Hurry up, pull up the drawbridge. The invisible bees is here. Quick, get your magic key. Pretend this is magic. Touch it and we turn into dragons!'

It is important to remember that observation is not entirely neutral. The observer's perception of a situation can influence the observations, since they may unwittingly distort what they see or hear in line with their own pre-judgements or prejudices. Professional training and experience can also lead practitioners to see and interpret in particular ways. Sources of bias may arise from culture, from language differences, and may even be based on characteristics such as physical appearance or gender.

Johns (2004: 18) offers a number of models to support more structured reflection. He identifies several 'reflective cues', which include focusing on a description of an experience that seems significant in some way and reflecting on the following questions:

- What particular issues seem significant to pay attention to?
- How were others feeling and what made them feel that way?
- How was I feeling and what made me feel that way?
- What was I trying to achieve and did I respond effectively?
- What knowledge did or might have informed me?
- How does this situation connect with previous experiences?
- How might I respond more effectively given this situation again?
- What would be the consequences of alternative actions for others and myself?

You may find it helpful to try this approach to problem-solving in your own context. It can also be related to an analytical tool known as 'critical incident analysis'. This also involves personal reflection on a specific incident or problem that has arisen. The focus is on analysis rather than seeking solutions, trying to understand rather than leap to conclusions. This is one of a number of identified leadership styles or approaches.

Leadership styles

Rodd (1998: 16 citing Neugebauer 1985) identifies four key styles of leadership, relating them specifically to early childhood care and education:

1 *Task master*, who 'places heavy emphasis on results and little emphasis on relationships or morale'.
2 *Comrade*, who 'places heavy emphasis on relationships and morale but little emphasis on the task or results'.
3 *Motivator*, who 'places strong emphasis on both the task and relationships'.
4 *Unleader*, who 'places little emphasis on either results or relationships'.

Reflection point
Can you place yourself or leaders you have worked with in any of these categories? What are the advantages and disadvantages of each style? What impact do you think each of the above styles might have on team performance?

Goleman *et al.* (2002: 55) identify six leadership styles:

1 *Visionary*, which 'moves people toward shared dreams'.
2 *Coaching*, which 'connects what a person wants with the organization's goals'.
3 *Affiliative*, which 'creates harmony by connecting people to each other'.
4 *Democratic*, which 'values people's input and gets commitment through participation'.
5 *Pace-setting*, which 'meets challenging and exciting goals'.
6 *Commanding*, which 'soothes fears by giving clear directions in an emergency'.

Again, you might try to categorize yourself or someone you know into one of these styles. One of the problems with leadership theories of this sort is that an individual's leadership style may not or need not be fixed. Indeed it may be helpful if the leadership style can be changed to suit circumstances. Rodd (1998), for example, suggests that a young or inexperienced team may benefit from a directive style of leadership, while teams where there is a high degree of conflict might be improved by a more democratic style of leadership. Goleman *et al.* (2002: 55) contend that visionary leaders are needed when 'changes require a new vision or when a clear direction is needed'. Similarly, while we may not always think of commanding leadership (or being very direct in telling people what to do) as an empowering style, it may help in situations where managing change is proving difficult. It is, however, generally believed that effective organizations adopt empowering leadership styles at every tier or level of responsibility.

Approaching leadership in this way also overlooks the point made earlier, that distributed, shared or inclusive approaches to leadership and management are becoming increasingly important. Many organizations (including schools, children's centres and many other settings involved in the care and education of young children) are too complex to be in the hands of a single leader and many people, often in small and apparently insignificant ways, provide leadership of different kinds and perhaps different styles. In many walks of life, people have to operate as leaders. As discussed earlier, leadership and management are not solely the concern of the person at the top. In other words, leaders exercise leadership through their relations with other people. As the case study below shows, leadership is a relational and contextual process.

CASE STUDY

Sue's job title is nursery manager. She oversees the day-to-day running of a private nursery with her team who all have designated responsibilities. Each member of the team is a keyworker for a group of children. Planning takes place at nursery team meetings. Each practitioner helps to plan for an area of learning. Other duties – for example, greeting children and parents at the door – are allocated on a rota basis so everyone is participating. Staff are encouraged to contribute to and lead staff meetings and make suggestions for the agenda. There is an employee leaflet, a staff handbook and clear lines of communication.

Reflection point
Think about ways in which leadership is a relational and contextual process in your setting. What do you think makes an effective leader?

Effective leadership strategies

As you think about leadership, and in the light of experience, you will be aware that the effectiveness of leaders varies and is highly dependent on the context in which leadership takes place. The effective manager of a cinema, for example, will be judged on the number of people who come to the cinema, how much they spend, etc. An effective leader in an early years setting will be judged differently. Effectiveness in this field is not about how much money is spent (although the books must balance) or about how many children come through the door (since staff ratios must be maintained). An effective leader will be one who provides good quality care and education, or who addresses the well-being of staff, children and parents. The point is that effectiveness can only be judged by what you set out to do.

The problem for early years practitioners is that there are many different visions, aims or expectations for early years care and education. So perhaps the most important thing for a leader to do is to gain agreement among staff as to what their collective aims are. These aims need then to be displayed prominently so that everyone is clear about what the setting is offering. You could, for example, hold a staff meeting and ask the staff, in pairs, to write down what they think the aims of the setting are. You could note the points on a flipchart and summarize them into a setting mission statement which can then be displayed. This overall statement can later be broken down into individual aims and objectives which form the basis of the setting's policies and practice.

Whalley (2005: 8) draws some interesting parallels between effective learning and teaching with children and the strategies that effective leaders employ in motivating or supporting the development of team members. As Table 2.2 shows she compares the strategies used by practitioners (or pedagogues) with those successfully employed by leaders.

Sometimes, by reflecting, either informally or by writing a reflective diary, you can see that you could change your behaviour immediately. If, for example, you realize that you sometimes are too anxious to rush in and show children what to do, you can make a decision to try hard to stand back and make your interventions more focused and effective. It might take a while to remember to do that but you can begin to change right away. On the other hand, if you want to support others in intervening more subtly or respectfully, this may be a lengthier process. For example, Helen, a support assistant, was observed approaching Dana, a 2-year-old, from behind and dressing her in a fairy costume. Lena, a senior practitioner in the team, was distressed by this and realized that Helen, and perhaps other members of the team, would need training, and opportunities to discuss why this and other examples are disrespectful to children, and time to see why changes in their behaviour were necessary.

Table 2.2 Comparison of strategies used by leaders and practitioners

Effective pedagogic strategies	Effective leadership strategies	Examples (extracts from practitioners' reflective journals)
Ability to intervene subtly, rather than interfering	Leaders intervene respectfully and in an enabling way so that staff are left feeling that they did it themselves	Although Jack was taking a long time to do up his anorak, K managed to let him take the time and by not hurrying him but encouraging him to keep trying. He did succeed and was pleased with his own achievement. I was pleased with K too – a week ago she would have rushed in to do it for him
Recognition of the importance of the child's context and prior experience	Leaders know themselves and their staff well, they understand that the tensions, pressures and richness of their own life experiences inevitably have an impact on their professional life and continue to do so	M's father was rushed into hospital yesterday. Because she had planned and organized a training day, she came into work today. She insisted on staying but will need to take tomorrow off to organize care for her mother
Supporting communication through facial expression and physical closeness	Leaders are physically present a lot of the time and encourage and affirm through developing relationships with individuals	I overheard a member of staff who had been attending my language group responding to a child who was asking in Punjabi for her mummy. She responded in English, but the fact that she understood something of what the child was trying to communicate helped the child immensely. I was able to praise her at lunchtime and this really boosted her confidence in her ability to communicate with children in the early stages of learning English

Table 2.2 (continued)

Effective pedagogic strategies	Effective leadership strategies	Examples (extracts from practitioners' reflective journals)
Enabling the child to make choices and decisions, with appropriate support	Leaders want all staff to feel that they have the power to make decisions and lead in their own area	Although not starting with us until September, after joining us for a maths training day, E came in to bring us some boxes and stones she'd been collecting and has offered to take responsibility for creating some collections to use for maths activities
Supporting risk-taking	Leaders encourage staff to take risks and develop a culture that celebrates mistakes as an inevitable part of the learning process. If leaders get things wrong they are prepared to say they are sorry	Priti has been wanting to get to the top of the climbing frame with her friends but has been afraid to go beyond the first couple of rungs. By standing close beside her I was able to encourage her to attempt some higher rungs. In fact she did not need to hold my hand at all but just needed to know that I was close by
Encouraging the child to try new experiences, with support	Leaders are excited by staff who have new and challenging ideas and want to try them out. They are prepared to be uncomfortable and move from the familiar to the unfamiliar. They can be followers as well as leaders	When a team member suggested a new way to plan for story sessions, my initial thought was that it wouldn't work but I suggested that she try it out. We set a review date so that we can look at how things are working out – if it does work out that'll be great and we can all have a go

Awareness of the way in which the adult's attitudes and beliefs can affect learning	Leaders are aware of their own value base and are able to be critically reflective and modify their practice when necessary	Children's use of the workshop has not been very positive lately and some of the team want to limit children's choices so that they can't make so much mess. This is not really in the spirit of choice and decision-making – so the team have agreed to find a way of limiting for a time but then gradually build up resources, training children to use them as they do so. I'll monitor this because I want to be sure that we maintain good practice
		A parent asked me about the impact of music on children's development. I said I didn't know much about it but told him that I'd check it out and discuss it with him next week
Learning is viewed as a partnership and the adults demonstrate their commitment to learning	Leaders are excited about their own learning and generate excitement and enthusiasm about learning in their staff groups and the wider community. They are as comfortable in the role of learner as they are in the role of teacher/mediator	
		Pinder's family will be celebrating Diwali next week so I got a book out of the library so I could discuss what we might do knowledgeably with her parents

Source: based on Whalley (2005).

On occasion, you may have been in a situation where strategies for effective leadership and management have been thwarted by certain obstacles or barriers.

Barriers to effective leadership

Although some settings do manage to achieve 'outstanding' levels of leadership and management, leadership is not a simple or foolproof process and there are always a number of obstacles or barriers to effective leadership. Some settings face difficulties which arise from factors that are specific to the early years. These can be categorized into three broad areas: practical, political and philosophical. Many such problems are discussed later in this book but it is important to draw attention to some at this early stage. On a practical level, they include time for leadership, lack of training, trainers and ongoing support, and the fact that many leadership roles are assumed by accident rather than by design. The nature of the early childhood workforce (which is female dominated), together with the variety of backgrounds, levels of qualifications and experience of staff also has an influence. In addition, the wide range of functions undertaken in settings, such as children's centres, means that an even wider range of professionals have to co-operate towards the shared aim of their work with young children and their families. In a children's centre, for example, the team could include:

- teachers;
- practitioners holding NVQ2 and 3 awards in nursery nursing or social care;
- unqualified assistants;
- volunteers;
- students (from a range of disciplines);
- health practitioners;
- psychologists;
- therapists;
- counsellors and advisers in debt, employment, etc.;
- social workers;
- portage workers;
- community workers.

The challenge of working together in multi-agency contexts is discussed in Chapter 8.

Philosophically, there is a failure in society to have a single, clear view of the function of early childhood provision. There are various views relating to the vulnerability of young children and a wide range of interested parties in homes, communities and society at large, often with conflicting views. There is no clear definition of childhood and no clear understanding of the nature and purpose of early childhood education and care. Politically, change is taking place at a rapid pace, including the introduction of the EYFS, a legal imperative to work in multi-professional ways; the *Every Child Matters* agenda; the Children Act 2004; the Childcare Act 2006; the drive for graduate leadership via EYPS; and a host of other political initiatives. The management of change set against pressing timescales can be overwhelming for setting managers and staff.

In a climate of external pressure and a lack of resources, day-to-day crisis management may take prioriy over strategic leadership. However, Foskett and Lumby (2003: 73) note that:

> Managing staff is dependent on the same strategy as any other area of management, deciding the goals and finding the leverage to race or nudge painfully in the desired direction. Whatever the plan, fine-sounding commitment to people as central signifies nothing if the reality of educators' working lives and the reality of their culture is not taken as the starting point, rather than the latest clarion call for the current favoured approach.

On a positive note, the leadership process also brings rewards both in a personal and professional sense. For individual practitioners it can develop personal confidence and offer opportunities for collaborative learning. It can lead to further professional knowledge and skills and provide a valuable opportunity to work across professional boundaries. As the next chapter shows, leadership and management bring the advantages of building, leading and being part of a team with people at the centre.

Key points

- Leadership and management should be inclusive of all practitioners and not the domain of a privileged few.
- Leadership is concerned with inspiring improvement though reflection and collaborative action.
- Leadership is relational and contextual.
- There are a variety of leadership styles and strategies.
- Communication and interpersonal skills are of prime importance.
- Leadership brings challenges and rewards.

Practical tasks

1 In a staff meeting ask each member of staff to write down the talents and skills which they bring to their role. Look at the overall balance in the team and discuss how individuals could assume leadership and management responsibilities.

2 Discuss the idea of reflective practice with your team. Set up a system to encourage reflection on practice and suggestions for change, development and improvement.

3 Leader of leaders: developing a team culture

> Working in an early years setting whether it is large or small involves many interactions between adults ... These may be formal or informal. But these interactions are regarded as the building blocks of the service and the outcome of the service.
>
> (Rodd 1998: 42)

Introduction

Although early years settings are many and varied, the one common denominator is that a number of adults are involved. The responsibilities and demands of early childhood care and education are such that they cannot be adequately met by one person working alone. Even a childminder who may not appear to be in a 'team' is not working in isolation and may be working with other childminders, development workers, children's centres, parents and families. This chapter stems from the position that teamwork is more than just muddling through or completing given tasks. Rather, the 'team' is a powerful force with a crucial impact on the quality of provision. Early childhood services involve people, relationships and feelings. Understanding, developing and motivating people is a key feature in team leadership and the effectiveness or otherwise of a team can depend on the personal qualities, nature and interventions of the leader.

Responsibilities of leaders include both a responsibility *to* the team and a responsibility *for* the team. The role of team leader is ongoing and crucial in bringing individuals together and balancing their skills and qualities so that they perform as a whole. As Harpley and Roberts (2006: 9) point out, 'Good leadership enables a group of individuals to pull together as a team, to share their skills for the benefits of the setting and to meet the legal requirements'. In this chapter, we focus on the importance of building a 'team culture' where asking questions and checking understanding is the norm and where there is a comfortable climate of evaluation and reflection. We centre on the basic or 'core' team, the key practitioners working together on a regular or day-to-day basis. The broader, extended team which may be multidisciplinary in nature is discussed later in this book. We begin by discussing what is meant by 'team' and the nature of teams in the early years context. We move on to examine perspectives on the process of developing a team and the characteristics of effective teams. As well as continually building and motivating a team, the leader may need to act as a negotiator, as the successful negotiation of conflict is an integral feature of effective teamwork. We examine possible sources of conflict and change, and how to successfully manage such situations. The chapter concludes that teams can only be successful if they are built and shaped over time; if a collective, or consensus approach, built upon sharing and understanding of different viewpoints, is taken. The theme is extended in the next chapter which looks at roles and responsibilities of designated leaders and all those working with young children.

One of the most challenging aspects of the leadership role, and the one which causes most apprehension, is the idea of leading a 'team', particularly if you are new to the setting and the 'team' is already established. Although team leadership is one of the most important aspects of leadership it is one in which leaders receive limited training and support. The management of people can depend on a number of factors. First, there are environmental factors such as the legislative framework. In the early years field, as we have already seen, there have been a number of major national changes. Such developments inevitably impact on the roles and responsibilities of those working in the sector and have huge implications for the team leadership role. Second, the nature of teams will be influenced by cultural factors. Is the culture a collaborative one or is the process of working together under-emphasized? Third, the ways in which teams function can be determined by the structure of the organization and the competence of the leader. Leadership of a team not only involves technical requirements, such as knowing about legislation, it also demands certain social and emotional characteristics, including personal qualities, which enable the development and maintenance of successful relationships. It is well established that effective teamwork is a contributory factor to quality, but how can it be achieved? It is important to consider what is meant by 'team' in the early childhood context and who can be a team leader or a team member.

Thinking about teams

The nature and structure of a team will vary according to context. In the early childhood context, for example, a team may be different from a sporting context or a primary school. A team is generally understood to be a group of people organized to work together towards a common goal. This sounds relatively simple, but a closer look at various definitions reveals the complexity of a 'team'. Katzenbach and Smith (1993) suggest that a team is a small number of people with complementary skills who are committed to a common purpose, approach and performance goals for which they hold themselves mutually accountable. This is rather idealistic as a team may not necessarily be small, nor can it be assumed that their skills will be complementary. Few early childhood teams are evenly balanced in age, gender, qualifications and experience. Even where an employer attempts to deliberately select staff in order to maintain some balance it is not always possible to recruit the required combination of talents. As will be shown later in this chapter the team leader will need to develop the individuals in the team to achieve a balance of skills and knowledge. The idea of the team being mutually accountable is an interesting one. Usually, practitioners think of themselves as accountable to Ofsted, to parents and to children, perhaps even to the 'boss', but accountability to and responsibility for *each other* is not made explicit. In practice, it is important that each member of the team contributes to the whole and mutual accountability is felt.

Reflection point
To what extent do you encourage others to feel responsible for the work of the team by keeping people on track, facilitating input, raising questions about procedures and active listening? To what extent do you take responsibility for ensuring that this happens?

Where there is a team spirit, the needs of the group override the needs of individuals. Even though individuals may not necessarily agree with a certain point they will still remain loyal to the common goals. The leadership role is to create a team spirit, in which the needs of the team have priority over individuals. Rodd (2006: 146) describes teamwork as a process 'in which individual interests are subordinated in order to engage in joint, coordinated activity to achieve the common goals and purposes of a united group'. Consequently, the challenge for the team leader is to promote a corporate feeling of unity of purpose where individual interests are subordinate to the needs of the team, while at the same time still valuing individual needs, opinions, aspirations and contributions. In taking responsibility for the team, a leader will play a key part in ensuring good relationships and creating a climate in which staff feel valued and strive to keep learning and developing. Team leadership is about relationships with others and interpersonal skills. Effective team leaders display genuine empathy and understand the concerns of those in the team. They listen and try to understand how staff perceive things, they give genuine praise for achievements and support when needed. They support staff development through on-the-job training and mentoring, develop potential and delegate responsibilities. They have strong and clear personal values and are able to communicate a clear vision. Team leaders should be willing to admit mistakes and modify their ideas after listening to others. They need to empower staff by trusting them to take decisions or use their own initiative and discretion (DfES 2002b). As a leader, you may also be responsible for identifying and keeping central a set of core values or a vision for the setting as well as monitoring and developing the quality of provision.

Read and Rees (2003: 128) suggest that in order to operate successfully as a team, a group of individuals strive proactively toward positive ways of working together, and value individual contributions. They cite Handy (1990) who defines a team as a: '... collection of individuals gathered together because their talents are needed to perform a task or solve a problem. If the team wins, all those in it win. If the team loses they all lose. There is a common purpose, and the sense of camaraderie that should go with a common purpose'.

Reflection point
The notion of 'common purpose' is often used as a basis of successful teamwork. Do you have a 'common purpose', an articulated 'vision', a written 'mission statement' or a list of aims and objectives? What does it say? What does it mean to you? What are the shared understandings, values, attitudes and beliefs about how children learn and develop, written or unwritten, between you and those you work with? What are the key principles that underpin your practice? Are all of the team aware of the common purpose and shared goals? How is a sense of camaraderie promoted?

Structure and membership

Some teams may be put together almost at random, others are trained to a common standard. There can be self-managing teams, for example, a pre-school group may be a group of volunteers who share fundamental beliefs about the importance of play in early childhood. Conversely, there can be loosely-formed and temporary teams, put together to carry out a particular task. Much depends on the size, layout and structure of the organization. While the notion of 'team' implies a small group it may include everyone who works for an organization and be considerable in number. The size of the team will depend on the purpose, how many people are available and the task in hand. One small nursery chain, for example, may have only two people in the team, another can have over 50 staff, perhaps with smaller teams working in different rooms. Usually in early years settings there is a 'core' team, relative to staffing ratios. This might include the day-to-day supervisor or manager, a deputy and a number of assistants. The wider team or extended team may include lunchtime supervisors, supply staff, volunteers and students. The early childhood team is not a static entity but a fluid concept. As well as being composed of different personalities, the team may be part-time or full-time, they may be of different ages or at different stages in career or level of training and qualifications. Even a small core team could range from a young unqualified work experience student to a graduate with 10 or more years teaching experience.

Reflection point
What does the word 'team' mean to you? What are your experiences of being in a team, being led by a team leader or being a team leader? What is the difference between a group of people and a team? Who belongs in your core or extended team? In what ways do you or your team feel accountable?

Forming a team is more than just collecting a group of people together and calling them a team. It can be a lengthy, fragmented and complex process, depending on the circumstances. It has been suggested that teams move though a number of stages of development until the 'ethos' is achieved (Handy 1990). These are:

- forming;
- storming;
- norming;
- performing.

It is the role of the leader to support staff and help the team develop to the 'performing' stage – in other words, the point where they can work productively together. The process is non-linear in reality, but thinking about these stages provides a useful tool for evaluating your own team's coherence.

Reflection point

As you read through the descriptions of each stage think about the teams you work with or in. Can you identify a stage of development they have performed at in the recent past and which stage they are performing at now? How can the leader of the team help move them to the next stage?

Forming

At the forming stage the team is just beginning to find its identity. It may be at an initial stage or where a new person has joined or someone has left an established team. There is not yet a team, but a group of individual people who have been brought together. The team works as a group of individuals who contribute to discussions about the team's purposes and are beginning to have views on the other members, including the team leader. Some members will be more confident and established than others (e.g. new members who are not sure if they belong). They are becoming aware of what they do and how others respond to them. These feelings can be influenced by the personalities within the team. The leader at this stage will be assessing the individual strengths and weaknesses of individual characters, in order to move to the next stage. As members gradually start to feel more comfortable, signs of conflict may begin to occur. This indicates the team is moving to a new stage of team development.

Storming

This period is essential for the team to work effectively, with shared norms. The team is moving towards a general consensus. However, personal agendas are now exposed. Perhaps one or more individuals challenge others and express their individual view against the original flow. One member of staff, for example, may challenge the manager and say that there is not enough physical development provided, or that they should change the way snack time is organized. Members may be critical of each other, as individuals begin to assert themselves. This can lead to explicit conflict. The leader will need to handle any disagreements tactfully using diplomacy to negotiate through the differences, even if this requires examining the priorities and purposes again or some modification of the planned objectives. Discussions might be concerned with quality, curriculum implementation or resource issues. There may be confrontation regarding policies and the values underpinning them. Hence, ideas relating to policies and procedures should be revised or discussed, especially if the team is new. Here, the team leader needs to communicate clearly and manage the conflict effectively or the team will remain at this stage for a long time. Constant change may also mean that teams stay at this stage for a period of time.

Norming

The identity of the team is being established. The team begins to normalize and feel more cohesive. They settle into the new ways of working which begin to become established and supported. Issues are raised openly and staff are more comfortable with each other. They may begin, for example, to meet socially or communicate outside working hours. The team leader may be drafting or redrafting agreed policies and procedures. At this stage there is a feeling of trust and members work more co-operatively as they start to think and feel like a team.

Performing

This is where the individuals really feel like part of a team. The ethos is productive and supportive with everyone pulling together and working alongside each other naturally. The team is mature and has usually been well established for a period of time. The leadership role at this stage is to support, discuss, reflect and review with the team to consolidate and develop their practice. Members help and support each other as the team becomes mature and efficient. Individuals respond to each other's needs, personalities, strengths and weaknesses.

Developing team performance

O'Sullivan (2003) suggests an additional stage, that of '***transforming***', where the team is continually reflecting and developing practices and seeking to improve though change. Alternatively the team may be '***dorming***' (Harpley and Roberts 2006), or too comfortable, not wishing to meet new challenges or consider change but being satisfied with past performance rather than look-ing forward. Rodd (2006) offers a similar model of the team building process using the terms 'connecting', 'confronting conflict', 'co-operating', 'colla-borating' and 'closure'. She notes that the final stage, closure, is an important one which is often neglected.

In an alternative model, Smith and Langston (1999) suggest that as a leader you build a team spirit by observing what is happening and analysing the situation in order to identify any underlying problem. You would con-sider alternative actions that could be taken and develop an action plan, which may or may not be written. The action plan should contain action points, action, timescales and monitoring arrangements. The action plan shown in Table 3.1 was drawn up by a day nursery team following their inspection report.

Neugebauer and Neugebauer (1998) present the team building process in terms of a five-step framework:

1 Set achievable goals.
2 Clarify roles.
3 Build supportive relationships.
4 Encourage active participation.
5 Monitor team effectiveness.

Edgington (2004: 15) draws on a business model, which emphasizes three overlapping areas of functioning for an EYFS team leader: 'achieving the task'; 'building the team'; and 'developing individuals'. First, the team and the leader need to establish the overall aim of the setting. This can be broken down into smaller tasks or objectives which can then be prioritized. A first step in the process is to clarify the principles which underpin your practice. Then tasks can be defined, broken down and prioritized by the team in line with the agreed principles. The ability to prioritize logically is a crucial skill in leadership and management. The second step involves developing a team approach based on shared understandings on which they will base their work. The role of the leader involves co-ordination and communication. Third, it is important to identify and meet the professional needs of individuals, and know and develop individuals within the team – for example, through appraisal, delegating responsibility and discussion. Leading a team needs to be people-orientated rather than simply task-orientated. It is important to get to know people individually and understand their strengths and weaknesses, showing you are interested in them as people and not just as the doers of a job.

Managing performance, or the way in which people carry out their work as individuals and teams within the setting, is an important part of leading a team. The team leader is clarifying the team objectives, steering new initiatives, checking progress and providing direction. At the same time the leader is modelling good practice, acting as a coach on the job and developing the team's knowledge and skills. One of the most common reasons for job dissatisfaction is a lack of control. To begin with, less qualified or new staff will need some supervision. However, once they have been with you for some time you can allow them more freedom. This will not be detrimental to quality provided they are clear about their roles and responsibilities and the standards expected. The manager has to work to establish a learning culture, so all staff feel they can develop, by delegating responsibility where staff have particular skills or interests. The outdoor area, for example, could be one

Table 3.1   Post-inspection action plan

Actions required	Action to be taken	Who	By when	Monitoring
1 Review space in playroom	Revise layout of room, remove some tables, create space, look at storage	All staff, Sarah to take responsibility	End of Summer term 2003	Julie/Angie
2 Ensure hygiene practices are clear and followed	Display nappy-changing routine and cleaning rotas	Sarah	Immediately	Angie
3 Provide adequate hand-washing facilities	Purchase new bowl for hand-washing after painting, separate bowl for hand-washing before lunch	Angie	End of next week	Sharon

Recommendations	Things we could do			
Consider introducing key worker system	Reconsider key worker system. Develop key worker groups for 2–3-year-olds initially and later for 3–4-year-olds	Sarah/Sharon with all staff	August 2004 in readiness for new intake	Julie
Revise planning and assessment system	Revise current system of assessment to incorporate observations and records for all children and show in current written plans how needs of under 3s are met	Julie/Angie and all staff	By start spring term 2004 and develop through the year (meeting on INSET day in Xmas hols)	Sarah/ Angie and Julie
Reorganize outdoor storage space	Tidy the shed and store things in a more organized fashion	Sharon to do and Sonya to maintain responsibility from now on	End of next week	Sharon
Door repair	Repair door to children's toilet	Mick	Tomorrow	Sarah

Table 3.1 (*continued*)

Actions required	Action to be taken	Who	By when	Monitoring
Develop staff awareness of equal opportunities	Integrate activities into normal routine. Staff to undertake training in equal opportunities	Sarah to ensure someone goes on training and implement further improvements	End of autumn term 2003	Angie
Improve and clarify paperwork for medical consent and child protection	Revise to ensure clarity	Sue in office to provide new forms	End of autumn term 2003	Sarah

person's responsibility. However, it is important not to compartmentalize too rigidly, or staff may become entrenched in their own role and not inclined to change or share with others.

Motivating people is a key function of the team leader. This involves creating a shared sense of achievement and of belonging to the team. The leader must be seen to persevere, showing trust in the team, while treating each member fairly as an individual. It is essential to acknowledge and praise achievements and avoid criticism of individuals. Through staff appraisal, challenging but realistic targets can be negotiated for all team members. In this way, personal and professional development become firmly embedded into the role of all practitioners. Feedback is also important and can take a number of forms, including incentive and bonus schemes. Feedback can encourage the team to reflect on practice, share good practice and learn from each other, bringing out the best in individuals, even after a setback, such as a complaint from a parent. You should give immediate praise for good performance, for example, during an inspection or for something you have noticed during your observations. Intrinsic rewards, such as a private or public words of praise, are as powerful as more extrinsic rewards, such as 'employee of the month' schemes. Recognition of personal achievements does not have to involve hefty financial outlay: a birthday card, a thank-you note or a book token for the employee of the month all help towards motivating individuals. Communicating with staff through a newsletter can also be effective for those who are not in day-to-day contact with their team.

Team members will be demotivated by factors such as poor induction and a lack of understanding of their roles, perceived unfairness in pay or workload, the unwillingness of a manager to listen to and respond to concerns and the existence of a blame culture.

Reflection point
How well do you know each individual in the team? Does each member of the team understand the principles upon which their work is based? Are there regular opportunities for team discussions relating to shared understandings of 'good practice'? How are individuals' contributions acknowledged?

You might also think about producing a list of rights for your team or employees. The list below (DfES 2002b: 6) brings team leadership into sharp focus and suggests team members should have the right to:

- have a clear understanding of roles and responsibilities;
- know what is expected in terms of standards, quality, etc.;
- know their legal rights;
- know how they are doing;
- feel that their contributions are recognized and valued;
- know how the team and organization are doing;
- feel part of the organization's team and share successes;
- be kept up to date with organizational plans and programmes;
- be consulted on decisions that affect them.

Which of these rights do your team feel they have? Which ones still need to be addressed?

Characteristics of effective teams

McCall and Lawlor (2000: 61) suggest that to be effective as a team the group has to do the following:

- accept a 'team culture' which implies working honestly and fairly for the team, rather than for oneself;
- develop the capacity to work together and be prepared to learn as a team;
- work towards consensus decision-making, as opposed to citing individual preference;
- be open-minded about tasks and obstacles, including facing change and trying out new ideas and methods;
- act responsibly together, without the need for headteacher or 'lead manager' supervision;

- be willing to explain and justify the team's manner and modes of working, and modify these as necessary;
- accept that teams, like individuals, are accountable for results.

McCall and Lawlor also list the principle features which contribute to a successful team. These are summarized below:

- shared vision and agreed priorities;
- members have good interpersonal skills;
- balanced membership;
- systems in place for exploring different views and opinions;
- open and clear lines of communication;
- access to support and necessary expertise;
- support structures (e.g. to handle conflict);
- time for planning and evaluation;
- recognition;
- able to problem-solve;
- team has a clear accepted purpose which is explicit and published.

Reflection point
Which of the above characteristics does your team display? Edgington (2004) suggests that team leaders might evaluate their teams against the following criteria for successful and effective teams. She suggests rating your team against each question below and scoring from 1 to 5 – with 5 being a strength and 1 an area needing development. How does your team measure up against this list? What actions could be taken to make your team more effective?

- Is the team value-driven?
- Does it have good communication?
- Is it collaborative?
- Does it build on the abilities of its members?
- Do members listen to others in an effective way?
- Is there a willingness to solve problems?
- Is membership enjoyable?
- Are team members well motivated?
- Is the team dynamic?

Successful teams are also characterized by finding time for professional dialogue and building or sustaining professional relationships. The leader needs to promote positive communication including listening and open expression of ideas. It is of paramount importance that roles and responsibilities are defined, established and clearly understood by team members. The characteristics of the team (or teams) for which you have responsibility will also affect how you seek to develop team performance. Edgington (2004) characterizes three types of team. She suggests that there are *rigorous and challenging teams* who work as professionals, who are never satisfied with what they do and for whom leaders may need to encourage team members to identify their strengths and help them to relax. *Turbulent teams* can appear to be getting on well but behind the scenes dissenters can undermine developments. Edgington suggests that in teams of this sort there needs to be an emphasis on team building; on monitoring policy decisions to ensure they are implemented; and perhaps on identifying and dealing with team members who are undermining group decisions. The third type of team that Edgington identifies is what she calls the *cosy team*. She characterizes such a team as being inward-looking and avoiding change by rejecting ideas, such as a change of environment, because 'they've already tried that and it didn't work then so why should it work now?' Handy (1999) describes teams with some similar characteristics as engaging in 'group-think'. He suggests that in such teams 'no bickering or conflict is allowed to spoil the cosy "we-feeling" of the group' (1999: 163). He lists symptoms of group-think as including over-optimism, dampening any doubts; explaining away inconvenient evidence; stereotyping other groups; and stifling anything which challenges unanimity. New leaders of cosy teams need to use persuasion and avoid sudden change. This could be done by developing revised policies based on frank discussions (see Chapter 5).

> **Reflection point**
> Does your team meet to decide priorities, agree who is doing what and develop clear action plans? Do members have the confidence to question judgements and decisions and seek clarification? Are there formal and informal opportunities for changes to be suggested?

Another factor influencing the success of a team is the personal qualities of the team leader. It is the team leader who provides the link which holds the team together, boosts morale, maintains and supports structures, reviews progress, evaluates and plans for the future. It is the leader who needs to be able to communicate links between theory and practice and to translate principles into action. This requires commitment, enthusiasm and humour as well as an ability to deal with others. It demands good communication skills, written and oral, consistency and a sense of fairness. It is essential that you gain respect by example, act as a good role model and demonstrate that you have professional knowledge and skills, are well informed and remain loyal to the team. You need to show commitment to the task in hand, the team and the individuals in the team.

Some teams may not be well developed – for example, where members are different in personality, skills and capabilities and hold differing opinions, perspectives and priorities. Members of a team may have different experiences and there may have been little time to develop as a team. Team members may only share the fact that they work with young children. You may be so busy with the day-to-day business of caring for the children that there is no time set aside to make contacts with other professionals or to have informal discussions. This can create tension between achieving whatever the team is setting out to achieve and achieving individual tasks and needs. A team will not perform effectively if it is 'dorming' and unwilling to undertake tasks outside the comfort zone. Team performance may also be inhibited by other constraints such as fear of reprisals.

Reflection point
What do you need to do to develop your team? Is the decision-making process understood and are accountability lines understood? How do you share or acknowledge successes? Does each member of your team know their roles and responsibilities? Is conflict dealt with openly or pushed under the carpet? Are there ongoing opportunities for feedback and professional development? Do you make meetings productive and a positive experience for staff?

Managing conflict and change

Rodd (2006: 105) defines conflict in the early childhood context as 'a form of interpersonal interaction in which two or more people struggle or compete over claims, beliefs, values, preferences, resources, power, status or any other desire'. It is important to recognize that *conflict is inevitable* in complex organizations and too little conflict is as undesirable as too much. Conflict can range from petty quarrelling to full-blown bullying and needs to be managed early and diplomatically to avoid escalation. It is important to behave ethically and not to be seen to be taking sides.

Conflict arises from a number of possible sources ranging from strategic objectives to working practices. For example:

- a lack of information;
- an inability to accept criticism;

- tension between individual and corporate values;
- disagreements about the way children learn or the way behaviour should be managed;
- differing cultural beliefs;
- personality clashes.

In one preschool, the new manager, Sarnjit, a former Reception teacher, believed in structured activities and direct teaching of formal skills such as reading. The deputy, Jill, had always believed in learning though play as the most important element of the preschool. This resulted in some heated debate but eventually compromise was reached, in that Sarnjit recognized her experience with under 5s was limited and Jill acknowledged that more balance between adult-led and child-initiated activities could result in improved experiences for the children. In another instance, a member of the team took an almost instant dislike to a newly-appointed assistant. The existing team member was calm and quiet whereas the new team member was loud, bubbly and enthusiastic. The manager had to work really hard to see that this personality clash did not affect the rest of the team and that positive relationships could be developed between the two staff, in spite of their different personalities. She persuaded the quieter member of staff of the need for a balance of approaches and highlighted the strengths of the new team member. She discussed the importance of quiet times in the day for children with the new team member and eventually things settled down.

The manager's response will depend on the situation and whether the conflict arises from black and white issues or more deeply-held personal values. Some managers may tackle the situation personally, using a problem-solving approach. They may focus on identifying the problem, gathering information, considering alternative solutions, and choosing what to do. Alternatively, others may prefer not to be directly involved and ask someone else to deal with it. A manager may contact a colleague or another manager for advice, or in more complex situations may seek legal advice or advice from a professional association. If the issues cannot be dealt with informally there may need to be a meeting where everyone can have their say and agree a way forward. The leader needs the skills to negotiate between individuals and help them see other perspectives. Any oral or written communication in relation to conflict needs to be clear and objective. Sometimes, however, you may need to act assertively and put an end to unacceptable behaviour rather than let it impact on the provision. There needs to be a system in place for airing views, with a no-blame ethos, where staff can share ideas and not take it personally if an idea is not taken up as a learning experience. In more serious cases, you may need to call upon more formal grievance or disciplinary procedures which should already be in place. Conflict can also be influenced by leadership style, with levels of conflict being reduced if there is an atmosphere of openness and trust. It is also likely to be limited where there are clear policies and where staff are aware of their roles and responsibilities.

Reflection point
Think of a time when conflict occurred in your team or a team you have worked in. What caused it, how was it handled and how it could have been handled differently? Was it a communication breakdown or a breakdown of interpersonal relationships within the team?

Another common source of tension in any organization is resistance to change. The challenge of change is faced by all early years practitioners but is particularly significant for the leader who is responsible for introducing, implementing, managing and monitoring the impact of change on an ongoing basis. Change involves dealing with 'new expectations, new situations, new problems, heightened uncertainty and increased ambiguity' (McCall and Lawlor 2000: 1). The responses to the change will depend on a number of factors. First, whether the change is fairly minor and being internally suggested or whether it is a major strategic change which has been externally imposed. Second, the speed at which it is introduced. Most resistance to change is related to insecurity. Hence, unless it is a matter of urgency, it is important to introduce change gradually and have valid reasons for it. This is a time to be realistic and persuade others of the potential *benefits* of change. Resistance will be less likely if change is seen as an opportunity for improvement. Third, the attitudes of individual team members towards change. Some individuals have an inbuilt low tolerance for change which can stem from the fear of not being able to live up to any new expectations arising from the change. Where staff know and understand the change they are more likely to welcome it. It is seeing change as a threat which leads to resistance. The leader needs to stay focused on explaining where the change will lead, which, in turn, will help staff feel involved and have some understanding and ownership of the change. It may be that you need to offer training (both external and internal) before introducing change.

CASE STUDY

Cathy (the manager) decided to change snack time from a traditional break in the middle of the session where all the children sat down together for a drink and snack. Instead she introduced a 'self-service' cafeteria-style snack bar where children helped themselves from a variety of drinks and snacks left on the table. Some of her staff did not like this idea. When she was off on holiday for a few days, they went back to the original away of working. When Cathy returned there was a big row about the fact they had changed the system back. Once they all sat down and discussed what had happened and the advantages and disadvantages of both ways of working, it was agreed to try the cafeteria for a month and then review it. If Cathy had prepared her staff for this change beforehand there would have been less resistance.

McCall and Lawlor (2000: 17) summarize the key points relating to change as follows:

- change is ever present and always will be;
- the expectation of a suitable professional response to changes is increasing;
- early years settings cannot control economic, social and technological changes;
- settings need to be proactive rather than reactive, seeking positive strategies for managing change;
- mandated change has to be complied with but settings should strive to maintain their own identity;
- knowing 'how' and 'why' is more important than knowing 'what';
- balance is required between external pressures and internal priorities;
- leadership of change involves self-reflection on values, beliefs, attitudes and patterns of professional behaviour.

As a manager you need to have fostered respect and credibility to convince others of the need for change and especially the potential benefits. Instead of a coercive approach you will need to adopt a collaborative one. Sometimes there will be instances where this is not possible and you have to make the change regardless. However, the more coercive the change the more likely it is to be resisted.

Reflection point

Think of some changes that you have been involved in. Have they been internal or external? Were they coercive or collaborative? Have they been welcomed or resisted? How has the impact of the change been monitored?

A leader needs to be able to recognize and respond to reactions to change. Barriers caused by resistance are very difficult to break down, especially where the change is of a fundamental nature. Resistance to change can stem from a number of sources. Do those implementing the change know how it will affect them as individuals and what the impact will be on their workload? If the answer is yes, then the change is more likely to be accepted. Team members may feel something will be lost as a result of the change or may have misunderstood the implications. Change is less likely to be resisted if it is viewed as part of reflective practice (see Chapter 2). A continuous cycle of observing and thinking about practice and suggesting improvements results in change being naturally embedded in day-to-day routines. In addition, it is essential to encourage those implementing change to be evaluative of the impact on the provision. If a change is not working then the leader needs to have the courage to abort it.

Finally, it is important to acknowledge that team leadership is a process that needs to be considered alongside other leadership tasks, roles and responsibilities. The next chapter looks at these in further detail.

Key points

- Appropriate leadership enables groups of workers to become teams.
- Team building is a complex process not a single event.
- Team building is concerned with an ethos that is based on positive relationships which preserve individual autonomy while meeting the priorities of the team.
- Effective teams have a shared philosophy about ways of working with young children.
- Roles and responsibilities need to be clear.
- Management of change and conflict is a critical leadership function.

Practical tasks

1   Think about other adults you interact with in your role as an early years practitioner. Draw a chart or diagrammatic representation showing:

   a)   the core team – those you work with on a daily or regular basis;
   b)   the wider team – those you come into contact with but not necessarily on a daily basis;
   c)   your position within the team.

   How would you describe your working relationships with the adults you have included in your chart?

2   Hold a team meeting to discuss your common purposes and draw up a mission statement written jointly by all staff.

4 The roles and responsibilities of leaders

We are all parties to leadership. Although it helps to have a sympathetic position leader ... we shouldn't wait for the go-ahead. There can be acts of compassionate leadership in every step you take. You may collaborate with others as soon as you begin to value their interests. You can be a collective leader when you vow to serve others and your community ...

(Raelin 2003: 252)

Introduction

As changes occur in the way in which schools and other early years settings are organized; childcare needs are addressed for children above and below statutory school age; as government priorities shift, the roles taken on by practitioners in all sectors of provision will need to change too. Those of you who have been designated leaders (or as Raelin terms it above, 'position leaders') will be well aware that what is expected of you changes all the time. Your title and salary may remain the same but your role frequently changes, as circumstances are altered by both national and local contexts. In this chapter we explore the changing roles and responsibilities of leaders. We consider the range of tasks, roles and responsibilities which early years practitioners have to assume and the relationship between them. We explore specific nature of leadership roles and responsibilities in the 'leaderful community' (Raelin 2003) of early years settings and identify the different groups to whom leaders in this sector are accountable. Responsibilities to and for the team with whom you work are examined and the chapter concludes by considering the responsibilities a professional leader has in terms of self-development and reflection.

Tasks, roles and responsibilities

We begin by considering not only the roles and relationships which leaders (and indeed all early years practitioners) must undertake but also the tasks that everyone is involved in and how these relate to their roles and responsibilities.

CASE STUDY

Claire is an assistant head in a children's centre which was formerly a maintained nursery school. Claire's role has changed and developed over several years. When her children were small and attending the nursery school she volunteered as a parent helper. Because she already had a qualification equivalent to NVQ3, Claire was able to take on a wider range of responsibilities than other parent helpers. She felt comfortable, for example, playing maths games with the children and was able to contribute ideas for art and for design technology activities. When a post in the nursery class became vacant, Claire applied for it and was appointed. Her roles in the centre inevitably broadened, and she began to take responsibility for ensuring that resources were well maintained, and that all areas of provision were inviting and stimulating. She took on areas of responsibility beyond the setting and was able to take a lead in community involvement and work with parents.

When it was decided to introduce an extended day scheme, Claire was very enthusiastic and sometimes helped out by covering for staff absence or other emergencies. She enjoyed the opportunity to spend time with children in a more relaxed atmosphere and found that this helped her to build a strong relationship with them. It also meant that she was able to meet parents that she would otherwise be unable to see on the regular and informal basis which she enjoyed with other parents. Working alongside the extended day team also gave Claire an opportunity to build a stronger relationship with staff there. Overall she was able to act as a bridge between home and school and between school staff and the extended day team.

When the nursery school was designated as a children's centre, Claire applied for an assistant head's post, with overall responsibility for children up to the age of 3. In this role she worked closely with other senior managers to set up and implement plans to provide full day care for a group of babies and toddlers. She was also given responsibility for the day-to-day wrap-around care for older children.

In spite of this high level of responsibility, Claire felt that some additional qualifications would help her to fulfil her roles more effectively and she enrolled initially for an early years foundation degree course. The successful completion of that course spurred her on further and she undertook the NPQICL course. She has found that her developing ability to reflect critically on her work has given her both new insights and increased confidence. These in turn have enabled her to gain support for aspects of provision which have sometimes been regarded among some team members and managers as peripheral to their work.

During her time at this centre, Claire has held a number of different roles. In those roles there may well be a high level of overlap in the tasks she undertakes – but her responsibility as she undertakes different tasks may vary. For example, in most of the roles which Claire has been in, she will have undertaken simple cleaning tasks.

- As a parent helper, her motive or sense of responsibility will have something to do with simply being the extra pair of hands, and something to do with demonstrating to her own child her commitment to the setting.
- As a member of staff, Claire may have decided to get involved out of a sense of responsibility to the team but may also have been driven by her sense of responsibility to children. She may have noticed that the child who was asked to mop up some spilt water is becoming frustrated and is on the verge of a tantrum, and clearly needs support to complete the task successfully. In her role as an educator she may have sought to promote a child's self-esteem, acknowledging her responsibility for supporting all-round development.
- However, as an assistant head seeing water spilt in a corridor, Claire might mop it up in order to demonstrate her responsibility for the smooth running of the school as a whole; for the safety and well-being of children; or to act as a role model for staff and children. Alternatively, if as assistant head Claire were, for example, showing the centre to a councillor, it might be more appropriate for her to exercise responsibility as a senior manager and request that someone else do the task so that she can concentrate on acting as an advocate for the centre by bending the politician's ear.

Claire has a large number of roles within the centre, contributing to the well-being or care of children throughout their time there. In collaboration with the qualified teacher she supports children's learning and development across the curriculum. She liaises between different teams within the centre, and between parents and staff. She takes responsibility for developments within the setting and beyond. She demonstrates leadership in a number of important aspects of life in a children's centre which is also a school – using both formal mechanisms where she has been given specific roles and responsibilities and informal ones where she must use influence to contribute to change within the institution.

Table 4.1 summarizes the varying roles and responsibilities assumed by Claire and her team as they undertake similar tasks.

Table 4.1 Roles, responsibilities and tasks

Tasks	Roles	Responsibilities
Playing a (maths) game	Parent helper	To own child, demonstrating commitment to what goes on in the setting To children playing the game
	Carer	To children who may have needed a diversion or some quiet time away from the crowd
	Educator	Responsibility for mathematical development, with a focus on accurate counting and/or developing appropriate strategies
	Pedagogue	Responsibility for mathematical development but strong focus on personal and social development
	Team member	Responsibility to other team members to address curriculum plans and learning objectives
	Assistant head	Demonstrating responsibility to parents, children, team and community. Playing the game may be part of monitoring provision, or it may simply be a way of demonstrating involvement to parents, staff and children
	Student	Responsibility to governors and staff who have given permission to undertake courses. While playing the game, the insights obtained about children's learning and development create an additional responsibility to act on those insights and enhance the quality of education. Study also requires a sense of responsibility to self – taking time to study properly, acknowledging the gains for the centre as well as self. Not taking appropriate amounts of time for study and reflection sells everyone short
	Leader	Responsibility to children and staff, acting as role model to both groups
Changing nappies	Carer	To the well-being of the child, fulfilling responsibility to parents
	Pedagogue	To the well-being of the child but with a recognition that talking and singing as you undertake the task, the way in which you touch the child and so on, all contribute to the child's care and education
	Team member	Covering colleague's absence
	Assistant head	Responsible to child, parents and team but in addition may act in capacity as strategist and be trying to determine how to improve procedures for children and staff
	Leader	Responsibility for staff development, acting as a role model

Reflection point

As you go about your daily tasks, make some notes on the role you are playing and the responsibility you are exercising. Do not forget your responsibility to yourself as a developing professional. Note the changes as you move from task to task.

Within differing roles, leaders undertake a wide variety of different tasks. The sense of responsibility involved in carrying out even apparently similar tasks may vary. Beth, for example, regularly works in a nursery alongside other members of her team. At different times she may see a simple task like reading a story as part of her role as officer in charge, maintaining day-to-day contact with children so that she can fulfil her responsibility to have a clear overview of the children's needs and interests. Sometimes she is covering a staff leave or absence. Her role and prime responsibility in that case will be to take on the roles and responsibilities of the missing team member. At other times she may want to observe a particular child about whom a parent has expressed concerns – her role may be that of an observer or assessor and her responsibility will be to the child and family. In all of these cases however, Beth is acting in her role as a leader and whatever her focus, she recognizes her multiple roles and responsibilities to staff, to children and families, and to society in general.

Leadership roles

Leadership has been described as a 'differentiated role' (Pierce and Newstrom 2006: 9). This description contributes to the view that everyone in an early years team has sometimes to act as a leader. In the view of Pierce and Newstrom, different members of a team act in response to the needs of the group and take on different leadership roles. It then becomes the role of the designated leader to orchestrate the work of the group in achieving its aims. In short, the role of leaders is seen to be evolving into 'leading others to lead themselves' (Pierce and Newstrom 2006: 11 citing Manz and Sims 1991). This fits well with a proposition put forward in the National College of School Leadership's framework for leadership development (cited by Crow 2005: 71–2) which states that 'school leadership must be a function that is distributed throughout the school community'.

Shared or distributed leadership may take a variety of forms (Gronn 2003). Leadership may be shared in the sense that everyone working in a centre sees themselves as being leaders by representing the centre to the outside world as well as 'reflecting pictures of the outside world back into the system' (Gronn 2003: 34). This has the distinct advantage in complex early years and integrated centres of not needing what Yukl has called a 'heroic leader' (1999 cited in Gronn 2003: 34) because the team can undertake all the necessary roles, actions and functions. It may also be compared to what Handy has termed role culture (1984 cited by Bush 2003). Role culture is characterized by a reliance on charts demonstrating the hierarchical nature of roles within an institution and indicating with whom each role and level of employment may communicate. Bush (2003) suggests that structures of this sort may be appropriate in periods of stability but are much less so in periods of rapid change.

Ideally, distributed leadership should be the result of conscious and deliberate action by the designated leader. Often it occurs spontaneously and the wise leader will nurture this. In a children's centre Laura, an experienced nursery officer, took a strong lead in improving the quality of interactions with children. Her skill in talking to children and in communicating with them was recognized by the whole staff, her advice was sought and she was acknowledged by all as being a leader in this area of work. The head was frequently asked to talk at national conferences and to write articles about the centre's high quality of work in intervening in children's play. She began by involving Laura but over time, as her confidence grew, writing and speaking on the subject was delegated entirely to Laura.

Gronn (2003) also describes some distributed leadership as intuitive. The way in which, within groups, different roles emerge and different people take up different roles has been well documented. Belbin (1981 cited by Handy 1999), for example, identifies eight distinct but unofficial roles which emerge in effective groups. These include the chair (whom Belbin describes as working through others); the shaper – the spur to action, passionate and dominant; the company worker, who is methodical and good at setting up administrative systems; the team worker (not always noticed except when he or she is not there); and the finisher, who makes sure that deadlines are met.

Reflection point

Think about teams you are involved in. In some you may not be the designated leader but in others you will be. Reflect on the roles you adopt in different teams and the contribution that you make to the work of the group. As a leader, it will also be helpful for you to think about the roles being adopted by others. Can you build on strengths you identify or can you support others who may be (wittingly or unwittingly) adopting unhelpful roles? Handy (1999) describes the hidden agendas of team members who may be acting to protect some vested interest, may be out to impress or get at you or someone else, or may be covering up their own feelings of inadequacy. Do these sound familiar?

There are many difficulties in having the role of a designated leader. Not least among these is that others hold particular expectations of you as a leader. Anne, a newly-appointed headteacher in a nursery school, held strong views of distributed leadership and was keen to encourage others to exercise decision-making. However, she was taking over from a long-standing and very traditional headteacher who had made all the decisions. In the first week of her headship, Anne was approached by a member of staff who asked whether the children should be brought in from the rain. She replied that she would be happy for the members of staff in the garden to make that decision. This was not well received since the nursery nurse involved felt unable to take responsibility. It is very easy to see how the expectations of others can lock you into certain behaviours or responses. As Handy (1999: 62) remarks:

> Individuals often find it hard to escape from the role that cultural traditions have defined for them. Not only with doctors or lawyers is the required role model behaviour so constrained that if you are in that role for long it eventually becomes part of you, part of your personality. Hence there is some likelihood that all accountants will be alike or that all blondes are similar – they are forced that way by the expectations of their role.

It may also be the case that designated leaders misuse the notion of distributed leadership. Amy, for example, is a manager who talks at length about her belief in distributed leadership – believing that in handing out responsibilities her role is finished. But designated leaders have responsibilities to team members to support them in taking on additional roles, to give constructive feedback on how things are progressing and above all to notice improvements and developments. Amy does not do this and as a result her team, initially happy to take on new areas and new initiatives, are left feeling disaffected. A vicious circle of disaffection has developed – Amy does not emerge often from her room and therefore does not even see developments let alone comment on them. It is important to be clear that the purpose of distributed leadership is not to make the leader's life easier but to provide a better service – by using everyone's talents to the full.

The gender of leaders in early childhood settings is interesting when considering roles, expectations and conflicts. Women may suffer from the same problem as women leaders in many other sectors – being expected 'to fulfil at one and the same time the expectations attached to being a woman and the expectations attached to a male stereotype of successful executives' (Handy 1999: 65). Men working as designated leaders in early years settings, on the other hand, may also have to contend with the fact that the care and education of young children is not always seen as an appropriate area for men to be employed in. Moreover, the expectation is that they will:

- act as role models for boys in undertaking traditionally male and female tasks;
- provide a balance within the ethos of early childhood care and education which is dominated by women.

Role ambiguity can be particularly troublesome when, as is so often the case, there is more than one view of what the leader's role is or should be. This is likely to occur in situations that are fluid and subject to frequent change – as many of your roles are likely to be. Role ambiguity leaves you uncertain about your actual areas of responsibility and others' expectations of you. It can lead to uncertainty about how your competence is judged or valued. This in turn may make you feel insecure about whether you will be considered for promotion (Handy 1999).

Many leaders also suffer from role overload (Handy 1999). Again this is particularly prevalent in situations involving high levels of change. Gronn (2003) suggests that with change, leaders may find themselves being given more and more roles to fulfil. Any salary enhancement becomes like an overtime payment as leaders struggle to deal with all that they are asked to do.

As discussed in Chapter 2, while management may be one of the roles of a leader, it is by no means the whole story. Pierce and Newstrom (2006: 11) remind us of this when they write:

> an increasing number of management gurus are suggesting that many of today's organizations are 'over managed and under led.' Increasingly, organizations are modifying the role of yesterday's manager, changing the role to that of a leader charged with the responsibility to gain follower recognition and acceptance and become a facilitator and orchestrator of group activity, while also serving as coach and cheerleader. It is feasible that many of those roles (e.g. servant, teacher, coach, cheerleader) will become a common part of the conceptualization of leader and leadership as the twenty-first century continues to unfold.

Reflection point
Reflect carefully on these comments about leadership roles. Do you see yourself as coach and cheerleader? In what ways do you feel that you are enabling others to lead themselves?

The responsibilities of leaders

Everyone involved in work with children and their families carries a heavy burden of responsibility. It is important, amid all this talk of responsibilities, to remember that in working with children, practitioners have the privilege of working in a rewarding and hopeful area of work. In dealing with the most vulnerable and impressionable members of our society, we clearly have a responsibility to the children themselves. As the emphasis in early childhood care and education has shifted to focus on the needs of working parents and the Extended Schools Initiative has emerged, the debate about the extent to which practitioners' responsibility is to parents or children has also developed. In addition to these day-to-day responsibilities there is a broader responsibility to society at large which is sometimes seen as more nebulous.

As a member of a staff team, you have responsibilities not just to your line manager, but to the rest of the team. Increasingly, as you develop and take on more responsible roles, you will become aware of the need to take responsibility for the development of staff and many complex aspects of the setting itself. You should also not lose sight of the fact that your developing role brings with it the responsibility to develop your skills and competence as a leader, in order to maintain 'the excitement and enthusiasm' for learning, which Whalley (2005) suggests is an important aspect of both effective leadership and pedagogy.

Accountable to society or children?

Although the accountability provided by inspection can sometimes seem removed from day-to-day concerns, the debate focused around *Every Child Matters* (DfES 2003) has sharpened the level of accountability to aspects which clearly impact on children's well-being. In the 2005 version of the Ofsted framework (in England) for nursery and primary schools (Ofsted 2005b), self-evaluation forms (SEFs) were introduced as an important step forward in promoting a professional approach to self-assessment. Leaders are asked to take increased responsibility for assessing their own performance. Head-teachers are asked to comment in their SEFs on a number of things, including the extent to which learners:

- adopt healthy lifestyles;
- feel safe and adopt safe practices;
- enjoy their education;
- make a positive contribution to the community;
- prepare for their future economic well-being.

The final point is replaced for non-maintained early years settings by a focus on the effectiveness of the organization of childcare. Advice on and strategies for completing an SEF are provided in Chapter 10.

Responsibilities to children and families

Practitioners' responsibilities to children are so much an inbuilt part of day-to-day practice that it can be difficult to take the necessary time and space to reflect on what is entailed in addressing those responsibilities. Elfer *et al.* (2003: 8 citing Manning-Morton and Thorp 2003), for example, identify a list of tasks or roles that a key person working with children under 3 needs to undertake if he or she is to meet the full implication of his or her responsibilities. The list includes the need for key persons to develop trusting relationships with children and parents; interacting with children in ways which build on their preferences and ensure that they feel safe enough to explore the world around them; acknowledging all their feelings including those that are seen as negative; settling children gently and being with them at key points, such as eating and toileting; and seeking support to ensure that key workers' emotional needs are also addressed. This range of responsibilities indicates just how complex the role of a key person is. It involves taking a high level of responsibility for all aspects of the children's development and well-being but inevitably will involve overlap with the responsibilities of parents and principal carers.

Responsibilities to families will be developed more fully in Chapter 9 but at this stage it is important to recognize that young children are closely bound to their parents, emotionally. Part of all practitioners' responsibility for children's development is the need to work in partnership with parents. Failure to do this can place unnecessary and unhelpful pressure on the children themselves (Jowett and Baginsky 1991). Both as a leader and as a practitioner, your role will be to take a lead in this, modelling good practice and providing training for other staff members who find this difficult (Moylett and Holyman 2006). As will be seen in the next chapter, you should also take responsibility for ensuring that policies are clear and explicit since these make expectations clear to parents and provide support for staff. When they act outside policy, staff may lay themselves open to criticism from parents.

Whalley (2001) praises the role of the *Start Right* report (Ball 1994) in acknowledging the importance of parents' contributions and commitment to their children's learning and development. She suggests that it is the responsibility of early childhood practitioners to give support to parents by modelling effective practice and giving them information about research and opportunities to enhance their knowledge about the personal development of children. Manning-Morton and Thorp (2003) add that practitioners need to examine the attitudes they hold towards families if they are to develop warm and trusting relationships. As a leader, you carry a responsibility to help staff address any negative or conflicting views of parents, since they will damage relationships not only with parents but also with children.

Responsibilities to the community

While in a small village it may be possible to define a community, in large cities this may be more difficult to achieve. Even in rural areas many members of the community may travel long distances to work in neighbouring areas, giving a dislocated feel to what are often termed dormitory towns and villages. In large towns and cities, a sense of community may not exist because residents may move frequently, may not know their neighbours and may prefer to keep themselves to themselves. The community that you, as a professional, serve may not live in a single geographical area but may be widely scattered, perhaps defined as a community because they are working parents or because of high levels of socioeconomic need or disability.

> **Reflection point**
> Can you identify your community? Do you think you have a responsibility towards your community? Do you think communities can be self-defined? There are no clear-cut answers to questions of this sort but reflecting on the complexity of these issues may help you to clarify your roles and responsibilities.

The care and education of young children in Reggio Emilia in northern Italy is widely acknowledged as a model of high quality provision (e.g. see Moss 2001). One of the many interesting aspects of provision there is that the nurseries are built on models of distributed leadership. This in part arises from their origin in postwar communist and feminist activism but is also seen as an important part of the nurseries' relationship with and responsibility towards the community. Every practitioner in Reggio Emilia is expected to have a clear sense of responsibility to the community and to be responsible for ensuring that there is a climate of trust and active listening between families, including children, practitioners and politicians (Scott 2001). The provision of good working conditions for practitioners is seen as an integral part of the climate of trust since it is believed this contributes to both the self-esteem and well-being of children and staff.

As a leader it may often be important to view the community's perspectives critically. While the work of educators in Reggio Emilia is exemplary in many ways, this does not mean that it can be simply imported into other communities. Moss (2001: 133) reminds us that looking at work there can help us to be more critical by providing 'a lens which helps to make the invisible visible and to see what is visible in a different light'. Commenting on practice in Reggio Emilia, Browne (2004: 49) draws attention to an aspect which she feels is invisible there. She highlights the fact 'that an individual's identity develops as a result of the interaction of gender, class and "race"' and suggests that the political and parental lenses available to practitioners in Reggio Emilia have not led them to take full account of these aspects of community which challenge the status quo. Similar issues may need to be explored if, for example, you work in a disadvantaged working-class community where there is overt and violent evidence of racism.

Responsibilities to society

Traditionally the responsibilities of practitioners working in the field of the care and education of young children have been seen as relatively narrow, focusing mainly on children and their families. The government's childcare agenda, which is primarily designed to support working parents, has broadened the level of responsibility since this has been set in a context of broader social and fiscal policy. Making provision for children which ensures that parents get to work on time has always been the duty of childminders and nannies, but for many practitioners this is an entirely new experience.

The climate of trust which has been commented on as being a feature of work in Reggio Emilia seems not to exist in the UK. Developments in the 1990s, such as the introduction of the National Curriculum, Standard Attainment Tasks (SATs) and other testing procedures, and the creation of Ofsted inspections, were an attempt to monitor (on society's behalf) the way in which schools were addressing their responsibilities. This may have arisen from media pressure; concerns about unequal levels of achievement; a focus on value for money; calls for higher of accountability across many professional sectors; or a perceived effort to shift the balance of power from teachers to politicians. Just as many early years practitioners have felt the pressure of unannounced inspections and have seen this as a mistrust of their professionalism, so one of the most persistent objections to increased levels of monitoring came from teachers concerned about the erosion of their professionalism.

Ofsted's field of work has always included nursery and Reception classes in maintained schools but in 1997 its sphere of influence was extended. The Conservative government issued vouchers for nursery education. In order that the effects of funding could be seen, a set of objectives often known as the Desirable Learning Outcomes (DLOs) were published (SCAA 1996), against which Ofsted-trained inspectors assessed provision. From that point on Ofsted inspections occurred in not only maintained settings but in non-maintained private and voluntary settings where free education places were offered for 4-year-olds. Funding was dependent on an inspection process devised and managed by Ofsted. Since that time there have been a number of changes in the process of inspection and its scope, including the introduction of free education places for 3-year-olds. There is in addition a pilot scheme to try out free education places for 2-year-olds. The whole process of inspection is discussed in more detail in Chapter 10.

Responsibilities to and for the team

Even as a leader, you are likely to be a member of one or more teams. The team might be focused around meeting the needs of children with SEN. It might be a class-based team focusing on the needs of one set or cohort of children. Frequently practitioners find themselves in a range of teams – an extended day team, a management group, an action committee and so on. As suggested in Chapter 2 the responsibilities of leaders include both responsibility *to* the team and responsibility *for* the team. In taking responsibility for the team, you will, for example, take a lead in:

- promoting positive relationships;
- creating an ethos in which staff feel valued and want to learn more and develop further;
- keeping core values at the heart of the setting's work;
- monitoring, maintaining and developing the quality of provision.

In addressing these responsibilities you will be taking responsibility for the team but also demonstrating your responsibilities to the team, for developing effective practice.

These things cannot be achieved by the leader alone. Sam, recently appointed head of a small day nursery, was anxious to ensure that her staff team were fully engaged in a shared responsibility for what happened throughout the setting. She was greatly inspired by the work of Goleman *et al.* (2002) on the subject of emotional intelligence and leadership, and decided to begin team meetings with a reminder of the need to ensure that everyone stick to the point. She asked team members not only to monitor their own behaviour but also to monitor what others said and did so that meeting times were purposeful and productive. This is important in all areas of work but particularly so where shift work is involved since it is often very difficult to get everyone together. Staff came to value this approach and became highly disciplined and skilful in raising questions about procedures and building on the contributions of one another.

Reflection point

Goleman *et al.* (2002: 180) indicate that teams can be helped to share responsibility by:

- raising questions about ... procedures (e.g. asking the group to clarify where it is going and offering summaries of the issues being discussed to make sure we have a shared understanding of them);
- using good listening skills: either build on the ongoing discussion or clearly signal that we want to change the subject, and ask if that is ok...

To what extent do you think procedures of this sort would improve the effectiveness of leadership in your setting? How could they be introduced? What help might the team need to prevent such a change feeling too challenging or confrontational?

Responsibilities to and for yourself

It has been suggested (see, for example, Whalley 2004) that the purpose of education, including the care and education of young children, is transformation. An approach to leadership which results in transformation places 'self-examination' at its heart. This, it is claimed, can inform a range of new ideas; will build competence and confidence; support plans and their implementation; and enable leaders to take on new roles and evaluate and act on feedback (Whalley 2004 citing Mezirow 1975, 1982).

Self-examination involves reflective practice which is the subject of many current publications. Bolton (2005) emphasizes the importance of the writing process in aiding reflection for a range of professionals, including those in 'medicine, education, clinical psychology, nursing, therapy and leadership'. (back cover). In Chapter 2 we highlighted the view of Johns (2004) on self-examination or reflective practice.

An effective process of reflection is inevitably linked to action, or as Freire (2005: 15), a highly influential educationalist of the twentieth century, suggests, 'authentic reflection cannot exist apart from action'. John Dewey, again a highly influential writer working in the early part of the twentieth century, expresses this slightly differently: 'Reflection', he suggests, 'involves not simply a sequence of ideas, but a consequence' (Dewey [1910] 1991: 2). Observation is an essential element of reflective practice. However, as Drummond (1993) reminds us, looking and listening are not neutral or objective activities. The observer's mind or perception of a situation may create errors in observations.

Sometimes observations can become formalized and lead us to a form of practitioner or action research. Rodd (1998: 174) comments that 'research is also important for leadership . . . because it is a recognized means of gathering the facts and information which carry weight in arguments for change'. Clark and Moss (2001) make the point that research brings responsibilities – meaning that if you have identified problems or issues for the child, then you have a responsibility to act on the knowledge. Mary, as part of her foundation degree study, gave a group of children disposable cameras to photograph the aspects of provision which were important or significant to them. She was shocked to find that several of them took photographs of the bathrooms – which they said they found dark, and even scary. Mary realized that she had to convince senior management of the need to redecorate and refurbish this area.

Graham, responsible for under 3s in a children's centre, was studying for the NPQICL and was anxious to develop his ability to reflect on his practice, and that of his team. He found the leadership or reflective journal which he was required to keep increasingly helpful. At the beginning of the course he had found it a chore and had not expected to agree with the comments (quoted below) of students cited by Bolton (2005: 165), but as the course drew to a close he discovered just how much he had come to depend on his journal. One student, for example, wrote:

> This journal . . . has given me intellectual space and opportunity – physical space from work and social group – spiritual space . . . also psychological space to rethink my responses, reactions, motivations, expectation and hopes . . . I'm more able to take risks and I have thought of things I'd like to do which I've previously not thought of as possibilities . . .

In a similar vein, another student wrote: 'I will continue to write a log because . . . [t]hings come out differently when written down. Feelings and thoughts can creep up and surprise you in writing. I will always be grateful to this course for giving me the space to discover this'.

In addition to written reflection, Graham found that he was more aware of things going on around him. He observed interactions between staff, or between staff and parents, more accurately. He found that he was more likely to take responsibility for his actions and to consider their likely outcomes more fully, and was more likely to question and analyse what would previously have been automatic and largely unquestioned decisions.

Developing professionalism

Rodd (2006: 54) has identified three stages of professionalism in leadership in early childhood services: direct care/novice; direct care/advanced; and indirect care. For each of these she identifies two sets of roles and responsibilities. She suggests that the roles and responsibilities of the novice professional are:

- to deliver and be accountable for a quality service;
- to develop and articulate a philosophy, values and vision.

Thus, even inexperienced or novice practitioners can only be seen as professional if they are both accountable and sufficiently reflective to engage in developing a vision which informs their practice.

Lucy had recently completed an NVQ3 qualification and was working in a private nursery. She demonstrated a warmth which children, parents and fellow team members alike found attractive. She was willing to take the initiative but also ready to ask advice when she needed to. Leadership qualities showed themselves in situations where she acted as a mentor for students undertaking work experience – not merely indicating what had to be done, but explaining the particular importance of helping children to feel secure, competent and valued.

As Lucy became more experienced she undertook an increased range of roles and responsibilities (described by Rodd as advanced direct care) and was appointed deputy head. In this role she was able:

- to engage in a collaborative and partnership approach to leadership;
- to engage in ongoing professional development and to encourage it in all staff.

She demonstrated good administrative capabilities, getting letters out on time, maintaining records efficiently and responding in good time to requests for information. Staff felt that she dealt sympathetically and fairly with issues which they raised and she was able to communicate effectively. In this role Lucy also undertook an increasing amount of responsibility for financial management.

The third stage of professionalism identified by Rodd, namely that belonging to those not directly responsible for day-to-day care, demands the ability:

- to be sensitive and responsive to the need for change and to lead change effectively;
- to act as an advocate for children, parents, carers, staff, the profession and the general community.

Lucy's line manager was ill for a period of time, and during her months of absence Lucy was given the opportunity to lead the team. She found that she enjoyed the experience and was good at helping the team to embrace change. She gained a great deal from the opportunity to raise the profile of the setting in the wider community.

> **Reflection point**
> Which of these aspects of professionalism do you feel able to demonstrate? Which do you enjoy? Which do you feel you need to get better at?

Moyles (2006: 16) adds another perspective on learning to become a leader. In her framework for the evaluation of leaders, shown in an adapted form below, she identifies four levels of competence:

1 *Intuitive and pragmatic.* Working from a sound knowledge base, but intuitively, instinctively and somewhat spontaneously, rather than from the basis of deep thought or reflection.
2 *Reasoned and articulate.* A more thoughtful stance from the basis of thinking through and articulating the needs of any situation, using experience, sound knowledge and explanation skills.
3 *Involved and collaborative.* A different level of operation altogether, seeking expert advice from others within and beyond the setting and working in close collaboration with others whose knowledge and opinions are valued, discussed, considered and used as relevant.
4 *Reflective and philosophic.* Definitely the most thoughtful, cognitive level, using all one's powers of thinking to scrutinize one's beliefs and values and those of others, and to explore concepts such as change and vision for one's particular setting as broadly and innovatively as possible.

Many practitioners, both experienced and inexperienced, are intuitive and pragmatic. They think on their feet, they know what feels right and they often get things right. Graham had been just such a leader and he was for this reason reluctant to begin a leadership course. He was regarded by the team and by parents as a good leader but, contrary to his expectations, he found that having to explain and spell out his actions gave him more confidence, and made his presentations more thoughtful, reasoned and articulate. His increased confidence made it easier for him to seek advice, making his a more collaborative style, being less afraid of looking inexpert. The course gave him the opportunity to develop his powers of reflection, to understand different perspectives and above all to develop a vision or philosophy for the centre. He did not lose the intuitive understanding which he had initially brought to his professional role as a leader, but he was better able to explain his reasons to others and to check out his own motives for himself.

One key role for an early years professional in transforming both self and institution lies in exciting the enthusiasm of other practitioners, both within and beyond the team. McGregor (2003: 126) suggests that 'the role of leadership is ... in facilitating engagement, imagination and alignment'. Crompton (1997) suggests that community leadership requires commitment and Owen (2005) highlights his view that effective emerging leaders focus on three Ps – people, positivity and professionalism (which he suggests includes loyalty and reliability).

It is clear from this that becoming a professional is a *process*. Experience and reflections gradually lead the aspiring professional towards becoming what have been called mature or influential professionals (see Pound in press). According to Pound, the characteristics of these professionals are that they:

- have 'long experience in a range of roles and functions';
- 'hold composite, high level, professional leadership roles';
- 'strive for "professional insight, perspective and realism"'.

Gardner offers yet another stimulating perspective on the nature of professionalism. He differentiates between those who are members of professions and those who act professionally. He writes:

> Many individuals designated as professionals and dressed in expensive suits do not act in a professional manner; they cut corners, pursue their own interests, fail to honor the central precepts and strictures of their calling ... On the other hand, many individuals who are not so designated officially behave in an admirable, professional-like manner. They are skilled, responsible, engaged, themselves worthy of respect.
>
> (Gardner 2006: 129)

For Gardner, professionalism of this sort involves what he terms 'an abstract attitude – the capacity to reflect explicitly on the ways in which one does, or does not, fulfil a certain role' (2006: 130). Leaders in the early years have a responsibility to ensure that they develop this capacity not only in themselves but in those they lead, since their ultimate responsibility is towards society's youngest and most vulnerable members; the future of society itself.

Key points

- Early years practitioners, whether designated leaders or not, often undertake some similar tasks, although their roles and responsibilities in doing so will vary.
- Becoming a leader is a developmental process which develops through experience and reflection.
- Professionalism lies at the heart of becoming an effective practitioner and leader and this too is a process of development.
- Reflective practice supports the process of development and is a vital tool in self-examination.

Practical task

Begin keeping a reflective journal, initially for a week. It is probably better to use a book than sheets of paper which more easily get lost and muddled. Simply spend five minutes (or perhaps longer when you get into it) writing down what occurs to you about the day, and your role as leader. This is not for anyone else's eyes so you can let off steam, spell any way you like, cross out what you like and say what you like. The point is to earmark some time for thinking back over what has happened during the day. Could you have done anything differently? What other courses of action were open to you?

At the end of a week think about what you have gained from this process and consider whether it might be a useful practice to continue.

5 Leadership, policy development and welfare requirements

> Group providers will be expected to have written copies of any policies and procedures which are required, for example, to safeguard children or promote equality of opportunity. Providers should ensure that all members of staff have been given copies of these policies and procedures as part of their induction, and that they are explained to, and accessible to parents.
>
> (DfES 2007: 20)

Introduction

This chapter links policy development, leadership and meeting the welfare requirements as set out in the EYFS statutory guidance (DfES 2007), effective from September 2008. It focuses on written and unwritten, essential and desirable policies. It suggests that policy development should involve the whole team and be regarded as a complex and proactive, rather than a simple and reactive, process. The chapter begins by looking at the rationale for and importance of policy development, not least in order to meet statutory responsibilities. It contends that policies should be seen as playing a key role in promoting shared beliefs and values, should underpin day-to-day practice and be used as a baseline for everyday decisions. We then move on to discuss frameworks for writing policies and strategies for leaders to ensure policies are implemented by all the staff. We centre on policy development as a dynamic and interactive process between five Ps – philosophy, principles, purposes, procedures and practice. Throughout the chapter, we use extracts from sample policies including equality of opportunities, safeguarding children and health and safety, which are underpinned by new legal responsibilities, to illustrate the complexity of policy development and provide guidance on what policies need to cover. We look at how policies can be used on an ongoing basis as working documents and the reasons for reviewing them.

Finally, we draw attention to the obligations of employers in relation to documentation required by employment law.

Reasons for policy development

In the current climate of accountability it is sometimes difficult to see beyond the need to have policies, procedures and other documentation in readiness for your inspection. However, there are some more important and fundamental reasons for policy development other than having the appropriate piece of paper in the right file for Ofsted. It would be impossible to operate at all without any accepted ways of working or shared ideas, written or unwritten. For the purposes of this chapter, policy is a collectively agreed statement of beliefs and is informed or guided by philosophy and principles. It is a course of action recommended or adopted by an organization. It is policies that inform procedures. Procedures, in turn, inform practice, as a procedure, or way of doing something, is a written method or a course of action to be taken in particular circumstances.

Policies serve the dual purpose of underpinning practice while at the same time meeting legal requirements. While some policies are desirable in that they clarify aspects of practice which need to be shared with others, certain policies and procedures are essential in order to meet legal obligations. It is a specific legal requirement, for example, that 'Providers must have an effective behaviour management policy which is adhered to by all members of staff' (DfES 2007: 28). Implicit in this requirement is not only the existence of a written policy but also that the policy is known, understood and implemented in practice by all the team. It also implies that the practice is monitored in terms of effectiveness. As leader, not only are you responsible for making sure the policy is developed but also that your team has the knowledge, understanding and skills necessary for effective implementation.

> **Reflection point**
> Do all your team have a shared understanding of what is meant by effective behaviour management? Is there a clear policy on behaviour management? Are you aware that failure to implement aspects of the requirements for behaviour management is a criminal offence?

Similarly, there is a requirement to draw up a health and safety policy which includes procedures for identifying, reporting and dealing with accidents, hazards and faulty equipment. This needs to cover the health and safety of the premises, children and adults. You will need a named health and safety person, risk assessment documents and to find out about local and national requirements. Again, it is not sufficient to just have the policy in place; it is a leadership role to ensure all staff have an understanding of requirements, for example, by providing a manual, meetings and training opportunities.

The *National Standards for Under Eights Daycare and Childminding* (DfES 2001a) will be replaced from September 2008 by the EYFS *Statutory Framework*, setting the standards for the care, learning and development of children from birth to 5 (DfES 2007). The framework establishes two sets of requirements – the learning and development requirements which are discussed in Chapters 6 and 7 and the welfare requirements which provide a rationale for the essential policies discussed in this chapter.

Meeting the welfare requirements

You should already have policies and written procedures in place to meet the national standards. The introduction of the EYFS welfare requirements heralds the need to review, revise and update your policies to ensure you continue to meet your statutory duties. Although you should have most of the required policies in place, the emphasis has shifted towards not just having a policy but having legal and effective compliance. Both the general and specific legal requirements have the force of regulations and therefore must be adhered to by all early years providers. It is an offence to fail to comply with certain requirements. As a consequence, it is essential that as a leader you keep your knowledge up to date, otherwise you may unwittingly be breaking the law. Alternatives to the statutory guidance may justifiably be put in place providing the requirements are being met.

While childminders are not compelled to have written policies, they are required to have policies which are clearly articulated to parents and others on request. Schools are not legally obligated to have separate policies for the EYFS, providing that requirements are met through the policies for children above statutory school age. Nevertheless, there will be some areas of practice, specific to the Foundation Stage, such as settling in procedures, learning through play and the outdoor curriculum, where it would be helpful to establish separate policies and procedures. As stated earlier, you will need to review your policies and ensure, as a minimum, that clear policies and procedures are in place that cover the welfare requirements. The *Statutory Framework* divides the welfare requirements into five areas of policy and practice:

1   Safeguarding and promoting children's welfare.
2   Suitable people.
3   Suitable premises, environment and equipment.

4   Organization.
5   Documentation

Each of these areas is then subdivided into a set of general welfare requirements as follows.

Safeguarding and promoting children's welfare

- The provider must take necessary steps to safeguard and promote the welfare of children.
- The provider must promote the good health of the children, take necessary steps to prevent the spread of infection, and take appropriate action when they are ill.
- Children's behaviour must be managed effectively and in a manner appropriate for their stage of development and particular individual needs.

Suitable people

- Providers must ensure that adults looking after children, or having unsupervised access to them, are suitable to do so.
- Adults looking after children must have appropriate qualifications, training, skills and knowledge.
- Staffing arrangements must be organized to ensure safety and to meet the needs of the children.

Suitable premises, environment and equipment

- Outdoor and indoor spaces, furniture, equipment and toys must be safe and suitable for their purpose.

Organization

- Providers must plan and organize their systems to ensure that every child receives an enjoyable, challenging learning and development experience that is tailored to meet their individual needs.

Documentation

- Providers must maintain records, **policies and procedures** (author's emphasis) required for the safe and efficient management of the settings and to meet the needs of the children.

Each of these welfare requirements is then set out in three sections:

1 Overarching legal requirements.
2 Specific legal requirements.
3 Statutory guidance which providers must have regard to and take into account in their endeavours to meet the general and specific requirements.

All providers must meet the welfare requirements by having up to date policies and procedures, as indicated in Table 5.1.

Apart from those areas of practice underpinned by legal responsibilities, in the longer term it is ideal to have a policies in place clarifying those aspects of practice which need to be shared with others. These should be developed and reviewed to reflect the ethos, aims, objectives and best practice of the

Table 5.1   Relationship between policies required by the EYFS (DfES 2007) and *National Standards for Under Eight Daycare and Childminding* (DfES 2001a)

EYFS requirement	National standards	Policy/procedures required
Safeguarding and promoting children's welfare	St 13 Child protection St 12 Partnership St 2 Organization St 9 Equal Opportunities St 6 Safety St 4 Physical environment St 10 Special needs St 7 Health St 8 Food and drink St 11 Behaviour	Child protection Complaints procedure Missing child procedure Failure to collect child procedure Admissions policy Equality of opportunity (including SEN) Administration of medicines No smoking policy Behaviour management policy
Suitable people	St 1 Suitable person	
Suitable premises, environment and equipment	St 4 Physical environment St 5 Toys, resources and equipment St 3 Care, learning and play St 7 Health St 6 Safety	Health and Safety Policy
Organization	St 2 Organization	
Documentation	St 14 Documentation	

setting. As you continue to reflect on practice you may add carefully formulated new policies in the light of experience.

> **Reflection point**
> Which of the policies specified in Table 5.1 have you already in place? Are they up to date? Are they known and implemented effectively by all staff?

A prime purpose of policy development is to share information. There are specific legal requirements which stipulate that certain policies must be shared with parents – for example, safeguarding children, admissions, and procedures to be followed if a child goes missing, if a parent complains or if a child is not collected at the appointed time. As well as parents, policies may need to be shared with inspectors, advisory teachers, development workers or other professionals. They may also need to be communicated to management committees or school governors. A useful strategy is to write a policy summary leaflet for parents, or include a summary of the required policies in a parents' information pack, clearly stating that the the full version is available on request.

Another fundamental reason for developing policies which reflect shared values and beliefs is to ensure equality of opportunities. They can be used to provide clear guidance to be followed by all staff and volunteers, to ensure equality and fair treatment of adults, children and parents. The following extract from a policy on equality of opportunities demonstrates the point.

Triangle Nursery Equality of Opportunities Policy

The company actively promotes equality of opportunity and anti-discriminatory practice for all children. This means all children are treated with equal respect and valued regardless of difference. It does *not mean* all children are treated the same. Some children may need to be treated differently in order to be given equality of opportunity.

The nursery has one member of staff [name] responsible for equal opportunities who has attended relevant training and passed information on to the company and its employees.

The purposes of this policy are to:

- ensure equality of opportunity;
- ensure that disadvantaged groups receive the same opportunities as others;
- comply with the spirit, as well as the letter, of the law;
- ensure the consistency of equality;
- avoid unfair discrimination;
- provide machinery for challenging unfair treatment.

Clear procedures and policy statements also ensure consistency of practice among different staff. This is particularly important in larger centres, including children's centres, where not all staff are working together all or even most of the time. Policies and procedures should form an essential part of staff induction and on-the-job training. Key policies such as health and safety, fire procedures and safeguarding children should be explained *before* new staff start work.

Policies provide a tool which can be used for training, monitoring and evaluating practice. Edgington (2004) suggests that teams could be prepared for developing certain policies by researching the relevant aspect of practice. You could provide the team with articles or chapters from books to read, or you could ask staff to attend training in the policy area. Visits to other settings could also prove a valuable source of ideas. The more knowledgeable the team is, the more effective the policy is likely to be. Well structured policies can provide clear success criteria to assess the effectiveness of your aims and objectives. Edgington suggests several ways in which policies can be used as a monitoring tool. First, you or your staff could select a policy or an idea within a policy and gather evidence to show the extent to which it is being implemented. Parents and children can also be consulted on how a policy is working in practice. Parents' views can be invaluable in monitoring the effectiveness of your settling-in procedures. Children can comment, for example, on resources and the environment. Second, you could discuss a policy at a team meeting and highlight those aspects which are being done well and those where there is room for improvement. Third, as well as the welfare requirements, you could use policies as a focus for leading, monitoring and evaluating the curriculum. Policies can be instrumental in informing the development of curriculum planning, assessment and the organization of the environment, a point developed in the next two chapters.

Policies provide necessary protection for the employer, for staff and for children. Children's safety, welfare and rights are protected by clear procedures and policies. Procedures offer parents the security of knowing what will happen in a certain situation, for example, if their child is ill. In the case of a complaint or a child protection issue, for example, staff decisions can be supported if they are based on a given procedure. An employer can turn to policies to help implement disciplinary or responding to grievance procedures.

According to Edgington (2004) policies should help teams to:

- clarify their beliefs, aims, objectives and vision for all aspects of their practice;
- develop shared understanding and expectations and therefore work more consistently;
- ensure that all children and parents have equal access to high quality experiences;

- communicate philosophy and practice to others;
- monitor and evaluate their practice using agreed criteria.

A professional approach to practice through policies and procedures not only helps to raise the status of your setting and the early years sector, but inevitably impacts upon the quality of the provision. Having examined why policies are important the next part of this chapter moves on to suggest how they can be developed, formulated and articulated.

From philosophy to practice – the five Ps

A critical success factor in policy development is the involvement of the whole team from the outset. If policies are to reflect shared values and beliefs about practice and in practice, they cannot simply be written and imposed. Neither can they be bought or adopted 'off the shelf', although it may be useful to look at other policies for information. In some settings staff may be totally unaware of the existence of any policies because they are not used as working documents to underpin practice. Policies may have been filed and subsequently ignored or sometimes the manager and the deputy may look at them but other staff, including students or assistants, are left out of the loop. It is essential that those who are going to be implementing the policy are involved in developing it, even if only for the first draft. In larger teams you could divide staff into sub-groups and set tasks. Even if it is not possible to meet you can use other methods to consult staff, such as informal discussion or an anonymous questionnaire. Although time consuming and somewhat daunting, this process should not be rushed and will pay dividends in the long term, as without any ownership the staff will be reluctant to even read or implement the policy. Although everyone does not need to know every detail of every policy they do all need to be aware of the policies. Again a useful strategy is to provide a policy summary leaflet for every member of staff and have a full policy folder available as a reference point.

The process of policy development can be thought of as five interactive Ps:

- Philosophy
- Principles
- Purposes
- Procedures
- Practice

The setting's *philosophy* or shared values and beliefs need to underpin any written or unwritten policy. Therefore a consensus view needs to be reached at the initial stages of the policy development process. Once the philosophy has been established, key *principles* can be developed. These will inform the *purposes* or objectives of the policy. Concrete guidance or *procedures* as to what the policy will look like in *practice* can then be added to provide the final piece of the puzzle.

> **Reflection point**
> How would you summarize your setting's philosophy on safeguarding children? Would all staff cite a similar view? Can you identify two or three key principles relating to safeguarding children and promoting their welfare? How are they reflected in policy and enacted in practice?

Policy content will be contextualized but firmly grounded in research, national expectations and law. Translating policies and procedures into practice cannot be left to compromise. There need to be clear systems in place to ensure all staff fulfil their obligations and to prevent serious deviation, especially from the statutory policies but also from other important aspects of practice. In order to ensure final drafts of policies are read, understood and used by staff, you could create a policy checklist which staff should sign as part of their induction to confirm they have read the policy. You would need to create a similar system in relation to revised, updated or new policies and procedures. You could also include a clause in the contract of employment stating that the employee agrees to follow the setting's policies and procedures. Alternatively, staff could sign a slip to say something like, 'I have read, understood and agree to implement the policies in the nursery policy folder'. You could include a statement on the front cover, particularly of statutory policies, that failure to implement this policy could lead to disciplinary action. The more times and places the existence and importance of policies are emphasized verbally and in writing, formally and informally, the more staff will see that they are not just there to be filed. Rather, they are statements of principle and documents which are intended to translate into, and be evident in, practice. Linda, a nursery manager, has a job description which makes this clear, stating that: 'The nursery manager needs to ensure that all staff work together in accordance with company policies, which in turn comply with national requirements.' The following job description extract also shows how the importance of a policy to practice can be highlighted in role descriptions. The assistant should:

- have high expectations of all children and be committed to inclusive practice; promote equality of opportunity in accordance with the equality of opportunity policy;

- support the management in providing balanced and flexible daily routines indoors and outdoors, which meet individual children's diverse needs in accordance with the planning and assessment policy;
- support, inform, respect and involve parents formally and informally in their child's care, well-being, development and learning both at home and in the setting; and support the management in implementing the parent partnership policy;
- undertake first aid training, know and comply with the company's health and safety policy and procedures.

Clear guidance should be available as to consequences of deviation either through follow-up training and support or disciplinary action.

CASE STUDY

The preschool group policy on outings clearly stated that the adult:child ratio for travelling on public transport was 1:3 and at least two qualified, vetted members of staff should be present at all times. Sue, the manager, asked Julie, the deputy, to take 12 children on a bus trip to the travel agent with two parent helpers. Julie knew this was contrary to policy and refused to go so the manager went instead.

This scenario is interesting in that the manager was determined to deviate from the policy even though the deputy had pointed out this would be the case. This caused conflict between the manager and her deputy, risked the safety of the children and contravened the policy which she had signed to say she would implement. Depending on the context this could have resulted in a verbal warning for the manager.

Similarly, if a nursery food and drink policy states that children should be given healthy choices and sugar-free drinks, a parent (aware of the policy) could complain if staff gave her child orange squash. The manager could only apologize to the parent and reiterate the policy and then use the policy itself to identify to staff that practice has been contrary to the policy. The manager could point out to staff that any further incidents which do not reflect policy may result in formal consequences.

The skill in writing policies is to be succinct while still communicating the main points. They should not be over lengthy or contain jargon, although some will by necessity be longer and more complex than others. A 'no smoking' policy, for example, is relatively straightforward. It will explain how you ensure that children are in a smoke-free environment. It will state that no one smokes in outside areas when children are present or about to be present. By contrast, an equality of opportunities policy will require far more thought and preparation. It will be longer and may need to be divided into clear sections. Some complex and possibly contentious issues will need discussing at the preparatory stage. What do your staff understand by the term 'equality of opportunity'? Are there established shared values and beliefs about 'inclusive practices'? What will the policy look like in practice?

In terms of welfare requirements, the statutory guidance can be used to set out the basic content, but should be contextualized to reflect your setting. The specific legal requirement is that all providers 'must have and implement an effective policy about ensuring equality of opportunities and for supporting children with learning difficulties and disabilities' (DfES 2007: 25). Providers in receipt of government funding must have regard to the SEN *Code of Practice* (DfES 2001b). The *Statutory Framework* (DfES 2007: 25) clearly defines the parameters. The policy on equality of opportunities should include:

- information about how the individual needs of all children will be met;
- information about how all children, including those who are disabled or have SEN, will be included, valued and supported, and how reasonable adjustments will be made for them;
- a commitment to working with parents and other agencies;
- information about how the SEN *Code of Practice* is put into practice in the provision (where appropriate);
- the name of the SEN co-ordinator (in group provision);
- arrangements for reviewing, monitoring and evaluating the effectiveness of inclusive practices;
- information about how the provision will promote and value diversity and differences;
- information about how inappropriate attitudes and practices will be challenged;
- information about how the provision will encourage children to value and respect others.

Reflection point
Look at your setting's equality of opportunities policy. Does it contain all the above information?

As part of the requirement to safeguard children and promote their welfare, providers must keep a statement of the arrangements in place for the protection of each child. Safeguarding and promoting the welfare of children is defined for the purpose of statutory guidance under the Children Acts 1989 and 2004 as:

- protecting children from maltreatment;
- preventing impairment of children's health or development;
- ensuring children are growing up in circumstances consistent with the provision of safe and effective care 'and undertaking that role so as to enable those children to have optimum life chances and to enter adulthood successfully' (HM Government 2006a: 34).

All staff need to be clear about the arrangements to safeguard children from abuse or neglect and the procedures to be followed in the event of allegations of abuse or neglect. The written statement should be based on the procedures laid out in *What to do if You're Worried a Child is Being Abused* (HM Government 2006b). It should include the following elements:

- your commitment to the protection of children;
- the responsibilities of all staff with regard to child protection matters;
- the steps to be taken when a concern is raised;
- the name of the designated person responsible for child protection liaison and their role/responsibilities;
- how and under what circumstances parents will be informed about any actions taken and how confidentiality will be managed;
- procedures to be followed in the event of an allegation being made against a member of staff or volunteer;
- arrangements for sharing these procedures with parents before their child starts attending the setting.

Polices for safeguarding children should also be in line with your Local Safeguarding Children Board (LSCB) guidance and procedures.

Setting managers can unite their team though policy development. It is the process of writing about practice which enables the team to understand it and communicate it to others. The process of being involved gives power to team members and working towards consensus is crucial if policy is to be consistently understood and enacted. Diversity in qualifications and experience may lead to differing views, and these need to be negotiated. You may have to persuade staff to accept that policy reflects a shared view, which sometimes has to override an individual view. For example, some staff may believe it does no harm for children to have sweets in lunchboxes, whereas the setting's healthy eating policy asks parents not to send sweets in lunchboxes unless it is a child's birthday. Clearly written policies will reduce the possibility of conflict.

Framework for writing policies

We now move on to explore and extend a framework for writing policies offered by Edgington (2004: 45). This useful model suggests policies should be written in three sections, each of which informs the others. These are:

1   Rationale.
2   Purposes.
3   Broad guidelines.

The rationale should inform what is included in the purposes and the guidelines should show how each purpose is being or can be achieved. Edgington points out the distinction between the policy and a set of more detailed guidelines. The policy can be regarded as a public document whereas the detailed guidelines are mainly of interest to those working with the children on a regular basis. You may have a policy which sets out briefly the approach to be taken when going on outings, with appendices detailing the actual procedures to be followed by staff when preparing for and going on an outing. The policy might state that children are taken for walks on a weekly basis and a trip using public transport is organized annually. The procedures would include all the fine detail as to how the actual outing will be conducted, such as ratios, visiting the venue beforehand to conduct a risk assessment, taking a mobile phone and taking children's registration forms. Relevant documentation should also be provided as appendices to the main policies. Hence, with the outings and medicine policy you would have the relevant parental consent form, with the health and safety policy you would have risk assessment pro formas.

The first section, **rationale**, sets out briefly the setting's beliefs in relation to the policy theme. It sets the tone for the rest of the policy and answers the 'why' questions. For example, why do we need to take care when children are collected from the premises? Why do we need to be inclusive in our equality of opportunities policy? Why do we need to safeguard children from harm or neglect? Why do we need to manage children's behaviour effectively? Why do we hold these beliefs? This first section only need provide a brief summary of principles and could include a well chosen quote. You could draw on principles underpinning early childhood care, learning and development, including those stated in national guidance. The following extract from an inclusion policy makes the rationale clear:

> Little Monkeys aims to include children with disabilities and or SEN wherever possible. We have regard to the fundamental principles in the DfES *Code of Practice*, (2001b) and related legislation. We work

closely with parents and other agencies to ensure children's individual needs are identified and met within a caring inclusive environment. Little Monkeys recognizes the right of all children to be equally valued and to participate fully in the life of the nursery and the before or after school clubs with appropriate support. We adopt a whole setting approach which recognizes that *all staff* are responsible for meeting the needs of *all children* including children with SEN.

This first section is probably the most difficult to write, as it needs to make clear the agreed philosophy of the setting in relation to the policy theme. Again, this extract from a policy on working with parents clearly states this setting's values and beliefs:

At Tender Years we work together with parents* at every opportunity. We believe that 'THERE IS NO SUBSTITUTE FOR THE PERSONAL TOUCH'. The relationship with parents should be one of mutual trust and respect. Parents should be provided with information and support. Their views and information about their child should be asked for, welcomed and taken into account. Communication with parents is at the heart of our successful partnership with parents. Although all staff will know all parents and children, each child should have a key worker who knows a particular group of children well and provides a point of contact for the parent. Parents should be told who their child's key worker is and key workers should exchange information with the parents.

*For 'parent' please take this to include parent/carer/grandparent or whoever is the child's main carer or carers.

Once the rationale is agreed, work needs to be done to develop a set of achievable objectives which reflect the underlying principles of the policy. The second section, **purposes,** could contain a clear statement or bullet-point list of what the setting hopes to achieve in the area of practice. This is the section which could be used as success criteria when monitoring and evaluating the effectiveness of the policy. It answers the 'what' questions by stating what the setting wants to achieve in relation to the policy themes. The list below clarifies a setting's objectives in relation to SEN and inclusion.

Our objectives are:

- To successfully implement the principles, procedures and practices recommended in the SEN *Code of Practice.*
- To remove barriers to admission and achievement and

ensure maximum participation and equality of opportunity for all children.

- To guide, inform and support all staff and parents on issues relating to children's individual needs.
- To ensure implementation of local guidelines on SEN and inclusion.
- To meet the needs of all children identified as having SEN, ensuring progress, confidence and increased independence in learning and development.
- To promote positive images of difference and encourage all children to feel they belong.
- To keep accurate records on all children's progress maintaining confidentiality at all times.

Third, the **broad guidelines,** can then address the 'how' questions. In other words, state what is being done or intended to be done to achieve the purposes. The 'food and drink' policy extract below sets out guidelines for various elements of the policy, such as the provision of water, snacks and the procedure to be followed if a child has an allergy.

Water – fresh drinking water is available to children at all times through:

a) water fountain or container with tap and plastic cups; or
b) a plastic jug of water (with lid) and cups on a tray accessible to children; or
c) offering regular drinks to children throughout the day.

Drinks and snacks – drinks and snacks are available at least once per session. Children are provided with milk (unless allergic) or water. On occasion children may be offered alternatives, such as milk shake or soup, but these should be 'special' rather than routine. Children who are allergic to milk, nuts or colourings, or who have any other allergies should *only drink liquids or eat food provided by the parent in a named container.*

If you are unsure always phone the parent before giving a child food or drink not provided by the parent.

Squashes will *not* be offered.

Children should be offered a *healthy* snack once per session. They should choose from two alternatives, for example: apple, banana or grapes (or other fruits and vegetables), carrot sticks or raisins, dried soft fruits, bread sticks, low fat crackers with low fat spread, plain low sugar biscuit, food from other cultures, wholemeal toast plain or with healthy topping.

Allergies and special dietary requirements

- Talk to the parent on initial visit about allergies or other dietary requirements and ensure they are recorded on the registration form.
- Display a list of children and their food allergies on a *coloured* sheet of paper in the kitchen and *draw it to the attention of ALL STAFF and helpers.*
- In the case of peanut allergy please inform the office and ensure you are trained and have consent to administer treatment before the child starts.

As mentioned earlier, it is important not to try to include every detail in the policy, but to separate the policy or public information from elements which are relevant mainly or solely to staff, in other words procedures, detailed guidelines and associated documentation. You could also keep policies for staff, such as the staff holiday policy, or dress code, in a separate staff handbook.

Reflection point
Think about each of your written policies. Are they brief and clear? Can you edit them? Can you separate the rationale, purposes, broad guidelines and detailed guidelines?

Policies are not static but constantly evolving and will need reviewing and updating. It is useful to set a timetable for review and insert the next review date at the end of each policy, leaving the previous review dates to record the frequency of reviews. Once the initial policy is formulated, reviewing and revising is not so onerous a task. How often you review policies will depend on the circumstances. A new policy could be reviewed 6 or 12 months after introduction. A long established policy could be reviewed every two to three years. You will need to review in response to national and local changes, including new legislation – for example, on disability, or data protection and statutory guidance. You may need to update in the light of a specific experience, a parental concern or as a result of monitoring observation of practice.

CASE STUDY

Justine, a nursery manager, received a complaint from a parent that children watched too much television. Although there was an unwritten policy that children in full day care could watch a maximum of 20 minutes a day, it was usually at the end of the day. When the parent came to collect his child, it looked as though all they did was watch television. The policy was changed so that sometimes children watched the television after lunch and some days not at all. The routine was revised and explained in full to parents who were reminded of the variety of activities during the rest of the day. The routine was written down and sent to all parents.

Alternatively, you may revise or add in certain elements to a policy as a result of advice from local support services or a recommendation from Ofsted. In one setting Ofsted recommended revision of the key worker system and the policy was subsequently changed. Changes in the physical environment such as a new sensory garden or an extension, changes of staff or in the nature of your intake may also necessitate some reworking of a policy. It is important to check that there is consistency between policies and cross-reference where appropriate. As well as having policies to meet national requirements in relation to children's care, learning and development, if you employ staff you will need to develop additional documentation relating to your employees and volunteers.

Employment law

Employment law is a rapidly changing field and we recommend that you take legal advice or advice from a professional association. Areas of employment law include:

- recruitment;
- contracts of employment;
- family rights;
- sickness benefits;
- discrimination;
- termination of employment.

In the area of age discrimination, for example, the first Employment Equality (Age) regulations came into force on 1 October 2006, representing a major change in employment law. There is a reverse burden of proof in that it is up to the employer to prove that they chose the person for the job on merit. The key for every employer is to record the recruitment decision-making process. Breaches could result in heavy financial penalties and ignorance is not acceptable as an excuse. You also need to be aware of the various types of age discrimination such as:

- *Direct discrimination* – where a decision is made because of a person's age or perceived age. It is irrelevant whether the discrimination is intentional or unintentional. For example, if you overlook a promotion opportunity for a person aged 57 because she will be retiring soon this would be direct discrimination.
- *Indirect discrimination* – where an employer applies provision which disadvantages a certain group of people on account of their age. For example, asking for six years' experience, which indirectly discriminates against younger people.
- *Harassment* – unwanted conduct which violates a person's dignity or creates an intimidating, hostile or offensive environment.

Age discrimination can sometimes be lawful if a person's age relates to a genuine occupational requirement. You must be 18, for instance, to work in a bar, or you must be over 17 to be counted in day nursery staffing ratios. It is important to review your recruitment and selection procedures, and documentation (including job advertisements) to ensure they are compliant with new regulations.

Reflection point
Are you an employer? Have you attended any employment law training? Are you confident you are not discriminatory in terms of sex, race, disability, sexual orientation, religion and age? Can you prove this to be the case? Are you an employee? Have you been informed of your rights?

Key points

- Policy development should involve all practitioners, and take account of parents' and children's views.
- Policies may be written, unwritten, legally required or optional.
- Policies need to reflect the setting's ethos and lead to effective practice.
- Leaders need to ensure policies are implemented and reviewed.

- Policies need to be in place to fulfil statutory obligations as a provider and employer (if applicable).

Practical tasks

1 Check through your policy folder. Draw up an action plan for developing, reviewing or revising the required policies in Table 5.1.
2 Hold a staff meeting. Explain the welfare requirements to staff. Ask staff to identify any issues which need addressing in relation to meeting the welfare requirements. Plan any changes that need to be made.
3 Give each member of staff an area of the welfare requirements to look at and think about in detail. Ask them to prepare a short statement about their focus area to the rest of the staff at the next meeting.
4 At a staff meeting ask groups of staff to work on sections of a policy. One pair or group could work on the rationale, another on the purposes and another on the broad guidelines. Put the sections together to form a first draft.

6 Perspectives on leading and assessing the curriculum

... an educational system is not worthy of its name unless its representatives can clearly articulate what that system is striving to achieve and what it seeks to avoid or curtail.

(Gardner 2006: 166)

Introduction

An important aspect of becoming a leader is learning to make clear to others – parents, staff, politicians, as well as other professionals – why you do what you do. In relation to pedagogy, the work you do with children, this is not always straightforward. This is in part because working with young children can look like intellectually undemanding work – anyone can play with children can't they? Work with young children is often regarded as having low status and this leads practitioners to undervalue what they do. It may also mean that when parents challenge practice or other professionals request particular strategies, practitioners often feel unable to determine the best course of action as they are not in the habit of articulating the reasons for the decisions they have made about effective practice.

In this chapter we will consider views on what a curriculum actually is and links between curriculum and pedagogy. The role that you and your staff team take, both in the development of the curriculum and in explaining it to parents and others, will be explored. As the quote above suggests, there will be an emphasis on reflective practice, and the need for practitioners and leaders to be able to identify and tell others about what is important and why. We will also examine the importance of ensuring that the curriculum is fully meshed with the needs and enthusiasms of the children with whom you work. We begin with an overview of understandings of what a curriculum is to encourage you to reflect on the curriculum that you offer, its rationale and how it supports the values your setting holds. The chapter goes on to consider a range of approaches to assessment and concludes by beginning to look at the role of the leader in supporting and developing the curriculum and assessment.

What do we mean by a curriculum?

There are many views on what a curriculum is. *The Rumbold Report* (DES 1990: 9) stated that:

> The curriculum – which we take to comprise the concepts, knowledge, understanding, attitudes and skills that a child needs to develop – can be defined and expressed in a number of different ways. These varying approaches include frameworks based on subjects, resource areas, broad themes or areas of learning.

A curriculum is often presented more simply as 'a definition of what is to be learned' (Ross 2001: 122). This may be interpreted in a variety of ways. The curriculum may, for example, be defined in terms of areas of provision. Many practitioners, for example, plan for activities and experiences within the role-play area, the cooking area, sand or water trays or more generally outdoors. While this form of planning supports organization – making it clear to the whole staff team what should happen where and when – it may lead practitioners (as well as parents and possibly even children) to think that mathematical learning, for example, is only planned for and happening in the maths resource area.

When working with other agencies, defining the curriculum in terms of areas of development may be preferred. Aspects of physical or linguistic development, for example, are commonly reported on but may be given a different emphasis by professionals with different experience and training. Many early childhood settings plan around broad themes – perhaps based on interesting or topical events or celebrations.

Schema form the basis of planning in many settings (Athey 2007). In each setting taking this approach to the curriculum, plans are made for individuals on the basis of their preferred ways of exploring space. Practitioners seek to identify through observation children who like to transport materials, or who are interested in, for example, trajectories or enveloping. They then seek to ensure that the available resources and experiences cater for children's preferred mode of activity.

Most commonly among those working with children over 3, practitioners within the Foundation Stage in England have been encouraged to define 'curriculum' as subject areas or areas of learning. The EYFS (DfES 2007) is set out in terms of areas of learning and development. These relate to children from birth and are linked to, but are not the same as, subject areas. The six areas of learning and development defined in the EYFS have clear connections with the subjects of the National Curriculum.

> **Reflection point**
> Take some time to reflect on the possible impact of the *Statutory Framework* (DfES 2007) on the lives of young children. A major rationale for the shift from two separate curriculum documents (*Birth to Three Matters* – DfES 2002a – and *Curriculum Guidance for the Foundation Stage* – QCA/DfES 2000) to a single EYFS document has been that it will offer children increased continuity in learning and development. Critics claim that the areas of learning and development offer a top-down model of the curriculum and that there is a danger of overlooking the needs of the youngest children. They would have preferred a curriculum which took as its starting point the needs of babies and toddlers. What do you think?

In England, the curriculum is defined by the EYFS. Communication, language and literacy (CLL), and problem-solving, reasoning and numeracy (PSRN; previously known as mathematical development) are directly linked to English (or literacy) and mathematics (or numeracy). Knowledge and understanding of the world subsumes design technology, information technology, science, history and geography. Creative development involves art and music – but also addresses other forms of creative media such as play and drama – which are not explicit parts of the National Curriculum. It also explores creativity which is, of course, not confined to creative media. Mathematicians and scientists are also creative. The EYFS underlines the way in which creativity underpins all learning. Physical development is linked to physical education but entails wider consideration of physical learning and development. Within the National Curriculum, both citizenship and personal, social, health and emotional education are not designated subjects, but the non-statutory guidance for both subjects offers continuity with the EYFS.

This way of organizing what should be learnt is not without critics. There is a danger that practitioners can assume that goals or learning intentions become a sort of syllabus, leading them to teach what is written rather than in ways that mesh with learning. The fact that we want children to be numerate does not mean that we must spend hour after hour teaching numbers. On the contrary, learning to count will involve much more than being taught – relevance and motivation, context and understanding must all be addressed.

Reflection point
In Scotland, within the Foundation Stage, mathematics is not a separate area of learning but is included in knowledge and understanding of the world. What advantages or disadvantages does this have? What are the implications of linking mathematics or numeracy to the development of the youngest children?

However, the outcomes required of all educators in relation to *Every Child Matters* (DfES 2003) demand a sharpened understanding of the need to go beyond subject-based knowledge and learning. The five outcomes required in *Every Child Matters* relate to healthy lifestyles, feeling safe, enjoyment and achievement in education, making a positive contribution to the community and preparing for future economic well-being. At first sight, you may feel that only the item relating to enjoyment and achievement is relevant in evaluating or assessing provision. However, given the wider view of the curriculum, adopted in these chapters, it becomes clear that all five aspects are relevant. In simple terms, health, safety and social awareness are all part of children's personal and social education. Future economic well-being is related to academic achievement but also to children's disposition for learning. The evidence that you seek in relation to your self-evaluation, described in Chapter 10, should demonstrate awareness of the links between curriculum provision and the five required outcomes of *Every Child Matters*.

Intended and unintended curricula

Mary Jane Drummond's view of curriculum (Drummond *et al.* 1989: 26) reflects this wider perspective. Her definition includes:

> the whole set of experiences from which children can learn, which we provide consciously – and unconsciously – in a whole variety of settings. The curriculum for young children includes:
>
> - all the activities and experiences provided for them by adults;
> - all the activities they devise for themselves;
> - the language that adults use to them and that they use to each other;
> - all that they see and hear in the environment around them.

This highlights the fact that young children are learning much that practitioners are often unaware that they are teaching (and that children may disregard things which educators believe they are offering). Much has been written about the 'hidden curriculum'. Since very young children are actively seeking to understand the culture within which they are living and growing, they are highly susceptible to the messages unconsciously communicated to them. Many aspects of practice, which practitioners may not readily associate with the curriculum, inform and shape children's learning. If, for example, practitioners leave the role-play area in a mess, with dirty dressing-up clothes and torn bedding, children pick up the message that imaginative play is of little value. If your team spends the great majority of time in the writing or drawing area, then children will perceive these as your priorities. These aspects of the hidden curriculum are generally unintended. Practitioners do not usually knowingly want to convey such messages.

Reflection point
What do you consider to be the curriculum in your setting? Which aspects are explicit? Which, do you think, are hidden or less apparent? Would your staff team agree with your view?

The current debate about the quality of school meals, for example, highlights an aspect of the hidden curriculum – which can be described as moving from an unintentional to an intentional part of what society wants children to learn, or the curriculum. If healthy, nourishing meals are served in relaxed and aesthetic surroundings, children learn not only about the importance of food but also about how they themselves are valued. Everything that practitioners do with children communicates to them what the adults around them think is important – what is of value and what is not. An American writer, Hurless (2004), writes incredulously of her experience accompanying a French preschool group to a farm. She recalls that promptly at 1 o'clock: 'A four-course meal is served, with breaks between courses. The three-year-olds proceed through courses of sliced tomatoes in vinaigrette dressing, Salisbury steak in mushroom sauce, and then are delighted when the chocolate mousse appears.'

A wide range of research (see e.g. Siegel 1999; Hobson 2002) has highlighted the fact that children's learning is modified and moderated by the adults around them. Babies and toddlers look to adults and older children who are important in their lives in order to know what to think about what they see, hear, taste and feel. They learn about themselves: whether they are valued and therefore valuable, loved and therefore loveable; whether they are noticed and cherished and therefore of worth or not. They also notice adults' responses to others – they see how we respond to a disabled adult, or an old person who is walking too slowly in the shopping aisle, or people who cannot communicate in English, or whose skin colour or dress is not that of the majority group. While these influences are not part of the intended curriculum, they are part of what is learnt: the unintended curriculum.

Unwritten curricula

The move towards written curricula or frameworks can lead us to overlook the fact that some effective programmes or approaches do not have written guidelines. The value of preschool provision in Reggio Emilia, for example, is internationally recognized but there are few written guidelines. The special emphasis of the approach in Reggio Emilia lies in the fact that the staff team of every setting includes a visual artist and the basis of the curriculum is symbolic representation. Despite the absence of a written curriculum there is a set of principles (see www.sightlines-initiative.com/index.php?id=15) which guide all decisions about support for children's learning. In addition to these principles, it has been suggested by Carla Rinaldi (2001: 53) that in Reggio Emilia:

> For us, the three subjects of education are the children, the teachers, and the families. These three subjects are in relationship with each other and are an interconnected system. This means that everything that happens to one affects the others. You cannot have a school in which the child doesn't feel right, in which the teacher doesn't feel right, in which the parent doesn't feel right. It is essential to create a school and infant-toddler center in which all the subjects feel welcomed, a place of relationships. Education is something that you try to create everyday.

A curriculum for babies?

Those who work with babies and toddlers often deny that they have a curriculum. This is largely because, as a society, curriculum is often regarded as synonymous with syllabus. What babies and toddlers learn is both biologically and culturally determined. Whatever the culture in which they grow up, babies and toddlers are undertaking biologically-determined learning – for example, learning to walk and to talk. This learning is a part of development – we can support it or impede it, but given most normal circumstances, walking and talking will be learnt in a fairly predictable order and at a reasonably predictable age.

But these are not the only things that babies and toddlers are learning. Like older children (and adults), they are also subject to the hidden curriculum, both intended and unintended. They are absorbing the important aspects of the culture in which they grow up. These are not taught formally but absorbed within the core of the brain (the amygdala) as emotional experience. The early stage in life at which this happens means that children are unlikely to be able to recall the experience in later life. They will not be able to easily eradicate or modify the learning because it is not readily open to language or reason (Siegel 1999; Gerhardt 2004). The aspects of culture that are learnt are not so much selected as absorbed. This means that there are specific difficulties in defining what babies and toddlers should learn.

As Ross (2001: 122) reminds us, 'everyone believes that they know what other people should learn'. At no age is this clearer than in early infancy where society in general believes that it knows precisely what babies and toddlers should learn. DeLoache and Gottlieb (2000: 5) remind us that: 'Every group thinks that its way of caring for infants is the obvious, correct, natural way – a simple matter of common sense. However ... what we easily call "common sense" is anything but common. Indeed, what people accept as common sense may be considered odd, exotic, or even barbaric in another'. This is illustrated in Barbara Rogoff's book *Apprenticeship in Thinking* (1990). Rogoff includes a photograph of an 11-month-old baby from Zaire cutting fruit with a machete. To the eyes of those of us from the minority world this appears shocking, but as Rogoff observes, 'this is not an unusual situation in this culture where infants are generally able to observe and participate in skilled cultural activities' (1990: 131). It is also echoed in Bruner's comment (in the foreword to DeLoache and Gottlieb 2000: x) that 'there may indeed be "universals" in childrearing – like keeping a baby out of harm's way – but these universals are subject to such culturally local expression that one needs to look at them almost like art forms, religious beliefs, or mythic representations'.

So knowing what babies should learn is not as straightforward as it may at first appear. The decisions we take about their learning are often largely invisible to us. We may not, for example, notice that we may be treating boys and girls differently, that baby girls are held for longer or that boys who are learning to walk are given more encouragement to go further afield. Children (including babies), however, *do* notice, often at an entirely subconscious level. Cathy Nutbrown (2001: 134) reminds us that 'children have an awesome capacity to observe in fine detail and they learn from what they see'.

Moreover, the decisions we take about children's learning have long-term consequences which we do not readily link to pedagogical decisions taken when children are in their infancy. In *Why Love Matters* (2004), Sue Gerhardt offers strong evidence, based on psychotherapeutic knowledge and neuroscientific research, about the long-term impact of curricular decisions. Gerhardt underlines the lifelong impact of the strategies that babies nurtured in what they perceive to be dangerous and unpredictable surroundings adapt in order to survive comfortably. These conditions do not need to be dangerous in adult terms – they merely need to be distressing, inconsistent or unresponsive for the child to adopt coping strategies. This in turn affects the development of the brain, which means that in later childhood and in adulthood an individual may lack the resilience needed to cope emotionally and socially in their everyday lives. By that stage in life, it may be too late to make up the ground lost. Moreover, as we now know, this will have consequences for both cognitive development (see e.g. Goleman 1996) and physical development and well-being (Martin 1998).

For these and other similar reasons, practitioners, parents and politicians have often been reluctant to define a curriculum for such young children. In *KeyTimes*, Manning-Morton and Thorp (2001) entitle their document a 'framework for developing high quality provision for children under three'. *Birth to Three Matters* (which was published by DfES Sure Start 2002a) was similarly described as a framework to support children in their earliest years. EYFS (DfES 2007) has taken the starting point of the *Curriculum Guidance for the Foundation Stage* (QCA/DfES 2000) and created a framework for the learning and development of children from birth. The new guidance links the four themes of:

1   The child as a unique and competent learner.
2   The importance of positive, secure and loving relationships.
3   The role of the environment in enabling, supporting and extending learning and development.
4   The six areas of learning and development.

Reflection point

Recognizing the contribution of children themselves, adults, peers and the environment to what is to be learnt is potentially very powerful in supporting the strong development and general well-being of children. To what extent does the centrality of the needs of the child together with the importance of relationships and environment inform the curriculum in your setting? Do children really come first in your setting? In what ways does the staff team work to develop strong relationships with children and families, and among themselves as a team? Is the environment exciting and stimulating and considered as integral to every child's learning and development?

Pedagogy

Until recently, the term *pedagogy* was relatively unknown in this country. It is however widely used today, perhaps because of the impact of research projects such as SPEEL (or the *Study of Pedagogical Effectiveness in Early Learning*) (Moyles *et al.* 2002) and REPEY (or *Researching Effective Pedagogy in the Early Years*) (Siraj-Blatchford *et al.* 2002). Both projects were funded by the Department for Education and Skills (DfES). The term 'pedagogy' encompasses not only what is or should be learnt (or the intended or planned curriculum) but consideration of how it should be learnt. Collins *et al.* (2001: 2) admit that the term has not been widely used in English but suggest that pedagogy includes:

- consideration of the effectiveness of educational practice;
- knowledge to help professionals with the difficulties arising from childrearing;
- appropriate and inappropriate approaches to learning;
- appropriate ways of teaching and supporting children.

Siraj-Blatchford *et al.* (2002: 28) give the following definition:

> *Pedagogy* refers to that set of instructional techniques and strategies which enable learning to take place and provide opportunities for the acquisition of knowledge, skills, attitudes and dispositions within a particular social and material context. It refers to the interactive process between teacher and learner and to the learning environment (which includes the concrete learning environment, the family and community).

Peter Moss has been particularly influential in promoting the use of the term 'pedagogy'. He identifies it as capturing the holistic nature of young children's development. He refers to the 'inseparable trinity of learning, care and upbringing' (2004: 4).

The New Zealand early years curriculum document, *Te Whariki* (Ministry of Education 1996), comments on these aspects of the curriculum and suggests that the distinctive nature of the curriculum for each setting is maintained by differences in:

- cultural perspectives (e.g. language groups, religious groups, etc.);
- structural differences (e.g. full- or part-time provision, extended hours, etc.);
- organizational differences (e.g. nursery school, day nursery, playgroup, etc.);

- different environments (e.g. home-based; centre-based);
- philosophical priorities (e.g. Montessori; High/Scope; Steiner, etc.);
- different resources which are available in urban and rural settings;
- the involvement of the community;
- special emphases, such as music, art, story or outdoor provision;
- the contexts and resources provided by the programme (e.g. forest schools, Montessori materials);
- the age range of the children included in the programme (the continuity of philosophy – Rinaldi 2001: 66 – includes 'a strong image of the child that cannot be fragmented in age levels but has a long range view and is capable of welcoming each child's differences and variety of experience and culture').

Te Whariki specifies that practitioners should include experiences which are:

- *Humanly appropriate – relating to equity and respect for rights.* In order to achieve this, practitioners need, for example, to plan activities and experiences which reflect the diversity found within not just the immediate community but the wider society in which we live. However, children also need to find their family life and experience reflected in the setting. Children need to feel comfortable (Brooker 2002) – they need to feel that their language, religion, lifestyle are understood and valued by the practitioners. This might involve learning and using the lullaby that helps a baby get to sleep; providing an interpreter for families and children who are new to English; or telling stories that reflect important events in children's lives.
- *Nationally appropriate – what needs to be known and valued within the country in which a child is growing up.* While every child's national heritage should be reflected, in the UK it is also vital that they have the opportunity to learn to speak English, to understand British culture and to be helped to grow up feeling like an insider in the country in which they are growing up.
- *Culturally appropriate – drawing on the cultural heritage of the children, linking families and community.* Celebrating a wide range of festivals is now commonplace in the UK but cultural heritage includes songs, rhymes and stories, food, art and music. Children should be given the opportunity to experience the rich cultural heritage which has existed in Britain over a long period.
- *Developmentally appropriate – an emphasis on play, learning by doing, adult support and encouragement, and making sense of the world through representations and symbols.* Planning for learning needs to take account of the developmental needs of children. Do you, for example, consider children's need for short periods of medium physical

exertion rather than the high levels of exertion required by older children and adults (Doherty and Bailey 2003)? Are staff aware of the discomfort suffered by young children asked to sit still for long periods (Ouvry 2003)? Is children's drive for mark-making and rhythmic movement incorporated into planning?

- *Individually appropriate.* Learning is most effective when practitioners take account of and plan to build on children's interests and enthusiasms. For example, Hannah's key person noticed that she spent a great deal of time with nesting toys and sets of boxes. Her drawings included concentric circles. In order to encourage Hannah to spend more time outdoors, the educator provided a number of different sized hoops. This led Hannah to extend her learning and to explore new areas of provision.

- *Educationally appropriate – an emphasis on process, children's interests, fun, what the child already knows, including discovery and creativity.* This should lead practitioners to consider whether the activities and experiences they offer are generally educative. Are children learning anything positive from colouring in – or are they simply learning that their own drawings are not good enough? While enjoyment is vital to effective learning, is the fact that children enjoy something sufficient? They may enjoy sweets that rot their teeth but that does not mean we should encourage such a diet. Careful consideration of what children are learning is essential in planning and evaluating the curriculum.

Reflection point

Which of the categories of experience (human, national, cultural, developmental, individual and educational) highlighted above do staff in your setting offer children? Which would you like to develop further?

Approaches to assessment in early years settings

In Britain, in the tradition of early childhood education, there is a holistic view of learning. Within that tradition, the view of Susan Isaacs (1929) was that assessments should be made informally through close observation of children's learning. Planning should build on children's interests – as required today within the *Statutory Framework* for the EYFS (DfES 2007). Isaacs and Piaget (1952) shared a view of the child as a scientist and both observed children assiduously in order to understand them better. Piaget's main

interest was in understanding the nature of knowledge (known as epistemology) while Isaacs' focus was children's development or perhaps 'what makes
them tick'. Her book *The Nursery Years* was subtitled *The Mind of the Child from
Birth to Six Years*. However, she 'did not just collect a mass of data ... the data
have been set to work, to construct a coherent account of the development of
children's intellectual and emotional powers' (Drummond *et al.* 1989: 4).
However, in terms of assessment for accountability, formal assessment *in that
era* was seen as unnecessary. The Hadow Report (Board of Education 1933)
suggested that no further evidence of the value of nursery education was
needed other than 'the evidence of our own eyes'.

Educators' beliefs (including their beliefs about children) and philosophy
shape the curriculum which they offer to children and in turn the curriculum
determines the form of assessment. However, MacNaughton (2003: 141 citing
Anning) reminds us that although 'More research is clearly needed to explore
how to link desirable curriculum goals with desirable learning outcomes,
[what] research does show is that early childhood teachers do change what
and how they teach when assessment tools make them accountable for what
children learn'.

> **Reflection point**
> Consider this conundrum – beliefs shape curriculum, curriculum
> should shape assessment but assessment also determines curriculum. As
> you read the sections that follow, try to reflect on the key beliefs of
> practitioners and the links between curriculum and assessment.

Assessments in practice

Drummond's (1993) description of assessment as involving

- seeing learning;
- understanding it; and
- putting understanding to good use

can be applied to other needs of young children and their families. Every
professional who comes into contact with children and families needs to
observe, understand and make decisions for the good of the child and family
based on that understanding. Early childhood educators' focus is on learning
and development; that of a social worker might be on the emotional or
physical well-being of the child or the mental health of the parents; a health
visitor may focus on sound overall development or perhaps on milestones in
physical development. The CAF has been developed in an attempt to bring

these different areas of assessment together into a more cohesive whole. It is too early to say how effective it will be but it may serve to make professionals more aware of one another's priorities.

All judgements are subject to observer-bias. Health visitors' developmental checklists and psychologists' or speech therapists' tests may have been developed from an unrepresentative sample of the population. The birth weight of the child of a white European family or of a south Asian family may differ markedly and risk factors need to be considered appropriately. The way in which children's independence is fostered depends on cultural values and professionals have to remember that there are many perfectly acceptable childrearing practices. (The book entitled *A World of Babies* by DeLoache and Gottlieb 2000 offers some fascinating insights in this field.)

Children in British schools, in particular those in England, are probably among the most heavily assessed in the world. In the early years this begins with the Foundation Stage Profile. Assessment of this kind rests on an assumption that it is 'an objective, mechanical process of measurement. It suggests checklists, precision, explicit criteria, incontrovertible facts and figures' (Drummond 1993: 13). This view of assessment sits uncomfortably alongside day-to-day assessment in early childhood practice which Drummond (1993: 14) suggests is 'partial, tentative, exploratory and, inevitably, incomplete'.

It is also important to remember that it is no simple matter to identify the value added at each stage of education. This is because:

- Attempts at creating value added scores in the early years, which try to measure the progress made by children, rather than simply the early learning goals achieved, are relying on data which is not readily compatible with National Curriculum levels.
- Insufficient attention may be paid to the levels of parental support or the impact of socioeconomic disadvantage on children's achievement. This debate centres on two distinct views. On one hand, some groups of researchers (see e.g. Stoll *et al.* 2003) claim that schools can and do make a difference and that socioeconomic disadvantage should not be allowed to stand in the way of children's achievement. Alternatively there is a strong view that the social class of the children in a school defines the levels of attainment (see e.g. Hart and Risley 1995). Work currently being undertaken at King's College and University College London appears to confirm this view.
- Young children are likely to perform well below their optimum level of achievement in the artificial context of anything resembling a test – no matter how cheerfully or benignly presented.

Early years settings are not required to complete the Profile until the child's last year in the Foundation Stage. In most cases this will occur in the

Reception class. (Managers should not lose sight of the fact that children are not required to attend school until the term after their fifth birthday. This means that summer-born children do not become of statutory school age until the September in which they will normally enter Year 1.)

> **Reflection point**
> The *Statutory Framework* (DfES 2007: 16) requires early years settings to 'make systematic observations and assessments' of children's enthusiasms as well as their achievements, and to use these observations to inform planning. Are your staff team doing this? What help and guidance do they need to develop practice further in assessment and planning?

Identifying schema

There are a number of current approaches to assessing learning. Many settings, including Pen Green Children's Centre in Corby, use an approach which is based on schema or repeated patterns of behaviour. Tina Bruce (2005) and Cathy Nutbrown (2006) have been highly influential in making groups of practitioners and parents aware of schema and in encouraging both groups to 'spot schemas'. Despite the somewhat trivializing effect of the term 'schema-spotting', the approach has been very effective in encouraging the involvement of parents in assessments of their children. It is also very helpful in explaining the behaviour of young children.

Pen Green has developed some innovative and exciting assessment practice. Staff plan and support children's learning through their observations of children's interests and schema. Whalley (1994: 96) describes 3-year-old Jacob who attended Pen Green. Jacob had, according to his parents, shown an interest in string since the age of 12 months. The nursery provision included lots of balls of string which Jacob found fascinating. He persisted in unravelling and ravelling the string and winding it between chairs and furniture, and outside among the trees. He was particularly interested in length; how far would the string stretch? He enjoyed cutting different lengths of string and tied it to door handles. He was very concerned that the string would not touch the ground and was distressed when other children followed his string-tail and walked on it.

In more recent work Pen Green staff refer to clusters of schemas, which they see as combining and co-ordinating (Pen Green 2000). William, for example, was assessed as demonstrating an interest in trajectory, containing, transporting and scattering schemas. A visit to a duck pond, a trip to a viaduct and opportunities to play out the story of the three little pigs were planned for him to promote his interest in these schema and thus his learning and development.

Observing and assessing children up to 3

The *Early Years Foundation Stage* (DfES 2007), drawing on the *Birth to Three Matters* framework (DfES 2002a), includes advice for practitioners entitled *'Look, listen and note'*. Specific things which practitioners might observe in order to assess children's progress are suggested for each of the six areas of learning and development, at each stage of development. The difficulty with this segmented approach is that there is a danger of overlooking the child's overall well-being, of forgetting the need for a holistic approach. Managers will need to monitor practitioners in order to ensure that they are making clear connections in their assessments of different areas of learning and development.

At Fortune Park Children's Centre, profile books have been developed (Driscoll and Rudge). These began with the youngest children and include photographs, drawings and verbal accounts – all may be contributed by parents, staff or children. Driscoll and Rudge (2005: 103) explain:

> We have been using profile books at Fortune Park for nine years. They grew organically from the baby room. The children who came up through the centre brought their books with them ... We have also been fortunate to get feedback from teachers at local primary schools. They have told us that a profile book is easier to read and is more meaningful than the written reports we have sent about children in the past. As a result of this feedback, we have developed a system that takes the essential elements of the profile book – photographs, children's words and parents' voices – to create a synopsis of a child's development ... This format is accessible to children and their new teachers.

Play-based assessment

Practitioners are most likely to gain good insight into what children can actually do when activity is self-chosen or, in other words, when they are playing. This was evident in the work of Vygotsky (1978) who is widely quoted as highlighting the extent to which children appear to perform or achieve at a level well beyond that achieved in directed or even day-to-day tasks. Play situations are used by therapists and practitioners of various sorts to assess children's learning or understanding. Adult-directed tasks all too often define the limits of what can be learnt and do not therefore allow the child to demonstrate the limits of *their* learning. Sayeed and Guerin (2000) have developed an approach to assessment which they term 'play-based assessment' (PBA). The authors underline the value of intervention in children's play and the opportunities which interaction offers to both assess and develop learning.

Well-being and involvement

Ferre Laevers (1997: 17–9) has developed a theory of assessment or monitoring which rests on the assumption that learning will occur if children are in an overall state of well-being. In addition he proposes that the quality of learning is dictated by the child's level of involvement in any task – whether self-initiated or adult-directed. He suggests that the signs of well-being are as follows:

- openness and receptivity;
- flexibility;
- self-confidence and self-esteem;
- being able to defend oneself, assertiveness;
- vitality;
- relaxation and inner peace;
- enjoyment without restraint;
- being in touch with oneself.

If most of these signs are demonstrated and the child seems able to express a range of feelings including anger, excitement and sadness, well-being is likely to be high. Laevers developed this as a screening procedure and offers a scale for adults to rate children. It is used in this way at Pen Green and as part of the EEL project (Pascal and Bertram 1997). Children scoring a 3 or lower are discussed and strategies to support them identified.

Similarly there is a scale for assessing involvement. The following indicators for involvement have been suggested by Laevers (1997: 20–1):

- concentration;
- energy;
- complexity and creativity;
- facial expression and composure;
- persistence;
- precision;
- reaction time;
- verbal expression;
- satisfaction.

One of the criticisms of this approach is that it can appear very subjective. Although practitioners are experienced in gauging children's mental or emotional state, as MacNaughton (2003: 202) reminds us:

> Through our observation and assessment practices, we can see the biases in our relationships with children and we can see possibilities for collaborating with children ... To do this we must be able to see more than one view of the child and our relationships with the child ... educators often use audiotape or videotape to capture their observations (perhaps transcribing them) so that they can revisit their observations to explore the different ways that children and educators learn and make meaning.

She goes on to suggest that observing from multiple perspectives – observing with others, discussing observations with others and so on, can help to break down bias. The important point that she wishes to emphasize is that all observation is subjective – recognizing that as fact helps us to see more clearly. From McNaughton's perspective objectivity is an illusion.

Learning stories

The New Zealand early years curriculum, *Te Whariki*, (Ministry of Education 1996) has at its heart a metaphor of strands of learning being woven together like a mat. Margaret Carr states that 'assessment is woven with curriculum' (1998: 11). She highlights the nature of assessment as:

- something that happens during everyday practice;
- observation-based;
- about children's learning;
- an interpretation that may include reflection and discussion (as we strive ... to understand our observations);
- purposeful (as we put our understanding to good use) (Carr 1998: 33).

Learning stories is the means used for children's assessment under *Te Whariki*. This is based on the assumption that to assess all aspects of learning is too complex and ultimately meaningless and disjointed. Carr suggests that learning is like an iceberg of which we can only see a small part. The five strands of the curriculum are said to be characterized by five visible aspects of learning:

Curriculum strand	**Aspect of learning**
• Belonging	• Taking an interest
• Well-being	• Being involved
• Exploration	• Persisting with difficulty, challenge and uncertainty
• Communication	• Expressing a point of view or feeling
• Contribution	• Taking responsibility

The process for completing learning stories is set out in four steps: describing, discussing, documenting and deciding (Carr 2001).

- **Describing** – practitioners are encouraged to describe what they see children doing in order to move away from a focus which refers to a standard list of goals or achievements (thus all too often focusing on what children *cannot* do). Carr talks of this as describing learning 'in credit terms'. Practitioners are also encouraged to use the structure of learning stories which provides consistency while taking account of local needs.

- **Discussing** is seen as an integral part of learning stories. Carr suggests that 'discussions ... make judgements and assessments public' (2001: 125) and that they help practitioners to agree on their use of terms as well as their judgements. Children and families are also included and this will be discussed further in Chapters 9 and 10. Carr's fieldnotes (2001: 136) following a staff meeting at an early years setting, highlight the strength of this part of the process of assessment: 'It is difficult to do justice to the quality and warmth of these discussions. These staff arrived at evening staff meetings, often very tired after a day with young children. Then they began to review and plan with the children's Learning Stories, amusing anecdotes were told to supplement the written stories, side stories were shared and the exchanges became lively, funny and affectionate. Negative stories were also told, and positive interpretations often given to them by others'.

- **Documenting** 'is the writing down or recording in some way of learning and assessments. It may include annotated collections of the children's work ... A significant issue for practitioners is that documenting takes time, and the time it takes will be balanced against the perceived educational value ... the practitioners' responses to this issue [suggest] that when documenting is enjoyable, integrated into everyday practice, useful in contributing to children's learning and in providing feedback for families, then the time required is seen as worthwhile' (Carr 2001: 137). Carr also points out that documenting the learning stories makes them not only public but permanent, accessible to other professionals, families and children.

- **Deciding** is the point at which next steps are planned, progress is monitored and interventions and responses considered. Carr writes that 'in many contexts, this is called planning, but deciding also includes intuitive and spontaneous responding' (2001: 158). Carr's section on 'What next?' makes these stories formative but the role of practitioners as researchers and learners is also highlighted. Progress can be identified in three ways (Carr 1998: 27–8):

- Deciding to encourage a child or children to move onto the next step in a learning story. This involves noticing and scaffolding episodes when children shift from interest to involvement, from involvement and familiarity to challenge, from individual exploration to joint attention – communicating with others and listening to another point of view.
- Deciding to celebrate, consolidate and encourage existing and emerging behaviours so that they become habits and dispositions (e.g. taking responsibility for others in a range of situations).
- Increasing the complexity at any one step by allowing activities to take longer; increasing the challenge and uncertainty; making the media more complex or the communication on the topic range over a variety of media; making joint attention episodes demand more from each person.

Documentation in Reggio Emilia

Just as Carr and others responsible for the development of *Te Whariki* believed that assessment would be over complex and meaningless if it attempted to focus on all aspects, so in Reggio Emilia there is a belief that it is only necessary to make formal assessments if you believe that learning is not visible. In the introduction to the book entitled *Making Learning Visible*, produced jointly by Project Zero and Reggio Children (Guidici *et al.* 2001: 23), it is stated that:

> Our research is based on the notions that theory can result from as well as contribute to classroom practice, and that documentation of learning processes is critical to the research enterprise, as is the presence of multiple perspectives and languages. Rather than prescriptions we have tried to provide a set of educational points of reference or orientation. By making individual and group learning visible we hope to contribute to the collective inquiry into teaching and learning and to the creation of what Carla Rinaldi terms 'a culture of research'.

So what is documentation? Rinaldi (2005: 25), a senior figure in Reggio Emilia, describes it as a 'narrative form'. She suggests that it involves videos, tape recordings, notes, as well as photographs of children involved in their work and of the end products of their investigations, creations and efforts. It involves the discussion integral to learning stories but may refer to individuals or groups of children. It may also involve consideration of the nature of learning and epistemology or knowledge. Rinaldi (2005: 25) refers to the objectivity discussed earlier in this chapter:

The notes, the recordings, the slides and photographs represent fragments of a memory that seem thereby to become 'objective'. While each fragment is imbued with the subjectivity of the documenter, it is offered to the interpretive subjectivity of others in order to be known or reknown, created and recreated, also as a collective knowledge-building event.

Listening to children

Rinaldi (2005) goes on to suggest that assessment is just one part of documentation. She refers to the 'pedagogy of listening' and describes the way in which assessments emerge from a culture of valuing children and colleagues, ensuring that what they have to say is heard. In addition to offering opportunities for assessment, listening to children is now viewed as an effective way to promote independence, communication and learning. Listening to children goes beyond simply listening to the words they use; it is concerned with trying to understand what they mean and may involve interpreting gestures, facial expressions and body language as well as spoken language. Where practitioners develop their ability to listen they gain a 'clearer understanding' of the child's world (Lancaster 2003: 4) and engage more effectively with children.

Vivian Gussin Paley (1990) writes movingly of her experiences of listening to children. Her approach to curriculum involves story-writing/story-acting – with adults scribing children's stories and providing opportunities for them to be acted out. She listens to the words, daily transcribing conversations. She does not however merely listen to the words but seeks to *hear* them – to understand and to offer 'opportunities ... to communicate their experiences, views, concerns and aspirations' (Lancaster 2003: 4). Similarly, Hall and Martello (1996: v) remind us that children's 'talk offers a special access into their thinking ... [which adults] have to hear beyond the apparently seamless flow of sound and appreciate what is being revealed'.

Reflection point
Many practitioners are looking for ways to listen to children more effectively. This often requires a review of the organization to ensure that practitioners have the time and opportunity to interact with children. What do you need to do to support your team in listening to children?

Metacognition and assessment

Getting children to reflect on and judge their own learning is widely seen as important to progress. In addition to giving insight to their thinking, children's words can provide insight into their metacognition, or their understanding of their own learning. The *Foundation Stage Profile* (QCA 2003) gives space for children to comment on their learning. Hutchin (2003) comments on the importance of capturing this kind of awareness. It may be directly given as the result of a question, such as 'What are you good at?' or 'What do you like doing at school/nursery?' However, frequently such comments are heard when children themselves identify a new achievement. Hutchin (2003: 74) highlights Jessica, a child in a Reception class who, when asked about her writing, comments, 'I just try and try it'. Later, after enormous efforts to master hopping, Jessica says excitedly, 'I can hop and do it. Look, I CAN do it!'

Curriculum, assessment and leadership

> Which approach is the best one is a value decision that the individual educator must make ... One cannot choose not to choose, because to accept the status quo is also to make a choice.
>
> (Sleeter and Green cited by MacNaughton 2003: 2)

What you want children to learn, and how you believe they should be helped to learn, depend on the philosophy you hold. Even practitioners who claim to know nothing about philosophy nonetheless do hold a philosophy of their own. Every one of us has a set of views and beliefs about children, learning and curriculum. The philosophy which underpins a curriculum involves both views of learning and principles by which action is determined. It may or may not be in sympathy with government policy, with cultural views or with the views of parents. The view of learning may be based on current research, or current and possibly outmoded theories. The principles it includes need to be in sympathy with the goals that are set.

Discrepancies between what practitioners do and what they believe are surprisingly common. The current debate about phonics offers many examples of such a mismatch – with those who believe in structured approaches holding very different views to those who believe that children learn in much more individual ways. Similarly, members of a team may hold very differing views about toilet training. Some may focus on children taking responsibility for themselves and delay training until children can take an active role in the process. Other members of the team may feel that adults should take a stronger lead, as that will in the long run give children greater independence. The impact of these beliefs will determine how policies are interpreted.

MacNaughton (2003: 115) identifies the benefits of reflecting on and gaining a clear understanding of the philosophy that underpins your practice 'and on the role of early childhood education in society'. She suggests that reflecting on your understanding of principles and views of learning can help you as a practitioner to:

- prioritize the goals you have for teaching and learning in your setting;
- decide what actions will bring you a sense of personal meaning, purpose and accomplishment in your work with young children;
- choose among competing understandings and interpretations of classroom events;
- develop 'goals, values, and attitudes to strive for' that motivate and energize you on a daily basis;
- explore with parents and colleagues what you are trying to achieve in your work with children and why you organize things in the way that you do;
- enter into discussions with colleagues and provide a basis for an agreed team approach to your work with children.

CASE STUDY

Celine is undertaking a pathway to EYPS and is trying hard to develop reflective practice, in herself and in team members. She found the notion of an informal philosophy of education interesting. She considered the way in which the team prioritized and found that although she believed that developing oral communication was of fundamental importance, a relatively small amount of time was observed to be spent in developing shared, sustained conversations. It became clear that finding ways to promote conversation between staff and children would help her to bring a closer link between the aims and practice of the centre. She resolved to refocus the team and the parents in order to place oral communication at the heart of the curriculum. This entailed creating an action plan including staff training sessions.

Reflection point
What do you think your philosophy of learning and education is? Do other team members share this view do you think? Would observations challenge this view? What, for example, do staff actually spend most time on?

The four themes underpinning the EYFS are related to four key principles, as shown in Table 6.1.

Table 6.1 Themes and principles underpinning the EYFS

Theme	Related principle
A unique child	Every child is a competent learner from birth who can be resilient, capable, confident and self-assured
Positive relationships	Children learn to be strong and independent from a base of loving and secure relationships with parents and/or a key person
Enabling environments	The environment plays a key role in supporting and extending children's development and learning
Learning and development	Children develop and learn in different ways and at different rates, and all areas of learning and development are equally important and interconnected

Because of the complexities of both curriculum and pedagogy, curriculum leaders who are aware of the fact that children are learning much more than is actually or explicitly taught are essential to effective provision. As we saw in Chapter 2 there are many similarities between effective pedagogy and effective leadership. This means that leaders will benefit from increased awareness of curriculum and pedagogy, not just in their dealings with children but in their work with staff teams and parents.

In order to lead the curriculum effectively you and the whole staff team will need to become leaderful. Curriculum and pedagogy are much too big to be led by one person alone. Schools and many other early years settings frequently appoint curriculum managers – although their titles may vary. Sometimes their responsibilities cover one or more areas of learning, such as communication, language and literacy, or physical and creative development. Sometimes several people will take on responsibility for different aspects of an area of learning, so co-ordinators for music, dance and art may, for example, share responsibility for managing creative development. Some curriculum responsibilities are not linked to areas of learning but to aspects of provision. The appointment of someone to take responsibility for outdoor provision is very common. On a broader level, an important part of the role of special educational needs co-ordinators (SENCOs) or inclusion managers is to ensure high quality provision across the curriculum.

Reflection point

How is responsibility for curriculum in your setting divided up? In a setting with large numbers of children, it is unrealistic to expect one person (even you as the leader) to take the lead across the whole curriculum. If you work alone you may find it helpful to team up with other practitioners in a similar situation, learning from one another and sharing expertise. It is quite difficult to keep up with initiatives, research and writing about all aspects of the curriculum. What steps might you take to share responsibilities so that the demands made on members of a staff team are more equitable?

Your role as leader, whether designated or not, simply in fulfilling your responsibilities to children is to support other members of staff in understanding the complex nature of curriculum and pedagogy. You will also be seeking to ensure consistent provision within a particular aspect of the curriculum. As a team of curriculum managers or leaders, all practitioners should be striving to create consistency across all areas of learning and aspects of provision.

Key points

- Curriculum is a complex issue. It may be written or unwritten, intended or unintended. It is not the same as a syllabus, which merely focuses on what is to be taught. Curriculum is affected by a number of aspects.
- The unique nature of children, the impact of relationships and the environment have an impact on what is taught and learnt, as does the philosophy held by practitioners.
- Assessment is linked to curriculum and philosophy. In deciding what and how to assess, practitioners demonstrate what they value.
- Leaders have a crucial role to play in supporting the development of curriculum and assessment in being sufficiently reflective and insightful to articulate why practitioners do what they do.

Practical tasks

In order to reflect on these issues, undertake some or all of the following activities.

1 Spend some time observing the learning that children are engaged in. Is their learning part of the intended curriculum and/or are they more exercised by aspects of the unintended curriculum?

2 Review your curriculum planning to reflect on the way in which it is organized. Does your agreed planning format encourage practitioners to consider the intended but hidden part of the curriculum?

3 Encourage the staff team to spend some time observing one another. Encourage discussion about points at which unintended aspects of the curriculum may have been unintentionally reinforced.

4 Talk to staff and list all the situations in which you feel that the hidden curriculum is operating in a positive way.

5 Discuss with staff the extent to which assessment practice in your setting supports the intended curriculum. Does it tap into the learning which you most value or does it encourage staff to seek out things which you feel are of less importance?

7 The role of the leader in supporting learning and development

> The central mission of early childhood programs is to ensure that the quality of the day-to-day lives of the participating children supports and enhances their growth, development and learning.
>
> (Katz 1997: 17)

Introduction

In this chapter, the focus shifts to the role of the leader or manager in supporting staff in planning, providing and evaluating an appropriate curriculum. This key role is essential in ensuring that effective support for children's care, learning and development is provided. The role of the leader in creating a learning community among children, parents and staff is highlighted. A number of approaches to monitoring and evaluating provision and learning are examined, and tools to support monitoring and evaluation are provided. The importance of the relationship between the assessment of learning and planning the curriculum is highlighted. Aspects of curriculum organization will be examined, and this will include consideration of learning and teaching strategies; activities and experiences; materials and resources – both indoors and out; and the organization of time and space. The vital relationship between assessment and planning will be explored. Finally the chapter will examine the leader's responsibilities in ensuring that the EYFS and *Every Child Matters* are addressed within the curriculum.

Leading learning

The focus of this chapter is children's learning and development. You may therefore be surprised that we begin by highlighting the role of leaders in early years settings in supporting *adult* learning. Adults who regard themselves as lifelong learners provide excellent role models for children and help to create a learning culture. (In Chapter 9, opportunities to further parents' learning will be discussed.) The setting may offer family literacy sessions which offer opportunities for parents to develop their own basic skills and to enhance their understanding of how their children are becoming literate and numerate. Computer classes may be provided to enable parents to develop skills to improve their chances of gaining employment. Alternatively, something as simple as an informal knitting group may give some parents the confidence to meet with other people and may be a step towards taking on something more challenging. The role of parents in demonstrating to their children that learning is a lifelong process cannot be underestimated.

An essential element in establishing your setting as a learning community lies in creating a professional staff team that keeps on wanting to learn. This may be formal learning – undertaking courses and gaining additional qualifications – of it may include informal processes – discussion, reading and so on – but above all it must involve reflective practice. Gardner (2006: 39) goes so far as to say that 'those who are unable to ... become "reflective practitioners" should be counseled out of the profession'. Leaders need to support practitioners at all levels in evaluating learning, teaching, provision and organization. Some of this will be done through formal planning, assessment and evaluation procedures but some demands individual thought and analysis. Reflective or mindful practice has been likened to looking through a window: 'Many people remain trapped at the one window, looking out every day at the same scene in the same way. Real growth is experienced when you draw back from that one window, turn and walk around the inner tower of the soul and see all the different windows that await your gaze' (Johns 2004: 5 citing O'Donohue).

Leaders, like parents, need to model or demonstrate their own learning. While striving for effective practice requires you to undertake monitoring and evaluation, as the leader of a learning community your enthusiasm and professionalism should lead you to seek further learning and knowledge. Gardner (2006: 41) suggests that leaders for the future will need to want to continue to learn because they know that knowledge is changing all the time and that therefore the only way to keep up to date is to become 'a lifelong student'. Citing Plato, he goes on to stress the importance of enjoyment, of becoming 'passionate' about learning.

> **Reflection point**
> In what ways are you helping to create a learning community? What opportunities are you providing to encourage parents to continue to learn? How are you supporting practitioners in becoming reflective? Are you passionate about learning?

Leaders also have a role in helping others – parents, community, politicians and so on – to understand young children's learning and the development of appropriate provision to support it. This will involve leaders in reading and interpreting relevant research. It will also involve effective communication in helping lay people to understand why practitioners do what they do. This process may become more effective when leaders can encourage staff to develop action research, reducing the gap between practitioners and researchers and promoting reflection; getting teams to find answers to their own professional questions.

CASE STUDY

A small group of managers applied for and received funding from the local authority to undertake small-scale research on intervention in children's imaginative play. Each setting identified a particular focus and staff members were released to observe, reflect, discuss and develop practice. In one setting the focus was on the use of questions in interactions with children. In another it was on improving the quality of provision in role-play areas. Regular meetings to identify progress and obstacles encouraged staff to continue to meet and the network became a forum for problem-airing and -solving.

A head of a large children's centre recognized the need to provide training for the large team of professionals from different backgrounds. In discussion with her senior management team, she was able to identify a set of core learning opportunities for all members of staff which would enhance multiprofessional working. The group identified which aspects could be provided from within the team and which would need outside input and funding. A staff development plan was then constructed incorporating and prioritizing the core training programme.

Leading children's learning and development

Leaders in early childhood settings play an important part in supporting children's learning and development. As Ofsted (2007: 18) note in their survey of 144 settings, leading, rather than simply managing, the curriculum had 'a significant impact on the quality of provision and children's achievement. Rigorous monitoring was a feature of the best settings. It identified clearly what was working well, where practitioners needed to improve and what needed to be done'. On the other hand, weak leadership was associated with 'weaker teaching and learning', poorly managed assessment procedures and a curriculum that 'lacked coherence' (Ofsted 2007: 18).

Reflection point
Use Table 7.1 to reflect on curriculum leadership in your setting. Do you and your team know what is working well, what needs to improve and what needs to be done?

In the sections that follow, we will examine ways in which you can support the development of increasingly effective provision, learning and development. In addition to considering the management of assessment procedures we will look at ways of monitoring provision, including learning and teaching.

Monitoring and evaluating provision

Monitoring and evaluating are closely linked but are not exactly the same process. When you monitor provision you may observe interactions between children and adults, you may scrutinize planning or you may look to see which areas of provision are being well used and which appear neglected. Monitoring involves collecting data: fact-finding. Evaluation is the step which follows – the use you make of the data in order to form judgements about your practice.

Inspection frameworks and quality assurance

Ofsted inspections, Joint Area Reviews (JARs) and local authority reviews are all examples of externally driven monitoring procedures. In the current climate of top-down accountability, quality assurance has increasingly been seen as something which is done *to* you. A danger in this is that some practitioners may abdicate their professional responsibilities and may feel that their assessment of their own practice is not good enough. Professionalism demands that practitioners aim to do their best in order to raise standards. Fortunately, recent changes in Ofsted regulations, including self-evaluation, are taking a step back towards greater professionalism. These issues are explored in greater detail in Chapter 10. Suffice it to say at this point however that the key to establishing greater professionalism and leaderful qualities in assessing provision lies in:

- taking more responsibility for assessing your own provision;
- comparing your philosophy with your findings by being clear about what you are aiming to do and the extent to which you have matched that;

Table 7.1 Monitoring and supporting teaching and learning in the Foundation Stage

	Sources of evidence and ideas for questions to use when evaluating data	Observation and judgements
Teaching	*Observation* Is the teaching (both informal and formal) stimulating, enthusiastic and challenging? Are the relationships with children good/respectful? Are support staff (and volunteers including parents) usefully deployed? Are the planned activities and experiences appropriate to the age and stage of the children? Are tasks/activities sufficiently open-ended to allow children to respond at an appropriate level? *Planning, observation and discussion* Are adults clear about the aims of the activity in which they are engaged?	
Learning	*Observation* Are significant numbers of children engrossed in what they are doing? Are there opportunities and encouragement for children to collaborate with others? *Observation, planning and children's records* Can you identify purpose in what children who appear to be off-task are doing? (e.g. tracking a child will tell you if, for example, he or she is following a particular interest or schema) *Provision and observation* Are children encouraged to act independently?	
Achievement and progress	*Children's records and observation* Is there evidence of progress of learning in what children do and/or say? *Provision* What evidence of progress can you find in wall displays, home-made books, etc.? *Observation* Are the relationships between children good/respectful?	

Table 7.1 (continued)

	Sources of evidence and ideas for questions to use when evaluating data	Observation and judgements
Environment and resources	*Provision* Is the environment orderly and attractive? *Observation* Does it support children in finding the resources they need? Is it comfortable? *Observation and planning* Are indoor and outdoor activities linked? *Observation and provision* Are there sufficient resources for children's needs? Are they appropriate?	

- becoming practised and confident at articulating your successes and recognizing (and dealing with) areas in which you need to develop practice.

Research and the quality of provision

Large-scale research such as the EPPE project (Sammons *et al.* 2002) or the REPEY project (Siraj-Blatchford *et al.* 2002) can provide material against which practitioners can question and evaluate what they do. Findings about the involvement of parents or the qualifications of staff can, for example, lead settings to think about the implications for them.

The EPPE project used tools which are described as ECERS and ECERS-E. The original Early Childhood Environment Rating Scale (ECERS) (Harms and Clifford 1980) focused on personal care routines, furnishings and displays, language-reasoning, fine and gross motor activities, creative activities, social development and adult needs. The EPPE team decided to make use of this scale in their research but felt that it did not altogether meet the needs of the project. They therefore developed an additional, extended, scale which they entitled ECERS-E (Sylva *et al.* 2003). ECERS-E covers aspects of literacy, mathematics, science and the natural environment, and diversity.

Each scale has a seven-point rating scale with descriptors, with 1 being inadequate and 7 excellent. The extracts below give a flavour of what is involved.

Social development

1 = Free play (free choice) Child is permitted to select materials, companions and as far as possible to manage play independently. Adult interaction is in response to child's needs.

7 = Ample opportunity for supervised free play outdoors and indoors with wide range of toys, games and equipment. Supervision used as an educational interaction. New materials/experiences for free play added periodically.

(Harms and Clifford 1980: 31)

Race equality

1 = Books, pictures, dolls and displays show no or little evidence of ethnic diversity in our society or the wider world.

7 = Staff develop activities with the express purpose of promoting cultural understanding, e.g. attention is drawn to similarities and

differences in things and people, different cultures are routinely brought into topic work, and visitors and performers reflect a range of cultures.

Children's attention is specifically drawn to books, pictures, dolls, etc. that show black and ethnic minority people in non-stereotypical roles and familiar situations. Specific activities are developed to promote understanding of difference, e.g. paints are mixed to match skin tones to visibly show subtle differences.

In multi-ethnic areas, ethnic minority educators are employed in the centre. Elsewhere, black and ethnic minority people are sometimes invited into the setting to work with the children.

(Sylva *et al.* 2003: 33)

Reflection point

In reading the extracts from the ECERS-E do you notice any aspects of provision for social development and for diversity that are not addressed in your setting? What action might you take to promote developments in practice? Remember that we have only shown the extremes identified in the scales – for a broader picture you will need to refer to the original texts.

Although the projects in which these scales were used were large-scale, many settings use them for small-scale investigation – perhaps focusing on particular aspects or sometimes using a particular scale as a starting point for discussion about improvements. Many developments in settings arise out of small-scale research – a group of practitioners wanting to find out more about aspects of their practice.

Monitoring aspects of provision

The sources of evidence you might use to inform your judgements might include: resources and materials; planned and actual activities and experiences; children's records including paintings, drawings, observations and photographs of their activities and experiences; written plans, evaluations and assessments; and the quality of interactions between children and adults, adults and adults (including parents), and children and children.

In the following sections we focus on four key areas of provision, namely: learning and teaching; activities and experiences; materials and resources; and organization. Monitoring and managing assessment (which is of course integral to effective provision) will be considered later in the chapter.

Learning and teaching strategies

Too often teaching is thought of as the direct and didactic transfer of knowledge. However, early childhood specialists identify a large number of strategies which reflect their role as pedagogues and their concern with the quality of learning as well as teaching. Pedagogy underlines the fact that teaching cannot be said to have occurred unless learning has taken place.

Analysis of four important documents in the field of early childhood care and education (QCA/DfES 2000; Moyles *et al.* 2002; Edgington 2004; Mac-Naughton and Williams 2004) highlights a wide range of possible teaching and learning strategies. We have synthesized this range into five broad categories:

1 Stimulating, sustaining and extending interests.
2 Modelling.
3 Direct teaching.
4 Interacting and communicating.
5 Playing.

Stimulating, sustaining and extending interests
Arguably the most important strategy was identified by Edgington (2004) as the process of stimulating and sustaining or extending children's interests. From infancy onwards this is undoubtedly a most effective strategy for promoting learning. It is, however, difficult to manage since it requires good knowledge of the children themselves, an understanding of children's development and sufficient flexibility, creativity and expertise to be able to select the most appropriate means of developing interests.

This may be achieved by adding equipment which will promote a particular interest to existing provision. Isabel had recently moved to a new house and for the first time was enjoying having a garden. Staff added flower pots of different sizes and empty seed packets to the digging area. With these props she was able to represent or play the situations she had enjoyed at home. Needless to say, staff also did some real planting with Isabel as part of a small group. At home Isabel had a pair of plastic secateurs which she found frustrating because they did not actually cut anything. One member of staff planned for her to help prune some bushes, using real secateurs – an activity she found exciting and stimulating.

Interests are often developed by educational visits. This can sometimes have surprising results. Rob was very quiet and spent most of his time playing with trains. Staff planned a train trip in an effort to help him to make contact with other children. This was achieved – but not in the way staff had predicted. On the way to the station they saw two yellow beetle cars. Rob was very excited – his mother commented that this was because his much-loved aunt had a similar car. He proved to be quite an expert and got several other children interested in his enthusiasm too. A display of pictures, miniatures and models which the enthusiasts had made developed from this.

The role of initiating new interests should not be overlooked. Displays, outings, new role-play areas and even a single new piece of equipment can stimulate new interests as can a new or unfamiliar book, current events and occasions (such as the Olympics) or changes in the environment (such as a neighbouring building site or the visit of a circus). The importance of reflecting these stimuli in curriculum planning will be developed in the next chapter.

Modelling

A further important pedagogical strategy is modelling. Practitioners are very conscious of this valuable (but often unconsciously performed) role. We have only to watch young children pretending to be mum or teacher to have a clear idea of how keenly they observe and imitate adult behaviour. Schools make use of this in order to promote literacy – persuading parents to read with their children has a strong effect on achievement because children respond to the models of readers offered by their parents. Modelling caring, gentle behaviour has lifelong importance. If children gain an impression that physical force has power over negotiation and compromise, that may all too easily lead them to become aggressive.

Models are not simply of personal and social behaviour or of literacy, important as these are. Adults are also modelling (negatively and positively, consciously or unconsciously) mathematical behaviour, scientific and technological behaviour, creativity, problem-solving and, it is to be hoped, anti-discriminatory behaviour (Edgington 2004; MacNaughton and Williams 2004). Adults need to monitor the model they are offering. The child who immediately says of a broken toy, 'We'll have to ask daddy to fix it' has probably been offered a narrow and ultimately unhelpful model of who can or cannot repair things.

Direct teaching

Contrary to many popular views, direct teaching does not simply mean telling. It may involve:

- *Describing* – perhaps sitting alongside a child describing what they are doing in order to make them more aware of the processes in which they are engaged.
- *Singing songs* which help children to remember things like number names, alphabet, sequences in stories or days of the week.
- *Giving feedback* – adults who do not simply admire something that children have made or done but telling them what is good about what they've done support learning very effectively. There is always a

temptation when we are busy or distracted to simply say 'that's nice' but it is more helpful to say something that gives specific feedback.

- *Scaffolding or breaking tasks down into small steps* – practitioners need to make sure that they don't do more than is necessary for children, ensuring that they hold back so that children can act as independently as possible.
- *Demonstrating skills, strategies or techniques* – this will sometimes involve metacognition, heightening children's awareness of what they know and can do (Moyles *et al.* 2002).
- *Questioning and intervening* – intervention may involve any of the strategies identified in this list, or may be about offering a particular piece of equipment or simply holding paper while children cut in order to help them complete or extend what they are doing.

Interacting and communicating

Interaction and communication may take many forms. Both are two-way processes – you cannot claim to have interacted or communicated unless another person has been involved. Interactions may be physical, verbal, gestural or aural. They may on occasion involve little more than smiling across the room to encourage a child who is engaged in an activity. For all children interaction and communication should sometimes involve sustained conversation which challenges and extends their thinking. Staffing levels sometimes make it difficult to achieve desirable levels of interaction and intervention. However, if staff model strongly as communicators, children's interactions with one another will be enhanced. Learning from peers is an important aspect of group care and education.

Playing

Play is by no means the least important of the learning and teaching strategies – in fact it is vital to learning throughout life. The *Curriculum Guidance for the Foundation Stage* (QCA/DfES 2000) requires a balance of adult-directed and child-initiated experiences. Many activities and experiences can be planned to be playful but genuine play opportunities need to be open-ended, self-initiated and involve physical action.

Research suggests that while children recognize these aspects of play, they sometimes mistakenly believe that it does not involve effort, does not include adults and does not promote learning (Gura 1996). In using play to promote learning, practitioners need to ensure that children gain awareness of the effort that goes into play – even when it is enjoyable – and that adults do get involved in children's play and that children have many opportunities for physical activity. Although play, like language, is innate, it too must be learnt from more experienced players. Practitioners need to offer children:

- *Models of how to play, by joining in and offering suggestions.* Pat played with children in the hospital role-play area and in the play was able to suggest possible symptoms and treatments which extended children's play.
- *Experiences which provide motivation to play.* Staff provided a range of drums and some similar improvised instruments including buckets and plastic bowls when an African drummer had been to visit a centre.
- *'Food for thought' in the course of play.* When Harpreet pretended to be a dog in the home corner, the nursery officer informally introduced conversation about the humane treatment of pets.
- *Challenge to their thinking during play.* Sam noticed that children playing firefighters were unaware of the function of helmets and began to talk about putting on her helmet in case any burning wood fell on her head, etc. This led to extended conversation and enhanced understanding.

Activities and experiences

In placing an emphasis on the outcomes of learning, there is a danger that the early learning goals included in the *Curriculum Guidance for the Foundation Stage* may cause practitioners to lose sight of children's entitlement to experiences. Perhaps all children should have the opportunity to climb trees, explore musical instruments, grow fruit and vegetables or paddle in the sea.

Reflection point
What experiences do you think all children should be entitled to? You might like to talk to colleagues about what experiences they think all children should have access to.

Practitioners frequently ask for advice on practical activities they can use with children. The problem with this approach is that it may overemphasize adult-directed activity at the expense of child-initiated learning. While planning seeks to shape or direct learning, setting up an activity in a particular way often means that adults are determining the teaching, which can become very narrowly focused, leaving many of the activities and experiences which children select for themselves under-supported.

The need for a balance between adult-directed and child-initiated activity means that adult time should be equitably divided between the two. Failure to do this will signal to children that the things they are interested in and choose to do are of less value in your eyes than the activities and experiences which you lead. Adult-led experiences which offer support for learning should include visitors and outings.

Materials and resources

The provision of materials and resources may be monitored in a number of ways. In the early years, the informal daily evaluations which highlight what is working well, what needs improving and what needs to be done to enable teams of practitioners to review and modify their practice continuously. There are also a number of more formal processes designed to monitor the way in which the team in your setting is supporting learning.

The extent to which the learning environment has been well prepared may be assessed by using checklists. Cartwright *et al.* (2002) suggest questions such as those that follow to focus your evaluation:

- Is this area inviting and stimulating?
- Do adults and children know both the possibilities and the limitations of things that may go on here?
- Has this provision been planned for today?
- Was the planning based on assessments of children's learning and/or on staff evaluation of previous learning and activity?
- Has everything been carefully maintained and replenished? Are pencils sharp, paint pots ready to use, dressing-up clothes clean?
- Is everything safe, clean and tidy?

There are many suggestions about the range of activities and experiences which should be available to young children. How does the list below compare with what you have on offer?

- Home corner and other forms of role and fantasy play such as shopping, hospitals, robbers or space travel. There should be dressing-up materials to support this and other forms of imaginary play.
- Malleable and tactile materials such as clay, dough and cornflour. Natural materials such as water and sand (dry, damp and wet) might be included as might peat, lentils, wood shavings, etc.
- Woodwork has been a long-standing aspect of traditional early years practice in this country. Anxieties about health and safety have led many practitioners to abandon its inclusion in the curriculum but it continues to offer children many important opportunities to learn a range of skills such as perseverance, self-esteem and a sense of agency.
- A creative workshop which makes accessible glue, scissors, papers, junk materials, boxes, fabric, paint, etc.

- A related graphics or drawing and writing area. This is sometimes known as an mark-making area and may include pencils, pens, crayons, chalks, pastels, small notebooks, envelopes, stapler, hole punch, cards, post-its and so on depending on the age of the children.
- Small construction toys such as Lego and Sticklebricks as well as large construction toys such as hollow blocks.
- Small world materials – farms, garages, dolls' houses, etc.
- Books.
- Collections of resources for science and technology; mathematics and information technology. All too often curriculum planning for these areas is limited to the resources themselves rather than identifying experiences and activities which would promote learning in these areas more broadly. For example, pegboards and numbers may be placed in the maths area, but no plans made for using and exploring numbers within other areas of provision, such as garaging wheeled toys in the outside area or using phone books and calendars in the home corner. Information technology resources should not be limited to computers.
- Music and sound-making materials.
- Materials for exploring and categorizing. For the youngest children this will involve the provision of treasure baskets and heuristic play materials. As children grow older, collections of shells, feathers, pegs and pebbles will fascinate them.
- Climbing opportunities should be provided to challenge all children. For the youngest children in the early stages of moving independently, there should be apparatus on which they can climb, both indoors and out.

Although not a specific area of provision, all young children need easy access to empty boxes, bags and trucks, using which they can transport, transfer and examine resources (Manning-Morton and Thorp 2001).

While not all settings are able to offer high quality outdoor provision, it is importance is increasingly recognized and settings which cannot make provision similar to that identified below should consider how they can compensate for its absence. Outdoor provision should be linked to, mirror and extend indoor provision. Garrick (2004) suggests that in the outside area the following elements should be provided:

- large construction materials;
- a quiet area;
- materials to promote creative and imaginative play;
- opportunities for music-making;

- dens;
- a large space for running;
- a growing area;
- natural materials;
- a range of small apparatuses, such as balls, hoops, etc. as appropriate to the age of the children you are working with;
- a roadway for vehicles;
- materials for role-play;
- opportunities for gross motor activity;
- a wildlife area.

Reflection point

Reflect on the items in the lists and consider the following questions. Think about your reasons for answering as you do.

- Which do you provide?
- Which do you regard as essential?
- How do you give children access to experiences and materials which you are unable to offer on a day-to-day basis?
- How do you monitor to ensure that all your resources continue to be attractive and stimulating to children?
- Does this equipment allow 'for the fluent, flexible way in which children engage with the environment'(Gura 1996: 28)?
- Does this equipment allow 'for originality and the elaboration of ideas' (Gura 1996: 28)?

Organizing time and space

At the beginning of the twentieth century, the McMillan sisters, who set up many of the first nursery schools, and who were responsible for the development of the school health service and school meals, regarded *time* and *space* as the most important aspects of successful learning. Their play-based curriculum, based on the principles developed by Froebel in the first half of the nineteenth century, gave children long periods of uninterrupted time for play in large areas of outdoor space.

Structuring time

The way in which the day is organized influences learning and teaching. Some curricula (such as High/Scope) allocate relatively short periods of time to a variety of different activities. Others allow long periods of unbroken time which children must learn to manage effectively. In general, if children are to be encouraged to play – in order to promote learning and development – they will need more extended periods of self-chosen activity. If a child is told to play for ten minutes, it is unlikely that anything productive will come from such a short session. Gura (1996: 75) suggests that practitioners should ask themselves how they can organize the day so that less time is wasted. In general the younger the child the less effective large group sessions are.

The organization of time promoted by the primary national strategies has led primary and Reception teachers to drastically restructure morning sessions. The two long periods of directed, adult-focused time, which take up virtually the whole of the morning session, and the long periods of time during which children have to sit on the carpet, are not without critics. They have impacted on the whole curriculum, leaving less time for other subjects and causing some teachers to narrow their range of teaching approaches to those found within the strategies. It is important to think about unintended curriculum messages – in some cases we may be teaching children that maths and reading are boring.

Reflection point
Daily routines from two nurseries have been included below. Think about the messages they give as to what is important within the setting. Does your routine convey similar messages? Are they the ones you want to convey?

If we come before 9.00 we choose activities and play together with our 'big school' friends.
After 9.00 we choose and play with the toys until all our friends arrive.
We 'chat on the mat', count and sing a song.
We paint, stick, draw, look at books, play number games, build models and explore music, sand and water. We learn to share and be kind, to listen, count, play games and do puzzles. The grown-ups help us to choose and talk to us a lot. Sometimes we go to the library or for a walk. We play with the cars, trains and all the other toys. We have fun and learn at the same time. We dress up and make cakes. We are very busy. We play inside and outside in groups. Sometimes we go on the computer. We are playing and learning all the time.
We tidy up our activities, wash our hands and get ready for our snack.
We choose a healthy snack and drink, and sit for a few minutes.

We go outside together to play. We learn to climb and balance, throw and catch, hop, skip, jump and ride bikes. We look at books and play in the tents or with the sand.
We come in and sit down to listen to a story, learn some songs or sing some number rhymes.
Some friends go home after the story, some stay for lunch.
After lunch we might watch *Postman Pat* or play outside again.
Some more of our friends arrive to chat on the mat. We play and learn indoors and outdoors all afternoon. We have another snack and story.
After 3.30 most of us go home, but if we stay we eat our tea and play with the 'big' children again.
At 5.30 everyone has gone home – nobody sleeps here!
We want to come again.

8.45	Classroom set up ready for planned child-initiated activities (indoors and out).
9.00	Welcome and free-flow activity.
9.30	Free-flow continues and planned focused activities begin. Doors open so that children can go outside.
10.45	Activities cleared away.
11.00	Story groups, singing, etc.
11.20	Part-time children return to tabletop activities so that staff can talk to their parents as they arrive. Full-time children play board games and/or join in movement activities and prepare for lunch.
11.45	Lunch begins.
12.30	Outdoor play and stories or videos for full-time children. May also help with setting up for afternoon children.
1.00	Part-time children arrive; welcome and free-flow activity.

1.30	Free-flow continues and planned focused activities begin. Doors open so that children can go outside.
2.45	Activities cleared away.
3.00	Story groups, singing, etc.
3.20	Children return to tabletop activities so that staff can talk to their parents as they arrive.

Structuring space

The way in which the learning environment is set up – indoors and out – influences the learning and play that occur. Colour influences the mood of everyone. Feeling crowded affects the atmosphere, as does music. In some settings there is continuous music of one particular type. There should be some silences and some times when different moods are evoked through music.

Open spaces may encourage children to run, but may not encourage them to observe or notice things of interest. If there are only large tables, children may not become engaged with another child. This is a problem since pairings are widely seen as productive in supporting thought and communication in young children. On the other hand if there are no spaces where larger groups can operate effectively, children may miss out on opportunities to develop socially. Children should be closely involved in any major re-arrangements of the room. They often have clear ideas about what is important to them and what they find difficult.

Reflection point
Consider these two questions from Gura (1996: 77):

- Is there anything we can learn from the child's-eye view of a good play-work environment presented in the first daily routine example.
- Are there any aspects of this that trouble you?

Take some time to reflect on this point and when you are working with children think about:

- the way in which children use the available space; and
- any possible changes that might be made to better reflect the way children prefer to use the available spaces.

There are a number of other aspects to consider in structuring space. Brooker (2002) reminds us that the simple everyday aspect of ensuring that children feel comfortable in the learning and teaching space should be addressed. Making it possible for children to act as independently as they are able in toileting and eating should be a consideration. While not wanting to make the space overcrowded, the inclusion of some adult-sized furniture such a comfy armchair or sofa (if you have room) can make the setting more homely and relaxed.

Health and safety does need to be borne in mind but risk assessments should be realistic and should not mean that children are denied important experiences. For every risk considered, practitioners need to be encouraged to take account of what children will be losing if deprived of particular experiences. Climbing does present some risk – but lack of opportunity to climb limits children's ability to have a sense of agency and independence. It also prevents them from developing a range of skills and confidence.

If there are babies and toddlers in rooms with older children, they should have some protected space. It would be unfair to limit their access to the floor space which is so essential to their development. Similarly, adults sometimes do not like going out in the cold or wet, but given appropriate clothing children benefit enormously from fresh air and the stimulation provided by outdoor play.

Monitoring and evaluating learning

The EYFS Profile is not intended to be used until the final year of the Foundation Stage. However the final term assessment should be a summative account of prior observations of learning. Three experts who acted as advisors in the development of the EYFS (Spencer *et al.* 2007: 10–1) have suggested that the records through which children's learning and progress is assessed should:

- be developed in partnership with parents;
- encourage children to reflect on and actively identify their own learning, using annotated photographs and written observations;
- be based on observational data, tracking the development of learning;
- help practitioners to evaluate provision and act on their evaluations to make improvements;
- inform planning, show progress and identify next steps;
- be set out in such a way as to be easy to review and summarize.

Reflection point

Do your assessment procedures match up to these ideas? Do you involve children and parents in the process of documenting learning? Do you regularly collect observations and use them to identify new achievements and possible next steps in learning? Do you use observations to help you decide on changes in provision? Is your system of assessment and record-keeping manageable for practitioners? Does it allow leaders to monitor the quality of provision?

While the prime purpose of children's records should be to track their progress and ensure that provision challenges and involves them, the data has other uses. Scrutiny of children's records should also enable leaders to:

- check that all areas of learning and development are planned for and accessed in a similar way;
- identify whether some children are having limited access to some aspects of provision;
- compare aspects of children's achievement levels with those for the local authority or national levels;
- improve the way in which the learning environment or resources are organized;
- make changes to the timetable in order to offer children a better experience;
- identify staff training needs.

CASE STUDY

The staff team at a preschool playgroup regularly monitored the quality of their interactions with children by sampling conversations with children. Once a week, at hourly intervals throughout a session, a designated member of the team would observe the interactions of another team member. At the end of the session, both members of staff were given time to discuss and evaluate the observations. This process was followed once a term by an evaluation in which team members identified key learning points and aspects of provision which they felt needed to be developed. Like assessment, evaluation involves making sense of data.

Shown below are some other examples of situations where settings have used assessments of children's learning to develop practice.

- Hettie analysed her observations of Pinder's behaviour. He had had a number of outbursts of aggressive behaviour but when the staff team analysed their observations they noticed that these mainly occurred when other children ran past his intricate block constructions. By moving the blocks into a quieter corner of the room, there were fewer accidents and a significant reduction in Pinder's outbursts.
- Lorraine's analysis of children's records led her to suggest to staff that since so many children were not being identified as having made good progress in their mathematical development, she should organize some in-service education and training (INSET) to support staff development in that area and release key members of staff to review curriculum provision, in order to identify areas where planning and provision might be strengthened.
- Graham, a care assistant, following discussion with fellow practitioners, agreed that Glen, a toddler for whom he was the key person, was often fractious in the mornings and still grumpy when he awoke from his late morning nap. By being allowed to sleep shortly after arriving rather than later in the morning as was the normal pattern in the group, Glen played more happily for the rest of the day and his opportunities for learning were enhanced.
- Shona, a childminder, identified her need to learn more about children's drawing and mark-making when the mother of one of the children she looked after was critical of what her child was doing. Shona felt comfortable with what she was doing but did not know how to explain her views in a way which convinced the parent that she had a competent grasp of this aspect of development.

Reflection point
Can you think of examples of this kind of use of assessment in your setting? In what ways do you use observations to evaluate provision?

Are your assessment procedures manageable and informative?

- ***Is your assessment based on your general knowledge or understanding of young children?*** For example, you may observe Renée at 10 months of age 'reading' a book, turning the pages and mouthing sounds. If you do not know her you may regard this, as highly significant because many other babies of this age do not do this. However, you may go to Renée's record and find that this is not significant for her since several similar observations have already been made. Identifying significant achievement needs to be based on prior judgements or assessments about children's learning and development.

- *Is evidence about children's progress collected but not assessed?* Samples (such as drawings, paintings, photographs of block play, etc.) may be accumulated in a child's record but without contextual information, analysis or assessment they become meaningless. Hutchin (1999 citing QCA 1998) reminds us that 'assessment reveals how far children have acquired learning' and goes on to suggest (citing Drummond 1993) that assessment involves seeing learning, understanding it and putting understanding to good use. The person who chose to put a child's string and card collage in the filing cabinet perhaps had a good idea why he or she regarded it as significant. They may have recorded the date when the sample was collected but unless there is other vital information the sample will be without value. If no one has recorded the context under which it was made, such as whether the child selected the materials from a broad range, whether it was an adult-directed or child-initiated task, whether or not he or she chose to undertake the activity without prompting, etc. it will be difficult six months later to assess what it means for learning and progress. Hutchin (1999) suggests that it may be helpful to record the context; the area(s) of learning; what the practitioner believes the sample says about the child's learning and development; and what the implications for planning are.

- *Do children and parents have regular and significant opportunities to contribute to records?* Hutchin (2003: 54) suggests that the process of annotating samples can offer children 'a useful self-assessment conversation starter, giving ... [the] child an opportunity to voice their own opinion'. Ways of involving parents in this process will be discussed in Chapter 9.

- *Are assessments used to inform planning?* The most effective planning is based on assessments of children's learning and interests. This is a central tenet of high quality early years provision and is in line with EYFS guidance (DfES 2007: 11). The section entitled '*Look, listen and note*' will help practitioners to observe and assess effectively across the curriculum. The *Foundation Stage Audit Materials* (TTA 2004) are aimed at school managers or governors but are helpful in highlighting ways of monitoring provision and learning more generally. Table 7.2 suggests ways in which evidence drawn from assessments of children may be used to improve opportunities for learning.

Table 7.2 Using assessment evidence to understand and improve learning

Statement	Related questions	Evidence
The Foundation curriculum is suitably broad, balanced and relevant, and designed to support progress	How do we make sure that both taught and self-selected activities help children to make progress towards achieving planned objectives?	
	How do we make sure that the activities we provide are interesting and well matched to children's capabilities and interests, so that all children are well motivated and are developing concentration?	
	How do we use the outside area to support the Foundation Stage curriculum in all areas of learning?	
	How do we use the community and the local environment to enrich curriculum experiences?	
The Foundation Stage curriculum is well planned, documented and reflected in practice	How manageable are our planning formats?	
	Does our planning refer to learning intentions? How do we adapt it in light of daily practice with children?	
	How do we plan opportunities for children to make their own decisions in play and self-selected activities?	
	How do we monitor children's choices of activity in order to ensure a balance across the curriculum over time?	

Source: TTA (2004: s1.3).

Monitoring planning

The guidance for the EYFS (DfES 2007: 12) emphasizes the role of planning in 'making children's learning effective, exciting, varied and progressive'. It also underlines the value of planning as a team or, for those who work alone, in discussion with others in similar circumstances. It is the role of leaders to ensure that planning is being used to promote learning. In general, long-term planning will simply underline the principles or philosophy which underpins the work of your setting, your agreed approach to learning and teaching and key diary dates for the year.

Medium-term planning will usually demonstrate the focus for a period of about a term or half term and show that there will be even coverage of curriculum areas. In many early years settings, practitioners review their observations and assessments at regular (perhaps half-termly) intervals and in that process identify learning priorities or targets for learning for individual children. Hutchin (2003) suggests that this process should be undertaken on a rolling programme rather than undertaking all the reviews in one go. Her recommendation is to choose five children a week and to ensure that the whole team reviews one each day or five at the end of one day each week. This has a clear advantage in making the process more manageable but has the disadvantage of making it more difficult to use these targets to inform medium-term planning.

Reflection point
What is your view of the pros and cons of Hutchin's advice? If you work in a centre which has a shift system or in which staff often undertake a range of different roles in different teams, it may be very difficult to achieve.

Generally, short-term planning will be the detailed plan for a week or two. It will identify specific learning intentions for that period and will be responsive to children's interests, reflecting other interesting unforeseen events. From the observations (whether formal or informal) collected during the day or over the course of a week, staff may plan with the needs of specific individuals or groups of children in mind. Carr (2001) suggests that this may include:

- Planning for interest and involvement. This may involve the addition of resources to stimulate further play and exploration; a decision to base an adult in a particular area of the classroom (indoors and out); a particular line of questioning or discussion; organizing a visit or asking a visitor to come and talk about something.
- Planning for difficulty. This might also be thought of as planning for challenge, which may be physical or cognitive. Activities might be affective – seeking to improve a child's emotional well-being by promoting self-esteem and encouraging risk-taking; or social – encouraging closer working or negotiating between children.

These three layers of planning should interconnect. There will be distinct variations in the way in which settings manage these components but in general, short- and medium-term planning should between them demonstrate the following characteristics:

- identification of opportunities for planned observations;
- a focus on a manageable number of major learning intentions – perhaps one for each area of learning and development for each week;
- indications of where evidence of learning and interests have been used to inform or modify planning;
- flexible use of plans, which may change to take account of unexpected events or interests;
- changing and flexible use of resources;
- flexible deployment of staff to ensure that adults are available to engage with children's spontaneous play and self-initiated experiences as well as to lead focused activities;
- regular and robust evaluation of practice;
- wide involvement of team members in the planning and evaluation process.

Reflection point
Do the planning documents in your setting demonstrate these characteristics? If not, what can you change to make them (or the process by which they are arrived at) more effective and more responsive to children's individual learning and development?

Leaders' responsibilities in leading learning

Leaders have a responsibility to ensure that the provision they offer meets the requirements not only of the EYFS but also of *Every Child Matters*, the five outcomes of which require practitioners not only to assess enjoyment and achievement in the six areas of learning, but also to evaluate the extent to which children are staying healthy and are able to deal with risk in order to keep safe. This in turn requires organization within the setting which allows adults time to observe and interact. Emotional health requires play opportunities and the security of key working systems which require both careful planning, provision and assessment. Table 7.3 (a–d) underline the links between aspects of provision and the themes which form the basis of the EYFS. As you read them consider the ways in which you need to develop as a leader.

Table 7.3a The relationships between the four themes of EYFS and aspects of provision and learning

	Assessment	Learning and teaching strategies	Activities and experiences	Materials and resources	Organization
A unique child					
Child development	Sound knowledge of child development should inform all aspects of teaching and learning, including assessment				
Inclusive practice	Assessment should help practitioners to make sound judgements about children's needs and interests	Learning and teaching strategies should be identified on the basis of improving access to a wide range of learning experiences for all children		Are some additional resources needed to ensure access for all? Do resources reflect the experience of all children and the wider community?	Do some organizational practices (such as extended periods in large groups) cause particular difficulties for some children?
Keeping safe		Risk assessments should be carried out but should be balanced by a clear assessment of opportunities for learning and development that may be lost. Tree-climbing has its dangers – but not learning how to climb trees means that children may not learn to manage risks	The activities and experiences, materials and resources that we offer children should challenge and engage them. Being too intellectually safe undermines creativity		In order to risk making mistakes children need to feel secure. A predictable (but not boring) routine can help children to feel safe enough to take the risks that they need to in order to become effective learners

Table 7.3a (continued)

| Health and well-being | see references to Laevers' scales for well-being and involvement in Chapter 6 | The way in which practitioners support learning, the materials they provide and the experiences they plan should all demonstrate and model healthy lifestyles. Opportunities for sustained shared conversations about related topics should be exploited to promote children's interest | Organization should pay attention to children's right to physical health (e.g. toileting, eating, hand-washing routines) but should also pay attention to their need for emotional health |

Table 7.3b Positive relationships: the relationships between the four themes of EYFS and aspects of provision and learning

	Assessment	Learning and teaching strategies	Activities and experiences	Materials and resources	Organization
Positive relationships					
Respecting each other		Learning and teaching needs to focus on respectful interactions, beginning with the way in which practitioners listen to and support children facing behavioural challenges. Practitioners also need to model respect for each other and for other adults		Do resources reflect the experience of all children and the wider community and challenge unhelpful stereotypes?	
Parents as partners	Parents need to be closely involved in assessment of their children's learning, development and progress	Practitioners should engage parents in all aspects of provision – finding as many ways as possible to meet the needs of all parents, whether working, English-speaking, literate, etc.			Practitioners need to make time to talk to parents – both informally and in more formal planned contexts
Supporting learning	All these elements are vital to effective learning. Practitioners acting professionally will ensure that all are addressed through positive relationships with everyone involved in the care and education of children				

Table 7.3c Enabling environments: the relationships between the four themes of EYFS and aspects of provision and learning

	Assessment	Learning and teaching strategies	Activities and experiences	Materials and resources	Organization
Enabling environments					
Observation, assessment and planning	EYFS includes some clear guidance for assessment in the sections entitled *look, listen and note*				Time needs to be made to ensure that all members of the team can contribute to observation, assessment and planning
Supporting every child	In order to assess children's learning, practitioners need to be able to spend time with individuals and with small groups. This means that children who have additional support ought also to spend time with other adults so that they can benefit from different perspectives	Throughout the chapter we have identified a number of ways in which these three aspects of provision focus on supporting every child			Planning needs to ensure that all staff are deployed in the best interests of every child

Table 7.3c (continued)

	Assessment	Learning and teaching strategies	Activities and experiences	Materials and resources	Organization
The learning environment	A learning environment which allows for plenty of child-initiated activity supports assessment since practitioners can more easily identify what children can do and what they are struggling with				
The wider context	Observing children outdoors or in other contexts gives practitioners a more comprehensive view of children's achievements	Making use of other adults from the wider community helps to reflect the wider world	Activities and experiences, materials and resources all need to be real – to address children's concerns, reflect their experiences and widen their horizons. All children, but particularly those in settings with little or no outside provision, should spend time with other children and practitioners in the wider community – parks, museums, farms and so on		Planning needs to ensure that all staff are deployed in the best interests of every child. Opportunities for very small groups of children to go out also need to be planned

Table 7.3d Learning and development: the relationships between the four themes of EYFS and aspects of provision and learning

	Assessment	Learning and teaching strategies	Activities and experiences	Materials and resources	Organization
Learning and development					
Play and exploration Active learning	Active, playful learning offers the best insight into children's achievement	It is difficult to plan provision which flexibly supports play and exploration and builds on children's interests and enthusiasms. This has implications for the spontaneity with which practitioners can respond; the way in which resources are organized, and a routine which allows for extended periods of time in which children can learn to manage and direct their own learning			
Creativity and critical thinking	Extensive and flexible use of a wide range of materials is needed to assess creativity. Opportunities for sustained, shared conversation are needed to give practitioners insight into children's critical thinking	Similarly, creativity and critical thinking cannot be left to chance. They need similar levels and types of support. Making connections between aspects of provision supports creativity and critical thinking – using resources from one area to support play in another and so on. Take note of these words from EYFS (Card 4.3): 'It is difficult for children to make creative connections in learning when colouring in a worksheet or making a Diwali card just like everyone else's'			

Table 7.3d (continued)

	Assessment	Learning and teaching strategies	Activities and experiences	Materials and resources	Organization
Areas of learning and development	Achievement in all areas of learning and development needs to be highlighted and celebrated	A full range of learning and teaching strategies need to be used across all areas of learning and development. There is a danger that some areas may be based almost entirely on direct teaching, while others only arise in informal interactions and are rarely specifically planned	All areas of learning and development can be developed through a very wide range of activities and experiences. Problem-solving, reasoning and numeracy, for example, may be developed outdoors, in the home corner, the music area and so on. Similarly, resources designed to promote pattern-making may turn into food in the home corner and contribute to the development of creativity and imagination		Practitioners may need help to develop consistent and shared views but these will undoubtedly support learning across the curriculum

Key points

- Leaders have a responsibility to create within their setting a learning community which will include not only the children but staff and parents.
- Practitioners at all levels need to develop reflective practice and see themselves as lifelong learners.
- Reflective practice requires observation and assessment, monitoring and evaluation.
- Provision may be evaluated using a variety of tools.
- Monitoring children's learning and development requires sensitive listening and thorough systems and procedures in order to ensure consistency.
- Teaching must involve learning. It involves a very wide range of strategies which go beyond simply telling. Children learn through play, observation and talk – adults support the process by intervening in these processes to develop and extend thinking and understanding.
- In monitoring provision, leaders need to consider the activities or experiences offered, the materials and resources provided and the way in which time and space are organized as well as the responsibilities they have to address both the EYFS and *Every Child Matters*.

Practical tasks

1 Refer back to Tables 7.1 and 7.2 and try them out in your setting. Do they highlight any aspects of provision which you had not considered? Think about the way they could support you or members of the team in monitoring and evaluating provision and learning. What modifications would make them more relevant to your setting?

2 Using the questions below, evaluate the quality of the curriculum that you offer.

- Are children active and engaged or do they regularly appear listless or aimless?
- Are there similar amounts of time available for child-initiated and adult-directed activity?
- Does the curriculum build on prior learning and experiences, taking account of practitioners' observations and assessments of children?

- Is the curriculum relevant to children's age and stage of development?
- Are all children engaged by the activities provided with care and attention paid to their individual needs and experiences?

8 Leadership in a multi-agency context

> Does the involvement of a range of professional agencies, parents and the voluntary sector make complicated decisions easier or easy decisions more complicated?
>
> (Riddell and Tett 2001: 1)

Introduction

In Chapter 3 we discussed working together in terms of the 'core' team or those who are working together with children on a weekly or daily basis. This chapter extends the theme of teamwork by focusing on the notion of the 'wider' team in the context of multi-agency working. As a setting manager you will have worked with professionals from outside the setting in order to meet specific children's needs. In this chapter, we highlight the challenges and benefits for early years settings of working with 'outside' agencies. We suggest that effective implementation of multi-agency working is largely dependent on the co-operation of practitioners working with children in their settings. As a leader, it is part of your role to share information and skills as well as to develop positive working relationships with other professionals.

The chapter explores links between multi-agency working and improving outcomes for children. We then discuss the SENCO role, arguing that this is pivotal in the private, independent and voluntary sector. We argue that this role is not the sole remit of the designated SENCO but a shared set of roles and responsibilities. We move on to discuss issues relating the CAF, a generic tool to assess children's actual and potential 'additional needs' which relies on information sharing. The chapter concludes by looking a ways in which multi-agency working is being evaluated.

What is multi-agency working?

The drive towards 'partnership' working has gradually been replaced by the terms 'integrated' services, or 'integrated' working, encompassed in the notions of 'multi-agency' working and 'inter-agency' co-operation, used interchangeably in policy documents. There have been a number of attempts to define what is meant by multi-agency working and a variety of terms used, such as inter-agency, trans-disciplinary, interprofessional, multiprofessional, multidisciplinary and so on (Sanders 2004; Lumsden 2005). For the purposes of this chapter, we look at those professionals who, for whatever reason, come into contact with children in their settings and who should be working together and sharing information with each other, within the bounds of confidentiality.

The political basis for 'joined up' working and 'seamless' thinking is that it has inherent benefits for everyone involved. Common sense as well as more official channels dictate that members of different professions should share their knowledge and expertise. The commitment to the principle of working together stems from the belief that children's needs are not easily boxed into health, social or educational compartments and that children should be seen holistically within the context of a setting, a family and a community. As Wall (2006: 161) notes:

> We must work together in a collaborative manner sharing expertise, information and skills which need to be managed in a way that addresses the needs of families. Parents should not be responsible for passing on information from one professional to another. It is the responsibility of professionals.

Professionals should be working together to provide integrated, high quality support focused on the needs of the child. According to the DfES *Statutory Guidance on Inter-agency Co-operation* (2005: 13) such provision should be based on a shared perspective, effective communication systems and mutual understanding:

> Multi-agency working has a valuable role to play in improving outcomes for children and young people. Collaboration between people working in universal, targeted and specialist services strengthens inter-professional relationships, stimulates trust, promotes shared vision and values, increases knowledge of local services, provides alternative and creative intervention strategies, and addresses a wide range of risk factors. This, in turn, facilitates early identification, early intervention and preventative work.

The intention is that sectors should be working together at all levels, not only at ground level but at local and national levels. The Children Act 2004 requires each local authority to make clear arrangements for multi-agency working through establishing a Children's Trust (see Figure 8.1).

The Children Act 2004 also requires local authorities to establish a system of co-operation between 'relevant partners' in order to improve the well-being of children and young people and to safeguard and promote their welfare. Relevant partners include health and police authorities, and district councils. Children's well-being in the early years is defined as the mutually reinforcing *Every Child Matters* outcomes. As you saw in Chapter 4, for childcare and nursery education these are:

- helping children to be healthy;
- protecting children from harm or neglect and helping them to stay safe;

Figure 8.1 A Children's Trust in action
Source: DfES (2005: 7).

- helping children enjoy and achieve;
- helping children make a positive contribution to the provision and the wider community;
- organization.

Section 10(1)(c) of the *Statutory Guidance* (DfES 2005) states that other agencies engaged in activities for or with children and young people should be working co-operatively, including the children and families themselves, voluntary, private and community sector bodies, childcare and play organizations. The *Statutory Guidance* also suggests that multi-agency working arrangements should take place in and around places where children spend much of their time, such as schools or children's centres. Alternative settings might include village halls, sports centres, libraries and health centres.

Although few would disagree that there are potential benefits in working together to improve outcomes for children, it is important not to underestimate the complexity of creating multi-agency structures. It can present a number of challenges to delegated leaders, practitioners and parents. As Powell (2005: 81) notes, 'multi professional practices can be viewed as a comparatively uncomplicated, shared practitioner construction of children and their families'. The reality for many families is that different professionals only see bits of the child and do not see them holistically. This results in frustration for families as they struggle to find their way through a whole host of professionals, often having to repeat the same information over and over again.

According to Lumsden (2005) the embracing of other professionals, children, young people and their families is essential in developing shared meanings and working in collaboration. This implies that it is relationships between individual practitioners that will ultimately determine the reality of multi-agency working. It has been noted that the recent focus on the integration and co-ordination of early years settings and other professionals requires 'something more than benign co-operation across existing professions' (Abbott and Hevey 2001: 80). It seems that practitioners can no longer afford to stay within the 'comfort zone' of their own setting but must be prepared to listen to, and be listened to by, other professionals.

Harrison *et al.* (2003) consider the potential benefits of multi-agency working. They suggest that it centres energy and resources on a common problem, enabling a coherent and holistic approach to services for children. It can also lead to increased access to funding, and to greater credibility and authority. They list the characteristics of successful multi-agency working as:

- involving more than two agencies or groups, sometimes from more than one sector, for example, community health and education, and including key stakeholders;

- having common aims, acknowledging the existence of a common problem and having a shared vision of what the outcome should be;
- having an agreed plan of action;
- consulting with others including parents, children and the community;
- having agreed decision-making structures which are clearly articulated;
- striving to accommodate the different values and cultures of participating agencies;
- sharing resources and skills;
- the taking of risks;
- exchanging information using agreed communication systems;
- acknowledging and respecting the contribution that each agency can bring;
- establishing agreed roles and responsibilities, for example, through agreed sub-groups with terms of reference.

On the surface, some progress appears to have been made, notably the establishment of inter-agency early years centres, such as jointly funded Sure Start Centres, Integrated Children's Centres and Early Excellence Centres. However, there still appear to be some unresolved issues. Sloper (2004) concluded that there was little evidence of the effectiveness of multi-agency working in achieving improved outcomes for children and families. In a review of the work of Early Excellence Centres, Anning (2001) notes that teams of professionals from different agencies have been appointed with the brief to work in 'joined up' ways, although scant attention has been given to the challenge this creates for workers. The challenge is for practitioners to articulate and share their personal and professional knowledge of new ways of working. Other challenges include false perceptions of collaboration, commitment of time and resources, the need for positive personal relationships and clashes of beliefs between agencies.

A process of negotiation

Multi-agency working is a practical and evolving process of negotiation and communication between groups of professionals, occupations, sectors, agencies and disciplines. The term suggests that the children's workforce should work in a team context, forging and sustaining relationships across agencies and respecting the contribution of others working with children, young people and families. The implication is that all practitioners should actively seek and respect the knowledge and input of others. In the early years context there has been increasing intervention from 'outsiders' in recent years (e.g. advisory teachers, area SENCOs and development workers), each with their own message and each taking up precious time. In order to take full advantage of the knowledge, expertise and skills of each agency it is essential for practitioners to understand the roles and responsibilities of those working within each agency. This in turn requires a willingness of those working in schools or early years settings to accept the 'expertise' of others as an asset rather than a threat. However, forging shared perspectives with 'outside agencies' can be difficult to achieve when at best they may only visit from time to time and at worst may appear to see themselves as the 'professionals' on the basis of their experience, specific expertise and qualifications. A leader has to anticipate and manage possible sources of tension relating to differences in professional cultures including attitudes, values, beliefs and working practices. Positive relationships need to be encouraged if these visiting professionals are to be viewed as part of the wider team.

At the level of an individual early years setting, it is everyone's responsibility to ensure that the provision meets the needs of children and that each child reaches their full potential. For some children, this can only be achieved by input from several professionals. The most common reason for statutory or voluntary agencies to work with individual schools or early years settings is to support and advise practitioners in working with children who have been identified as needing extra support due to SEN.

Reflection point
How do you initiate and sustain contact with other professionals in a manner likely to promote trust and confidence in the relationship and the setting? How do you share information and skills with other professionals? What are the barriers to working effectively with other professionals? How could you improve your working relationships with other professionals?

The following scenario illustrates how easily tension may arise.

CASE STUDY

Isabel, a 4-year-old, diagnosed with autistic tendencies, has some behavioural and communication difficulties. She has spent over a year in a private nursery where the staff are experienced and trained in this field. With the support of a keyworker, she had been fully included in the life of the nursery, with few adaptations. The visiting SEN teacher suggested that Isabel would benefit from the use of a timeline and the staff were willing to try this strategy. However, on reflection after a period of time staff realized that Isabel was not benefiting from the timeline, and it was making her stand out as different to all the other children. The position of the timeline was also seen as exclusive as it highlighted to the other children and the parents that Isabel was a 'problem' and was special. The nursery manager telephoned the visiting SEN teacher and explained that she was going to remove the timeline from the wall. There was a rather heated discussion. When the visiting SEN teacher returned the situation was again discussed. The manager pointed out that they worked with Isabel every day and knew best, but the SEN teacher felt affronted that her idea had been rejected. After that point, no other children with SEN were referred to that nursery and the nursery manager lost confidence in the local SEN support services.

This case shows that multi-agency working involves a complex process of negotiation between individuals of which communication is an essential ingredient. By contrast, where there are positive relationships, the situation can be very productive. Support services can provide invaluable advice, in clarifying problems, in suggesting strategies for promoting learning and behaviour management and in liaising with parents. Outside specialists can help in the early identification of SEN and act as consultants, although it is still the SENCO who still has prime responsibility for co-ordinating the provision made for the child.

The role of the SENCO

The *Code of Practice* (DfES 2001b: 1.29) makes the important point that 'provision for children with special educational needs is a matter for everyone in the setting'. In addition to the headteacher or setting manager all other members of staff have important responsibilities. In practice, each setting can decide how to share day-to-day tasks and this will vary according to context. While the overall responsibility for implementing the *Code of Practice* lies with the setting's management group or head of setting, or in the case of schools with the governors and headteacher, the *Code* states that every setting or school should appoint a member of staff to assume responsibility for the day-to-day management of the provision for children with SEN. In non-maintained settings this may be the head of the setting. In the case of approved childminder networks the SENCO role may be shared between individual childminders or assumed by the co-ordinator of the network. Local authorities also appoint 'area SENCOs' to support settings in fulfilling their responsibilities. In local authority maintained nursery schools, the SENCO role is expected to be similar to that in the primary phase.

The *Code* promotes the SENCO to become a key decision-maker in the identification and assessment of young children perceived as having SEN. He or she is regarded as an important part of the management structure and organization. The *Code* provides a separate list of responsibilities for early years settings outside the local authority maintained sector in receipt of government funding to provide early education places. In these settings the SENCO should have responsibility for:

- ensuring liaison with parents and other professionals;
- advising and supporting practitioners in the setting;
- ensuring appropriate Individual Education Plans (IEPs) are in place;
- ensuring relevant information about children with SEN is collected, recorded and updated (DfES 2001b: 34).

Warwickshire County Council's (WCC 2002: 6) guidance for early education and childcare settings translates this into practice stating that:

> Each early education setting will need to identify a member of staff to act as the special educational needs co-ordinator or SENCO. This member of staff will be familiar with the *Code of Practice* and will lead and co-ordinate the staff in implementing the *Code* in the setting. The SENCO will be responsible for the following aspects of the SEN [policy] in practice.

It then provides a list of key responsibilities (2002: 6):

1 To manage the operation of the SEN policy and procedures in the setting.
2 To provide support so that all staff are informed and involved in SEN provision.
3 To liaise with parents of children with SEN and establish effective partnerships.
4 To ensure relevant background information about individual children with SEN is collected, recorded and updated.
5 To ensure that appropriate IEPs are in place and manage a cycle of IEP planning and review in accordance with the policy in the setting.
6 To liaise with all external agencies who may be involved with a child.
7 To set up and maintain a SEN register.
8 To contribute to the in-service training of staff.
9 To keep up to date with local and national changes in SEN practice and provision and keep all staff informed.
10 To monitor and review the SEN policy and practice in the setting.

This somewhat daunting list of management responsibilities can be divided into four areas. First, the SENCO is an administrator of the SEN assessment policy and procedures in the setting. He or she needs to plan, maintain, review and evaluate systems and policies relating to identification, assessment and provision for children with SEN. The day-to-day administrative tasks may include photocopying IEPs, making phone calls, filing, writing letters and record-keeping. SENCOs need to ensure appropriate records are kept at the stages of Early Years Action and Early Years Action Plus as well as for those children with statements of SEN.

Second, SENCOs provide the link between the setting, parents and external agencies. In this capacity they will be gathering information, talking to staff, parents and children, and chairing review meetings. They will be constantly monitoring, reviewing and evaluating children's progress in order to share information with parents and external agencies.

Third, the SENCO is expected to assume a leadership and management role, acting as a consultant to colleagues. Referring to primary school SENCOs, Moss (1996) points out that a large part of the role involves trying to ensure that colleagues do their part in assessing and making provision for all the children described as having SEN. A fundamental task for the early years SENCO is to support, guide and motivate early years workers, particularly in disseminating examples of effective practice. The role of all early years practitioners in identifying and assessing children perceived as having SEN is closely linked with the SENCO role, as they should be working together to address individual children's needs. The SENCO may also be expected to plan and deliver professional development to others, prepare for and manage documents for inspections including the SEN policy, the SEN register, information given to all parents on SEN provision and evidence of training and staff development relating to SEN and inclusion. The SENCO may be asked to manage finance and resources.

Fourth, the SENCO is assumed to be an expert in SEN practice and provision, directing the strategic development of teaching and learning. They are expected to co-ordinate assessment, provision and support for individual children with SEN, ensuring any child causing concern is followed through in terms of the *Code*. The SENCO should take the lead in further assessment of the child's needs, looking at both strengths and weaknesses. They should make sure that the child's individual education plan is appropriate in terms of targets and strategies. As Simmons (1994: 56–7) points out in relation to school SENCOs: 'This person will carry great responsibilities as well as a greatly increased workload ... who would consent to undertake this role? And how many will be able to fulfil the role adequately, without the training, resources and time needed to do the job properly?'

It is hardly surprising that the *Code* makes the point that in early education settings the SENCO will require sufficient time to undertake these responsibilities and suggests that settings 'may find it effective for the SENCO to be member of the senior management team' (DfES 2001b: 4.17). Undoubtedly, the setting manager must allow the SENCO dedicated time to carry out his or her duties. Time allocated should be in proportion to the number of children on the SEN register. It might also be useful to share some of the tasks with colleagues. Apart from the time management issue, the paperwork involved in administering the *Code* may be a source of anxiety for early education SENCOs.

The *National Standards for Special Educational Needs Co-ordinators* (TTA 1998) sets out some suggested additional knowledge, skills, attributes and expertise required by those co-ordinating provision in schools. These have been adapted below to apply to early education settings. SENCOs should have knowledge and understanding of:

- the characteristics of effective teaching and learning strategies and how they can support children with SEN and improve or maintain children's learning, behaviour and development;
- how to devise and evaluate systems for identifying, assessing and reviewing children's learning and developmental needs;
- the nature and purpose of IEPs, how they are formulated and how they can be used to best effect;
- how information technology can be used to help children gain access to the curriculum, learn and communicate;
- up-to-date relevant legislation, research and inspection evidence;
- the requirements to communicate information to local authorities, external agencies, parents and other schools or settings;
- the scope and role of local support services including voluntary schemes;
- the range of ways available for working in partnership with parents;
- how to contribute to the professional development of other staff.

According to the Teacher Training Agency (TTA 1998: 9–10), SENCOs should possess the following skills and attributes:

Leadership and decision-making skills in order to:

- create and fostering confidence and commitment among staff to meet the needs of all children;
- set standards and provide examples of good practice in identifying, assessing and meeting children's SEN;
- provide professional direction to the work of others;
- develop policy, record systems and procedures;
- manage resources;

- make decisions based on information/evidence;
- judge when there is a need to consult outside agencies.

Communication and self-management skills in order to:

- communicate effectively orally and in writing with children, colleagues and parents, and external agencies;
- negotiate and consult with parents and outside agencies;
- chair reviews, case conferences and meeting effectively;
- prioritize and manage own time;
- take responsibility for own professional development.

As with any leadership and management role, personal qualities are a key factor of the SENCO. The SENCO should have a personal impact on the setting, demonstrating enthusiasm and commitment, self-confidence, reliability and integrity as well as intellectual ability and the ability to adapt to a variety of situations. As mentioned earlier, SENCO responsibilities can be shared between practitioners. A nursery assistant, for example, could handle the one-on-one support in enabling children to achieve the IEP targets and be responsible for the record-keeping. The head of the setting could liaise with external agencies and write the SEN policy. A keyworker could be responsible for sharing information with parents. As well as identifying thier own professional development needs, the SENCO needs to find out what help and advice their colleagues need.

Reflection point
Have you discussed with staff their need for advice in supporting children with SEN? Is the designated SENCO viewed as a management role? Have you reflected on the skills and knowledge of your SENCO? How does your SENCO liaise with other professionals?

A more recent initiative known as the CAF (*Common Assessment Framework*) has been introduced to provide further impetus for information-sharing between professionals and multi-agency working. This will be implemented by schools, childcare providers, children's centres, health services and children's services including those in the voluntary sector.

The CAF

Since the publication of the Green Paper *Every Child Matters* (DfES 2003) and the Children Act 2004, managers of early years settings have been inundated with non-statutory guidance and policy documents. One initiative, the CAF, was specifically intended to 'drive multi-agency working by embedding a shared process, developing a shared language of need and improving the information flow between agencies' (DfES 2005: 15). It sets out to help practitioners develop shared understanding of children's needs and forms a basis for early intervention before problems reach crisis point. It can be used by practitioners who have been on training to assess the needs of unborn babies, infants, children and young people.

A common assessment is generic rather than specific. It is not concerned with measuring progress towards specific milestones or targets and can be used earlier than specialist assessments. It may also feed into other types of assessment, for example, the SEN *Code of Practice*. Common assessments are intended to be an easy and accessible process for all practitioners: holistic and voluntary, solution- and action-focused. They are transferable between services and areas based on developing a culture of understanding and trust. The common assessment process is based on the idea of a continuum of needs and services (see Figure 8.2), although the majority of children should not need a common assessment. A common assessment is not, for example, for situations where a child has obvious needs and a specialist or statutory assessment is required. Practitioners need to decide which children are at potential risk of

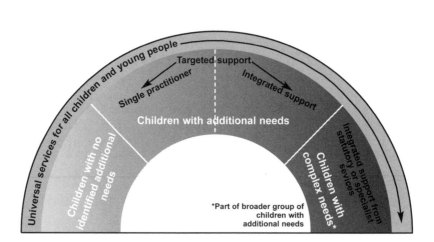

Figure 8.2 Continuum of needs and services (DfES 2006a: 7)

poor outcomes without extra services, although this does not guarantee the provision of those services.

As Figure 8.2 shows, children said to have 'additional' needs may require targeted support either from a single practitioner or a range of integrated services. However, children with complex needs (who are still part of the broad group with additional needs), require statutory or specialist services. These children may or may not have 'SEN' which are 'educational'.

How to do a common assessment

The CAF process consists of three steps, officially referred to as preparation, discussion and delivery (see Figure 8.3). First the practitioner needs to check if anyone else is working with the child as a common assessment may already be in place. This would normally be by asking the parent or carer or there may

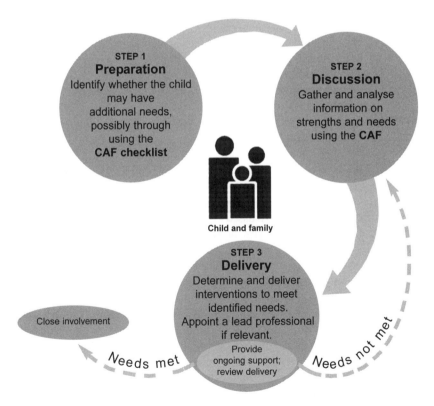

Figure 8.3 The three steps in the common assessment process (DfES 2006a: 17)

be a local system for logging common assessments. Discussion with a line manager and colleagues could also help decide if a common assessment is needed. If the practitioner is not sure whether an assessment is needed the CAF pre-assessment checklist can be used (DfES 2006b). It is intended to lead to better understanding as to whether an assessment is needed, a decision to be made jointly with the child and the child's parents or carers.

The information is recorded during the discussion with the child and family onto the CAF form. It is essential to ensure that parents understand what information is being recorded, what will be done with it and when. The CAF form is an instrument for recording the discussion, which has eight stages with discussion prompts provided for each. The practitioner is required to record the child's strengths as well as needs. The discussion prompts are listed below.

1   Explain the purpose of the assessment.
2   Complete the basic identifying details.
3   Assessment information.
4   Details of the parents/carers.
5   Current home and family situation.
6   Details of services working with the child.
7   Assessment summary
    a)   development of the child
    b)   parents and carers
    c)   family and environment.
8   Conclusions, solutions and actions.

Stage 7 is the basis of the discussion which is intended to be collaborative and based around the three domains of children, parents and environment. First, the development of the child, including areas such as health, behaviour, learning and self-esteem is discussed. The second element relates to parents and carers and is concerned with basic safety and care, emotional stability, guidance, boundaries and stimulation. Third, family and environmental factors form part of the assessment. This area covers aspects such as housing, finance and family well-being.

It may be that the child's needs are such that no additional action is required. If action is needed it could be by the family, within the service or setting carrying out the assessment, or there may be a need to try and access support from other agencies. Where it is agreed that the child has complex needs and integrated services are required, the practitioner will need to contact the relevant person in the local area.

Where appropriate, it is the lead professional who assumes responsibility for co-ordinating the provision of services. The lead professional stems from the CAF process where a child's needs are such that they require support from more than just one practitioner. One practitioner assumes the role of lead professional in co-ordinating the action identified as a result of the assessment process. In some cases, where the child's needs are more complex and they receive a specialist assessment, there may already be a single point of contact who will assume the role of lead professional (e.g. named social worker, keyworker).

Information-sharing

The non-statutory guidance on information-sharing intended for everyone working with children or young people, in the public, private and voluntary sectors, including volunteers, suggests that improving information-sharing is a 'cornerstone' of the government strategy to improve outcomes for children (DfES 2006c).

> **Reflection point**
> What are the purposes, advantages and disadvantages of information-sharing? What challenges does it present?

It is claimed that sharing information is essential to enable early intervention to help those who need additional services, thus reducing inequalities between disadvantaged children and others. The guidance sets out six key points (DfES 2006c: 5):

1   Practitioners should explain to children, young people and families from the beginning of the process which information will be shared, the reasons why and how it will be shared. The exception being that if an open explanation would put the child or others at risk of significant harm.
2   The safety and welfare of the child is paramount and must be an overriding consideration.
3   Whenever possible, if the child or family do not consent to have information shared, their wishes should be respected.
4   You should seek advice especially if you have concerns about a child's safety or welfare.
5   It is essential to check that information is accurate, up to date, necessary for the purpose, and shared securely with only those who need to see it.
6   Record decisions whether you decide to share information or not.

Although information should be shared on a 'need to know' basis the potential for sharing information is enormous, with implications not only for workload and time management but primarily in relation to consent and confidentiality. One daunting factor is the sheer number of professionals with whom practitioners may have to work in education, health and social services as well as the many voluntary organizations. Figure 8.4 shows the key agencies working with children or young people.

The hub shown has 13 sectors and each has its own internal communication network. Although maintained schools have been required for some time to publish information about their arrangements for working with health, social services, local authority support services and any relevant local

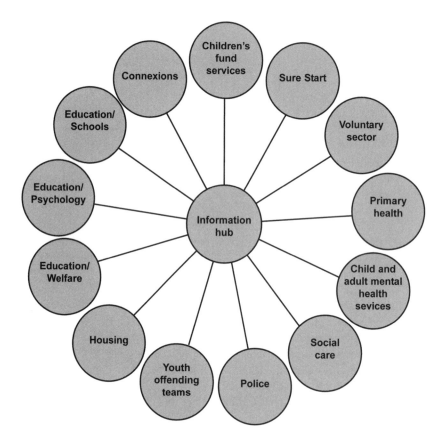

Figure 8.4 The information hub
Source: DfES (2003: 54).

and national voluntary organizations, it is a huge task for non-maintained early years settings to find out who the support services and agencies are and how to contact them. The list below is a typical non-exhaustive example:

- Speech and language therapist.
- Area SENCO.
- Development worker.
- Advisory teachers.
- Community nurse/health workers.
- Educational psychologist.
- Child Development Centre.
- General practitioner.
- Physiotherapist.
- Social workers.
- Education welfare officer.
- Family support worker.
- Specialist teachers (e.g. of sensory impairments).
- Parent Partnership Service.

CASE STUDY

A practitioner had been concerned for some time regarding 2-year-old David's health and nutrition. She had observed that the contents of his lunchbox were sparse and nearly always the same. When she tried to speak to his mother informally, she commented that all he ate at home was dog food (there were several dogs in the family flat) and how cheap it was. The practitioner reported her concerns to the manager. The manager contacted the social services. Discussions followed involving the health visitor and housing department, social services and the local Sure Start centre. Through information-sharing the professionals worked together with the parents to improve the child's living conditions and diet.

The Data Protection Act 1998 does not prevent the sharing of information but sets parameters for sharing information lawfully. Professionals need to record and update parental consent to share information with others, preferably in writing. Professionals need to be made aware of the nature of confidentiality, and when and why it is sometimes possible to pass on information *without* consent. This is a complex area and there are significant training implications.

Evaluation of multi-agency working

The success of multi-agency working will be continually evaluated at various levels. Statutory arrangements are in place for joint inspection of all children's services in a local authority. Ofsted and the Commission for Social Care Inspection are beginning to assess performance annually and give an overall rating of a council's children's services in improving the lives of children. Joint Area Reviews report on how well services are working together to secure positive outcomes for children and young people. They involve nine inspectorates and commissions in assessing how social, health, education and criminal justice services and systems combine to contribute to improved outcomes. Progress is monitored against priority national targets and other indicators. In primary schools, Ofsted inspectors judge the extent to which the education in the school meets the needs of the range of pupils and the contribution made by the school to the well-being of those pupils. Inspectors assess the overall effectiveness of the school, including how far the curriculum is responsive to external requirements and local circumstances. This would include any extended services, the effectiveness of links with other providers, services, employers and other organizations to promote the integration of care and education so as to enhance learning and promote well-being. In early years settings Ofsted inspectors also judge whether the childminding, day care and/or nursery education meet the needs of the range of children for whom it is provided and how well the organization promotes children's well-being. The clear message is that the entire children's workforce should be working together at every level – with each other and with parents and families to improve the lives of children.

For multi-agency working to be effective in practice, there needs to be a clear and explicit rationale as there may be deep-rooted cultural differences between professional groups, vested interests in maintaining boundaries and statutory restrictions undermining efforts. A number of key issues such as lack of time, lack of understanding of the purpose of multi-agency practice, professional rivalry and ownership of resources still need to be addressed. Challenges remain in the areas of planning, implementation and ongoing management. These include promoting an increased understanding and awareness of the roles and responsibilities of other professionals, joint funding, joint training, joint policies, rationalization of professional differences and joint planning (Wall 2006).

Key points

- The call for bringing together a range of professional identities, experiences and perspectives is not without its challenges.
- Individual practitioners need to promote an inclusive approach to professional difference and develop a range of different models enabling collaboration.
- The role of the SENCO is a leadership and management one which can be shared between practitioners.
- The CAF is a shared generic assessment tool to be used across all settings and services.

Practical tasks

1   Collect as much information as possible about your local support services and agencies. Read the information and store it in a file accessible to all staff.
2   Make contact with your nearest Children's Centre and explore ways of working together.
3   Invite local professionals such as the health visitor into your setting.

9 Leadership and parental involvement

> Family participation requires many things, but most of all it demands ... a multitude of adjustments. [Practitioners] must possess a habit of questioning their certainties, a growth of sensitivity, awareness, and availability, the assuming of a critical style of research and continually updated knowledge of children, an enriched evaluation of parental roles, and skills to talk, listen, and learn from parents.
>
> (Malaguzzi 1995: 63)

Introduction

In Chapter 4, the notion of a leader's responsibility to work in partnership with parents was discussed. In this chapter we will consider the importance of parents and professionals working closely together to support and enhance children's well-being. Malaguzzi's words cited above highlight the many skills that are required if practitioners are to be led to successful partnership with parents and families. The barriers to working with parents and what leaders can do to develop effective relationships with parents will be considered. The role of leaders in influencing both parents and staff members to enhance the quality of partnership will be explored. Finally, Whalley's (2001) analysis of the responsibilities of early years professionals towards parents will be examined and the role of leaders in supporting such partnerships will be considered.

Lightening the load

The idea that failure to establish positive relationships with parents can place unnecessary and unhelpful pressure on the children themselves (Jowett and

Baginsky 1991) is not a new one. However, all too often this can be forgotten. The effects of positive early experiences inevitably have a lifelong impact. Outcomes, both positive and negative, are not readily linked to the roots of success or failure. Recent research (Wood and Caulier-Grice 2006), for example, suggests that the long-term impact of early years initiatives is highly dependent on the quality of children's subsequent experiences at primary school.

In his review of research studies looking at the effects of parental involvement on children's education, Charles Desforges (2003) stresses that the fact that children themselves play an active part in bridging the gap between home and a school or early years setting. When children are very young this role as mediator can place a great deal of stress on them. As Martin Hughes (cited in Pound 2006: 140) comments:

> Children grow up within a closely linked network of people, based on their family, which makes up their community. Much of children's early learning takes place within this network. When they start school, children find themselves in a very different world, from which there are few links either to their own community or to the kind of knowledge they have acquired within that community. One of the tasks of school must be to help children create these links. This will not be an easy task, and schools will need all the help they can get – particularly from parents.

An outreach worker on a project involving parents in their young children's mathematical development commented on the additional stress placed on children when their parents are not familiar with the school system because they have not been educated in this country. She suggested that the project in which she was involved was 'lightening the load for the child' (Pound 2006) by educating parents.

Partnership with parents should lead professionals to consider what parents do at home with their children – working with them to develop what they do to make home life as supportive as possible for children's development and learning. The EPPE (Effective Provision of Preschool Education) project, which tracked the progress of 3000 young children through various forms of preschool provision draws attention to the impact of the home. As part of that work, researchers sought to identify the effect of the home learning environment on young children's progress (Melhuish *et al.* 2001). They characterized a positive home learning environment as one in which children and parents sing and recite nursery rhymes together, play with numbers and shapes (and letters), visit the library, and where there are rich opportunities for painting and drawing. In general, parents in such homes make learning a high profile and enjoyable part of day-to-day life.

What is especially striking about the EPPE study is that the quality of the home learning environment is highlighted as the variable in the early years which can be seen to have the most lasting effect on children's long-term achievement and progress (Desforges 2003). In earlier studies, the quality of preschool education received (see e.g. Sylva *et al.* 1999); the mother's level of education (see e.g. Tizard and Hughes 1984); or the socioeconomic status of the family (see e.g. Hart and Risley 1995) have all been regarded as being the most decisive factors in the learning and progress of young children.

While it is apparent that all of these factors have an enormous impact on subsequent achievement, the EPPE study maintains that the home learning environment has an even greater impact. Desforges (2003) suggests that this is because parents come to see themselves as having the ability to help their children. This in turn, he claims, has a positive effect on the child's own self-image as a learner.

Reflection point
In what ways are you able to help parents to recognize their abilities to support their own children's learning and development? As a leader, how do you help other team members to see the importance and value of involving parents in this way? Even if you work alone, and do not readily regard yourself as a leader, think about the ways in which you lead or influence parents to see themselves in this vital role.

Professionals as partners

We are used to talking about *parents as partners* but as Langford and Weissbourd (1997: 153) remind us, if we turn the phrase around and think of *professionals as partners*, we realize that we are not always thinking of an entirely equal relationship. This may heighten our awareness of the need to consider an alternative view of working with parents. Langford and Weissbourd go further, writing about a concept of parent leadership. They identify the possibility that a barrier to full participation may be low self-esteem or lack of confidence in parents.

In order to empower parents it is suggested that they be actively involved in governance or management of the setting or centre – not simply acting as representatives. Langford and Weissbourd suggest four steps to make empowerment of parents at this level a reality.

1   *Training for staff to develop the necessary skills and confidence to work on more equal terms with parents*. This ties in

well with Malaguzzi's suggestions cited at the beginning of the chapter about the range of skills or adjustments needed to engage fully with parents and families.

2 ***Opportunities for parents to access leadership training.*** This is a really radical suggestion, based on an assumption that the receivers of service – the families who are the primary advocates, protectors and nurturers of their children – have something important to contribute. Parents become leaders when they have the opportunity to do so and when the environment is sufficiently supportive for them to claim it as their own (Langford and Weissbourd 1997: 153).

3 ***Developing a more widespread consensus that 'policies must target the child and the family, not the child alone'*** (Langford and Weissbourd 1997: 153). This is very much in line with current policies being developed as part of the childcare agenda. There is a growing realization that young children cannot be seen in isolation.

4 ***Recognition of the need for increased staffing to cope with the the demands of 'a more comprehensive parent-support program'*** (Langford and Weissbourd 1997: 153). When policy-makers cite the long-term beneficial effects of high quality early education, they frequently draw on High/Scope research (Weikart 2000). This research suggests that for every dollar spent on such services, at least 7 dollars may be saved. However, the research does not mention that an important component of High/Scope provision included in the study was the involvement of parents.

Reflection point
Spend some time reflecting on these four points. It is probably beyond contention that staff benefit from training and that provision for young children must take account of the needs of families. Enhanced levels of staffing to make it possible to develop support programmes for parents are probably out of the question. Are there any ways in which you can get round this restriction? Perhaps you can use support staff from the local authority or perhaps you have some parents who are able to develop programmes for themselves. The most contentious of the points that Langford and Weissbourd make is that about parent leadership. Would that work or is it too idealistic?

CASE STUDY

Louise had been the head of an early years centre in an inner city area for some time. The setting included two distinct cliques or groups of parents – large numbers of young single mothers lived on the estate in which the setting was sited but many of the places at the nursery were taken up by children from more advantaged families in neighbouring areas. This was often because the more advantaged families were more settled, living in owner-occupied houses and able to get their children's names on the extensive waiting list very early. Most of the mothers living on the estate were moved frequently and rarely put their children's names on the waiting list as they did not expect to still be living in the area by the time their children were old enough to start nursery.

Louise realized that something had to be done to challenge the status quo but was surprised when she raised the issues with staff that most of them saw no problem. The consensus among the staff was that the waiting list was fair and that the parents who got their children's names down early really valued the places. Louise decided that some training was needed. In addition to pinpointing some relevant courses organized by the local authority and by private training companies, she organized a whole staff session to consider some of the reasons that staff felt more comfortable with the more advantaged parents. She realized that a genuine and lasting change in the attitudes of staff members would only be achieved over time.

At the same time she set up sessions for parents to help them learn more about children's learning and development. Sessions of this sort, organized in the past, had attracted the more articulate parents and this had not left room for many of the young parents that Louise now wanted to attract. She decided that the training would be linked to practical sessions – such as baby massage – so that a wider audience would feel able to join in. She employed an educational psychologist to run a regular surgery for parents facing sleep, feeding or behaviour problems. The most successful strategy was that of lending video cameras to parents and sharing and discussing with staff video footage taken in school and at home. Louise 'borrowed' this idea from something she had read about and was amazed at how effective it was.

Louise adopted yet another very helpful strategy. One member of the team, Sarah, had begun as a parent helper. She had been a very young mother and had over a period of seven or eight years undertaken a range of increasingly demanding paid roles in the school. She had successfully completed an NVQ2 qualification and had recently begun NVQ3 training. Louise decided to ask Sarah to take on the task of running some of these groups. Sarah's experience and credibility with both local parents and the staff team were major assets and she undertook this role very successfully. She was, moreover, able to take a lead among staff members, positively influencing any negative feelings and creating a much more equal partnership with parents.

Establishing effective relationships with parents

The preschools of Reggio Emilia have been listed among the best in the world by *Time* magazine. They also place a strong emphasis on working with parents. The ten key principles (www.sightlines.inititive.com/keyprinciples) include two which are of particular significance here. Parents are identified as partners and 'resource people'. A much more strongly worded principle is headed *'Children are connected'* and states: 'The child is a member of a family and a community rather than an isolated individual. The child learns through interaction with peers, adults, objects and symbols. Preschool centres are seen as a system of relations embedded in a wider social system'.

Historically, pioneers such as Margaret McMillan and Maria Montessori understood the importance of establishing strong relationships with parents. Over the last 50 years of British education there have been a number of developments in the involvement of parents in their children's education and it is accepted that failure to establish effective relationships with parents places an unnecessary burden on children. Sometimes team members find it easier to interact with some parents than with others. It is important to monitor interactions with parents to be certain that particular groups of parents are not being unwittingly excluded.

It is, of course, true that not all parents are as easy as others to engage in sound relationships. In a chapter entitled 'Persistence pays off: working with "hard to reach" parents', Arnold (2001: 110–1) presents two case studies of parents who had difficulty in building relationships with staff. Because of unhappy school experiences, the mothers had difficulty in feeling comfortable in their children's early years setting. Arnold lists the wide range of feelings and emotions that may be triggered by entry to a school building or similar institution and these include inadequacy, fear, anger and isolation.

CASE STUDY

Harpreet, a childminder, was well aware of the need (identified by Arnold 2001) to use a wide range of strategies in an effort to overcome such negative feelings in parents. She understood why it was difficult for some parents to accept suggestions about meal times or changes in sleeping patterns among the children she cared for, and she knew that it was important to overcome barriers connected to personal feelings. She worked hard at getting to know parents, particularly those who were not easy to communicate with and found that as she got to know them better she gained a better understanding of the difficulties they faced as working parents and also won them round by demonstrating how well she knew and cared about their children.

She learned to listen to complaints and to try to understand what was behind what appeared to her sometimes to be trivial issues. When, for example, Simon's dad picked him up one day he became angry about the fact that Simon had been changed into dry clothes. In calming him and talking it through, it became apparent to Harpreet that Simon's father was really upset because he was taking Simon to visit his grandmother and the clothes in which he had arrived in the morning were ones which had been a present from her. The issue was quickly resolved: the clothes had not been soiled, they were merely wet from helping with the washing-up and had already been dried. Had Harpreet reacted in the angry tone of the father rather than trying to find out what the problem was, the situation could have quickly escalated into an unpleasant confrontation. Her professionalism helped her to act in a leaderful fashion.

Reflection point
Think about an interaction with a parent that has been less successful than you would have liked. Think about why the parent responded as they did. Do you think he or she was feeling some of the emotions that Arnold highlights? You might consider:

- the parent's reason or motive;
- whether you responded in the most appropriate way;
- what you might have done to improve the relationship.

Disaffection or a reluctance to build relationships among parents can arise from a number of factors. 'Hard-to-reach' parents may include those: 'with mental health difficulties or the ones who are confronting drug dependency and/or alcohol-related issues. It also includes single parents (male and female) as well as refugees, travellers and others drawn from minority groups' (Jones *et al.* 2005: 65). In commenting on these groups and a group to whom they refer simply as 'the poor', Jones *et al.* add that some approaches to the involvement of parents are based on 'fear and the need to control the behaviour of diverse and less powerful others'. They further suggest that such approaches set out to standardize and regulate parents' behaviour. This view challenges the idea of support strategies such as parenting classes since the aim is seen as 'harnessing' or managing parents rather than seeking their active and democratic involvement. Jones *et al.* propose what they term a 'transforming' approach to the involvement of parents. They suggest that transforming approaches require that practitioners see themselves as part of a learning community alongside parents. This would mean that practitioners would avoid the use of over-technical language which may exclude parents and would not seek to educate parents into a way of interacting with their children which emphasizes a single style or approach to parenting. Hughes (2003 cited by Jones *et al.* 2005: 69) offers the following definition: 'A transforming approach to relationships between educators and parents promotes democratic citizenship by inviting parents and others to form policies, manage resources and evaluate services; and by devolving decisions about what and how children should learn.'

Reflection point
Do you think it would be possible (or desirable) for your workplace to develop transformative relationships with parents? If the approach adopted by early years settings towards parents were truly democratic, is it possible that decisions might become the prerogative of a small group of articulate parents determined to push through strategies and initiatives which meet the needs of their children but may not be in the interests of other children and their families?

Jones *et al.* (2005: 70) suggest that 'the key principles which underpin a transforming approach' to building effective relationships with parents include 'listening to parents; respecting parents' views concerning children and their learning; avoiding hierarchies by establishing equitable partnerships; and including parents at all stages of planning'. Arnold (2001: 111) reminds us of the ways in which institutions can unwittingly make it difficult to establish relationships with parents. She writes that:

> Organizations are usually run by powerful people who have succeeded in attaining a position of authority. Often they are run to suit the majority and this may exclude minorities. We are aware of 'institutional racism', that is when organizations have rules or structures that prevent minority ethnic groups from joining ... Schools sometimes have rules that prevent children from having an equal opportunity to attend, for example, an expensive uniform, which is obligatory. These sorts of barriers are structural.

It is also important to acknowledge that professionals' lack of knowledge can be at the root of a failure to build good relationships with parents. Different cultures have different ways of interacting and practitioners can easily misunderstand or be misunderstood in their communication with parents. Janet Gonzalez-Mena (2005: 29–30) reminds us that unless we have a full picture and know the meanings attached to certain behaviours it is easy to misinterpret what we see. She writes:

> The meaning you attach to the behaviour may not be even remotely related to the meaning the person you're encountering puts on it. A smile may not mean friendliness or even happiness; it may mean embarrassment. When you combine words, gestures, facial expressions, timing, proximity, and all other parts of an exchange, the meanings become even more complex.
>
> In any cross-cultural exchange, it is vital that you find out what meanings the behaviours have to the person performing them rather than doing what is natural – assigning meanings and values to the behaviour of others based on your own culture. It is also vital to understand that your behaviour doesn't necessarily convey your own meanings and values to the other person.

She continues by pointing out that when practitioners feel upset or angered by the actions of parents they should try to understand what is intended or meant. This aspect of relationships is part of being reflexive – it involves putting yourself in the parent's shoes and trying to understand the meaning of their actions. It will require increased understanding of patterns of communication in a range of cultures, including six factors that Gonzalez-Mena (2005: 38) identifies as supporting language:

1 *Personal space* – how close you sit or stand to communicate with someone you do not know well.
2 *Smiling* – what a smile means, when to smile, and how to interpret another's smile.
3 *Eye contact* – do you expect the person you are communicating with to look you in the eye? What is culturally appropriate for a family and its children?
4 *Touch* – touching someone can bring you closer or create barriers. Learning the cultural meanings of touch is important.
5 *Silence* – what is the meaning of silence and how much is too much? Silence has important cultural meanings.
6 *The language of time* – is a person late just because you think so? What does 'late' mean anyway? Is 'beating around the bush' a waste of time?

As a leader within your team, parents and other team members will often look to you to take a lead in developing negotiated agreements, conflict, resolution and mutual education. It is in no one's interest, least of all the child's, to allow difficult relationships between parents and staff to persist.

Reflection point
As a leading professional within your setting, it is for you to find strategies which will make interaction effective and comfortable for all. As the leader within a team or context what have you been able to do to make interactions increasingly comfortable?

Fulfilling professional responsibilities towards parents

Whalley (2001) praises the role of the *Start Right* report (Ball 1994) in acknowledging the unique nature of parents' contributions and commitment to their children's learning and development. She suggests that it is the responsibility of early childhood practitioners to give support to parents by modelling effective practice, giving them information about research and opportunities for enhancing their personal knowledge of children's development, and to develop self-esteem.

Responsibility to exemplify good practice

If leaders are to ensure that parents and families find good practice in relation to the development and well-being of young children, there are many steps they will need to take. Many settings run curriculum evenings and offer parents leaflets and displays illustrating and explaining aspects of effective practice. These alone however will not be sufficient since nothing is more powerful than day-to-day models of what effective practice looks like. Among the actions needed to ensure that teams address this responsibility, leaders will need to:

- ensure that all interactions between children and adults are positive and professional;
- develop policy so that there is consistent practice among staff;
- monitor practice to ensure that the highest standards are maintained;
- monitor planning and assessment to identify strengths and areas for development;
- create a climate within the setting where everyone feels able to make suggestions for improving and developing practice and for constructively challenging aspects of practice;

- ensure a learning culture where everyone seeks to continually develop their own knowledge and expertise.

Responsibility to provide information about current research

National policy and research into aspects of early childhood care and education often offer conflicting viewpoints. This can be both confusing and worrying for parents. The debate over the impact of day care on children's behaviour, for example, has led many parents to feel anxious and guilty. By ensuring that the staff team take time to explore and discuss relevant research, leaders can simultaneously support professional development and help to ensure that practitioners feel confident in discussing research findings with parents. Leaders can also create annotated displays of newspaper cuttings, since these are often misleading and such a display will allow parents to ask questions and consider conflicting views. A parents' reference library can help parents to become aware of current research on children's care and development.

Responsibility to offer appropriate parent education and professional support

Many early years settings offer classes and support groups for parents. Leaders can support this by encouraging staff to work with parents in identifying what is needed – and then evaluating the effectiveness of the offer. You may think that baby massage would be a nice addition to the services you provide but if no hard-to-reach parents attend, you may need to rethink. In one setting, a cookery class had been running but had to close because too few parents attended. A mother who had attended offered to take it on and was much more successful in recruiting parents. She knew the budgetary constraints under which many parents lived and was able to help them make cheap and nutritious meals.

Responsibility to help parents to develop and sustain their sense of self-esteem and self-efficacy

This may be achieved through many different strategies, including those identified above. Making parents more aware of what and why professionals do what they do can be empowering as can having additional opportunities to develop skills and knowledge. However, leaders might consider ways of improving partnership between parents and practitioners as a method of developing parents' self-esteem.

Partnership and conflict

Ronco and Ronco (2005) focus on partnership and describe the symptoms of what they call the Babel Problem. They suggest that when partnerships fail, people become confused and focus on their own problems rather than on shared goals. This often occurs where people speak a different language and is exacerbated because this means that people do not listen to one another. The authors are focusing on industry but the Babel Problem can be found in some early years settings. There may be confusion or at least a lack of clarity about the purpose of early years settings. This may lead to disagreements, with practitioners and parents unwilling or unable to see one another's point of view. Practitioners and parents often speak different languages and this can make it difficult to understand alternative perspectives. Ronco and Ronco (2005: 19) highlight the way in which too much or too little conflict can be a symptom of problems with partnership. They write that 'it's not that healthy organizations and alliances don't argue, but that they argue well'. Heads of centres who attempt to improve partnership with parents in schools or settings that do not have a strong history of parental involvement well understand this point.

CASE STUDY

Mary had been the head of a nursery school. In taking over the headship of a neighbouring primary school, she was surprised to find that many of the parents that she had known when their children were younger no longer came into school or contributed to fundraising events in the way that she has formerly known them to do. She took steps to improve their access to both staff and the building – which were very successful in raising parents' involvement. Before long, staff began to complain that parents were challenging many aspects of school life. Mary had to explain that she saw this as a positive step towards partnership and convince staff that this was the case.

Ineffective leadership is suggested by Ronco and Ronco (2005: 22) as one of the causes of failures in partnership. However, they add that 'little has been written and established about the nature of effective leadership in partnering situations'. This underlines the difficulties facing leaders in the early years who are required not only to develop partnerships with parents but with a range of other agencies. Ronco and Ronco (2005: 266–8) suggest some principles to follow in seeking partnering solutions. These are:

- *Suggest but never force.*
- *Encourage open dialog, but maintain discretion when asked.*
- *Go only as far as the work itself dictates.*
- *Reach out to people with whom you are in conflict.*
- *Embrace disagreement.*
- *Pay equal attention to what the group is telling you and what you yourself believe* . . . Work to see both the assets and weaknesses in your groups and teams, and work to balance these with your own convictions.
- *Sharpen your facilitation and collaboration skills.* Often, partnering groups fail to resolve problems not because the problems are difficult, but because they lack the conflict resolution and facilitation skills.
- *Work from the outset to move partnering from a 'programme' to 'the way we do business'.*

Reflection point
Using a situation in which you have been involved with a parent or group of parents, think over the points listed above. Consider the extent to which you felt able to interact with the parents in an open and genuinely collaborative way. Were you able to interact with them in ways that addressed their concerns, without feeling rattled or anxious?

Learning to listen

In Chapter 7 we considered the importance of listening to children and underlined the fact that genuine listening involves much more than verbal conversation. In just the same way, provision will be enhanced when staff take the time and make the effort to really listen to parents. Miles (1994 citing Peck) writes of the fact that in our society few people genuinely listen to children. She suggests that adults often fail to listen (perhaps because they're chattering on a mobile phone), pretend to listen (muttering things like 'did you?', 'that's nice' and so on) or listen selectively – simply tuning in to something that seems interesting. 'True listening, giving your full and complete attention, weighing each word and understanding each sentence' Miles (1994: 100) suggests rarely happens. Of course parents and carers of young children are busy, but perhaps practitioners are sometimes also too busy to listen.

Practitioners need to hear the 'experiences, views, concerns and aspirations' (Lancaster 2003: 4) of parents. Listening to them has many important benefits for parents, children and practitioners. Parents will feel more valued and more able to make the contribution to their children's development which research shows is so vital. Children's difficulty in bridging the gap between home and setting will be eased. Practitioners will have opportunities to model the importance of listening and are themselves more likely to be heard when trying to help parents understand the fundamental importance of communicating with their children. In learning to listen, practitioners can help parents and children to hear and be heard. You need to take a lead in developing improved communication at every level.

Key points

- Practitioners require a wide range of specific skills in order to work with parents professionally, effectively and in genuine partnership.
- Any failure to work in partnership with parents places an unnecessary burden on children, who have to work hard to make sense of their two worlds. Professional practice demands that partnership is made a reality.
- Not all parents are easy to work with and this is often because they had a difficult experience in their own education. It is the professional responsibility of practitioners to find ways to involve these hard-to-reach parents.
- Leaders need to help team members gain the necessary skills to make their work with parents effective and help parents undertake training which will enable them to develop a more equal partnership with staff.

Practical task

Analyse the attendance at the next event which you plan for parents (or one which you have recently held). Try to identify which parents came and which did not. Can you identify any reasons for attendance or non-attendance? Perhaps there was a burning issue which affected the parents of children with SEN more than other families. Maybe the parents who did not come needed crèche provision. Were they the most socioeconomically disadvantaged families? When you have made your analysis, identify some steps to broaden attendance next time you put on an event for parents and carers.

10 An inspector calls: leadership, evaluation and inspection

It is vitally important that the staff team who will undergo the inspection feel positive ... If staff are feeling positive they approach an inspection with confidence and clarity. Providing high-quality care and education should be seen as an everyday occurrence ... Staff who have positive leadership and support will have more energy and are able to cope better.

(Harpley and Roberts 2006: 10)

Introduction

In this chapter we look at the role of the leader in relation to managing the Ofsted inspection process and reducing the feeling of intimidation associated with the idea of an Ofsted inspection. Ofsted is an independent non-ministerial government department, currently responsible for the arrangement and inspection of a range of education and children's services, and for the inspection of early years provision and registered childcare. In April 2007 the organization's full title changed to the Office for Standards in Education, Children's Services and Skills, but it will continue to be known as Ofsted. We discuss ways in which the evaluation and inspection process can be used to enhance and demonstrate the quality of provision your setting offers. We begin by examining the background context, principles and purposes of inspection, noting that every day is an 'Ofsted day'. All staff should be enabled to take ownership of the inspection and its associated activities, as the inspection will involve everyone and will take place even if the manager is not present.

We go on to explain what you and your team can do in order to prepare positively for the inspection, reduce apprehension and ensure the inspection runs smoothly. We look at what needs to be done for you to demonstrate that you meet the requirements for learning and development and for promoting children's welfare as set out in the *Statutory Framework* (DfES 2007). We centre

on collecting together essential documents and completing the self-evaluation form (SEF). We suggest that all practitioners should always be prepared
and look at ways in which this can be achieved. The chapter moves on to
examine what inspectors are looking for and what to expect during the
inspection itself. We conclude by looking at what to expect in the written
reports, published on the Ofsted website, and how to respond to any actions
or recommendations for improvement in a positive way after the inspection.
The rest of this chapter is based on the view that the prime purpose of regulation and inspection of childminding and day care provision is to make
sure children are safe and well cared for. You should aim to see the inspection
as simply one part of a continual cyclical process of monitoring (or the process of checking that something agreed upon is actually happening) and
evaluation which asks not only whether something is being implemented but
whether or not it is working successfully.

From September 2008, providers will be inspected by Ofsted under Sections 49 and 50 of the Childcare Act 2006. Ofsted will have regard to the
Statutory Framework when they are carrying out their inspections. Nevertheless, throughout the chapter we make reference to the *National Standards*
(DfES 2001a) as they will continue to provide a useful reference point until
and beyond the time when the EYFS replaces them and becomes embedded
into day-to-day practice and the inspection process.

Inspection: background and context

In 1996 Ofsted began inspecting funded nursery education and since September 2001 the responsibility for the regulation and inspection of childminding and day care provision for children under 8 in England, including
nurseries, playgroups, crèches, after-school clubs and childminders trans-
ferred to Ofsted, now the single regulatory body. Following the introduction
of *Every Child Matters* (DfES 2003) a new inspection process was introduced
from April 2006, the most significant difference being that most group settings do not receive notice of inspection and the remainder, for example,
childminders, receive very limited notice. Depending on the size of the setting there may be one or two inspectors conducting the inspection. The
inspection will take place at least every three years or more frequently where
circumstances require it – if, for example, there is a number of staff changes, a
change of premises or a complaint which suggest national standards are not
being met. Ofsted's responsibilities include not only inspection but registration, investigation and enforcement.

As well as improving in quality, the size of the early years sector continues to increase in capacity. In 2005 there were approximately 105,000
settings offering almost 1.5 million registered childcare places, a growth of 15

per cent in two years. According to *Firm Foundations* (Ofsted 2005a), a report which covered the second programme of inspections against national standards over a two-year period from April 2003 to March 2005, almost half of the 94,000 registered childcare settings inspected provided good quality care. They met the national standards well overall, often exceeding them, with 4 per cent of settings being described as providing outstanding childcare. Good provision for children was reported across all types of setting and was particularly evident in full and sessional day care. In addition, around two thirds of settings were judged to be good in meeting the standards relating to caring for children's individual needs, offering play that promotes children's development, managing children's behaviour, ensuring a safe and stimulating environment for the children, and working in partnership with parents and carers. In relation to government-funded nursery education inspections, the report confirmed that of the 16,500 non-maintained education settings, a third of those inspected provided high quality education, with children making very good progress towards the early learning goals. The overall picture, therefore, is generally positive. Inspections should be seen as a way of maintaining and improving existing good practice rather than a threat. The vast majority of settings are not inadequate and have nothing to fear.

Principles and purposes

The *Framework for the Regulation of Daycare and Childminding* (Ofsted 2006: Annex D) sets out a number of clear principles which apply to all inspection activities carried out by, or on behalf of, Ofsted. These principles are intended to ensure that the findings of the inspection contribute to improvement and the process of inspection promotes inclusion. This in turn ensures that the inspection is carried out openly with those being inspected, and that the findings of an inspection are valid, reliable and consistent. The 12 principles are that:

1 Inspection acts in the interests of children, young people and adult learners and, where relevant, their parents, to encourage high quality provision that meets diverse needs and promotes equality.
2 Inspection is evaluative and diagnostic, assessing quality and compliance and providing a clear basis for improvement.
3 The purpose of inspection and the procedures to be used are communicated clearly to those involved.
4 Inspection invites and takes account of any self-evaluation by those inspected.
5 Inspection informs those responsible for taking decisions about provision.

6 Inspection is carried out by those who have sufficient and relevant professional expertise and training.
7 Evidence is recorded, and is of sufficient range and quality to secure and justify judgements.
8 Judgements are based on systematic evaluation requirements and criteria, are reached corporately where more than one inspector is involved, and reflect a common understanding in Ofsted about quality.
9 Effectiveness is central to judging the quality of provision and processes.
10 Inspection includes clear and helpful oral feedback and leads to written reporting that evaluates performance and quality and identifies strengths and areas for improvement.
11 The work of all inspectors reflects Ofsted's stated values and code of conduct.
12 Quality assurance is built into all inspection activities to ensure that these principles are met and inspection is improved.

The central purpose of the inspection is to report on the quality and standards of the childminding or day care provision and of the nursery education where applicable, and to check that the registered provider continues to be qualified to provide childminding or day care. Where a registered provider is on the local authority directory for the provision of free early education places, the inspection is usually 'integrated', incorporating the inspection of funded nursery education for children aged 3 and 4. In nursery education settings Ofsted also reports on whether children's spiritual, moral, social and cultural development is fostered and on the quality of leadership and management. Inspections are intended to be rigorous but with minimum bureaucracy and disruption. Ofsted currently reports on both the national standards and the nursery education under the *Every Child Matters* (DfES 2003) outcomes (enshrined in law in Section 10(2) of the Children Act 2004). Notably, Ofsted also reports on the organization of childminding and day care provision, as well as on how the childcare meets the needs of the range of children for whom the care and early education are provided.

Ofsted's (2006) stated aims for early years regulation and inspection are to:

- protect children;
- ensure that childminders and registered day care services provide good outcomes for children that ensure they are safe, well cared for and take part in activities that contribute to their development and learning;
- ensure that childminders and day care providers meet the *national standards*;

- promote high quality in the provision of care and early education;
- provide reassurance for parents.

Inspectors are expected to comment on several aspects of the provision. First, in order to put the report into context they write a factual description of the characteristics of the setting. This includes detail of the type and location of the setting, numbers of staff and qualification levels, and numbers of children provided for at the time of the inspection. An example is provided below.

What sort of setting is it?

Teddies preschool operates from within a classroom at St Peter's County Primary School. Children have access to a classroom, an adjacent toilet area and an enclosed outdoor play area.

The premises are situated within easy access of the village centre. The preschool setting operates from 09.00 until 11.30 Monday to Friday during term time with an optional lunch club from 11.30 until 12.30.

There are currently 34 children on roll of which 23 are in receipt of funding for nursery education. Children with disabilities, learning difficulties and English as a second language are welcomed into the setting. Presently, 2 children attend who have additional needs.

There are three full-time staff members whom hold childcare qualifications to Level 3 and one part-time staff member who has childcare training to Level 2. The setting receives support from the local authority and staff within the school.

Second, and of key importance, the inspectors are there to evaluate and report on the effectiveness of the provision. Inspectors must consider what it is like for a child in your setting, in terms of how the quality and standards of the childcare, taking account of the 14 *National Standards*, or forthcoming welfare requirements, and of the nursery education promote the following outcomes for children:

- being healthy (standards 7, 8);
- staying safe (standards 4, 5, 6, 13);
- enjoying and achieving (standard 3);
- making a positive contribution (standards 9, 10, 11, 12);
- how well the organization (standards 1, 2, 14) of childminding or day care promotes children's well-being.

Inspectors must also evaluate and report on:

- how well the organization of the childcare and, where applicable, the leadership and management of the nursery education, promotes the outcomes for children;
- whether the childminding, day care and/or nursery education meets the needs of the range of children for whom it is provides;
- how well the partnership with parents and carers promotes the nursery education;
- whether children's spiritual, moral, social and cultural development is fostered (nursery education only);
- improvements since the last inspection;
- any complaints about the quality of childcare since the last inspection.

Inspectors will record a judgement under each of the *Every Child Matters* outcomes and an overall judgement of one of four grades for the childcare, and where applicable, for the nursery education.

1   **Outstanding**. This applies to exceptional settings that have excellent outcomes over and above the norm. These settings are seen as being highly effective with exemplary childcare practice and children making very rapid progress towards the early learning goals. There will usually be no recommendations for improvement.

2   **Good**. This applies to strong settings, which are generally very effective in promoting the outcomes. If nursery education is provided, children are making good progress towards the early learning goals. Some recommendations for further improvement will be made.

3   **Satisfactory**. These settings will be working steadily towards effective childcare practice. Children will be making sound progress towards the early learning goals if nursery education is provided, but overall there is scope for some improvement.

4a   **Inadequate** (Category 1). This applies to a weak setting with unsatisfactory outcomes for children. If nursery education is provided the children are making limited progress and the quality of teaching and learning is unacceptable. The setting is causing concern but may be able to improve without external help. It may be that the setting fails to meet one of the *National Standards*, or there are significant weaknesses in the quality of teaching. A notice of action will be issued and a follow-up visit will take place. The setting will also have another inspection in 6 to 12 months. Ofsted informs the local authority.

4b   **Inadequate** (Category 2): This is where the setting causes such concern that serious attention needs to be given to improvement.

Childcare practice is such that one or more of the *National Standards* are not being met. Children are making little or no progress towards the early learning goals, if nursery education is provided. The setting is unable to improve without external enforcement or support. Ofsted will take enforcement action to require immediate improvement. For nursery education, the local authority is informed that external help is needed and a notice of action to improve is issued informing the setting of what they must do.

Third, inspectors need to set out what must be done to secure future improvement. Inspectors must report on **either** any recommendations to improve the quality and standards of care and, where applicable, of the nursery education **or** any provision where the quality and standards of care cause concern. They must specify any action required to ensure that the quality and standards of care are acceptable. Alternatively, they must state whether Ofsted intends to take enforcement action in respect of the provision.

While the manager may be the nominated contact person, it is the registered person who is responsible overall. Therefore, it is essential that the registered person (if different from the manager) ensures that the manager and staff are familiar with and implementing the *Statutory Framework* (DfES 2007). Staff need to be planning for and assessing children's learning and development across the EYFS (see Chapters 6 and 7) and show that everything is being done to help children progress towards the outcomes. Knowledge is power and the more you and your staff have secure knowledge of the *Every Child Matters* outcomes, the welfare standards and the EYFS curriculum, and the more you and they know about the inspection process, the less threatening it will seem. From 2008, you will need to ensure that staff knowledge is updated to take account of the EYFS.

> **Reflection point**
> Which of the welfare standards can your staff name and describe? Do all staff know the relevant EYFS curriculum content? Do staff know the ECM outcomes and can they describe how they are promoted in practice? Do the parent/s have information on the *Every Child Matters* outcomes? Are they encouraged to promote the outcomes at home?

In the next part of this chapter we discuss preparing for your inspection, in the sense of evaluating, improving and maintaining quality on an ongoing basis and hence always being ready for an unannounced inspection visit. One manager makes the point: 'I looked out of the window and saw a smartly dressed woman coming up the disabled ramp. I said to my staff (jokingly) "who's that?" She looks like an Ofsted inspector. I soon stopped smiling when I opened the door and found out that it was, especially as it was 2.30 in the afternoon. Well, I said to myself let's just get on with it.'

Preparing for inspection

It is the role of leaders, management and all senior staff to present a positive and confident attitude towards the inspection process, embedding a non-threatening climate of evaluation into the day-to-day life of the setting. Even well qualified and confident staff become worried about being observed and questioned by an outsider. If staff are used to being observed on a regular basis it becomes less daunting. Some local authorities and outside consultancies offer 'mock' Ofsted days.

A positive attitude toward inspection can be further promoted by regarding it as an opportunity to demonstrate and share what you do with the public domain. Inspections should be viewed as a constructive chance to obtain independent judgements and as paving a way for action to improve quality where necessary. As manager your role is to help staff see the process as a means of celebrating all the good things your setting provides. The more you and your staff are permanently prepared for an unannounced inspection visit, the more in control you will all feel, and the more likely that the outcome will be successful. At the end of the day, the inspector is looking to see whether you and your staff know what is expected and are doing what you can to provide it. Inspections are outcome-based and explicit, so if your quality is good and your staff are well prepared, there is no reason why you cannot be successful. We suggest that you concentrate your advance preparation in two key areas: organizing documentation, including the SEF and your policies; and staff development, including the enhancement of staff knowledge, skills and attitudes.

Organising documentation

Although inspectors will focus mainly on observing how you and your staff interact with the children and also talk to parents, they will want to see certain written policies and other information. As you saw in Chapter 5, there are a number of policies you will need to have ready, not only for the inspection but on an ongoing basis. It is your role to make sure that staff are aware of the policies, know how to access them and that one set of up-to-date policies is always on the premises. It is also your role to ensure that these policies are observed to be working effectively in practice and implemented by all staff. Early on in the inspection, the inspector will want to discuss the

SEF and if this has not been completed you will be asked to complete it on the day of the inspection. In addition there are a number of essential documents the inspector will need to check. You can have these ready in a file with your SEF. Make sure your staff know where the file is and what it contains (a contents page is always useful). Table 10.1 shows the information you should keep in this 'Ofsted essential documents file'. If all these documents are in one place it will save you or your staff having to search around for them on the day the inspector calls. It also makes the inspector's life easier and gives an immediate positive impression that you know what is required.

You can also check that your other files are up to date; for example, does the health and safety file contain up to date risk assessments and equipment checks? Are your SEN records complete and up to date? Are children's assessment records clear and linked to planning? Remember, having exemplary documentation will not, on its own, guarantee a favourable outcome. As you saw in chapter 5 it is the *practice arising from the policies* which is likely to be more effective, if written policies and procedures are in place to promote the aims of the setting.

Self-evaluation

The revised Ofsted framework requires settings to complete an SEF. The purpose is for the provider and staff to assess how well they meet the outcomes. The SEF looks straightforward at first glance, simply a matter of grading yourself against the *Every Child Matters* outcomes on the same scale as the Ofsted inspectors. However, self-evaluation is far more than a technical exercise. It involves analysing the progress made towards your objectives and deciding what else needs to be done. The crucial and complex question which all practitioners should constantly reflect upon, and inspectors will have uppermost in their minds, is **'What is it like for a child here?'** The role of the manager is to encourage staff to take a step back and keep this question in their minds on a day-to-day basis, reflecting and improving their practice accordingly. You could provide a checklist of prompts or questions to support their evaluation of each of the outcomes. In the outcome for children 'being healthy', for example, you might ask:

- Are children protected from infection and are well taken care of if they have an accident or become ill?
- Do children take part in regular physical play, both indoors and outside?
- Do children have an understanding of healthy eating?
- Are they encouraged to wash their hands and do they understand why?
- Are they offered healthy food and drink?

Table 10.1   Essential documentation required for an Ofsted inspection

For all childminders and day care providers	Additional documents for day care providers only
The name, home address and date of birth of each child who is looked after on the premises (not open access schemes)	The name, address and telephone number of the registered person and any other person living or employed on the premises
The name, home address and telephone number of a parent of each child (not open access schemes)	A statement of the procedure to be followed in the event of a fire or accident
The name, home address and telephone number of any person who will be looking after children on the premises	A statement of the procedure to be followed in the event of a child being lost or not collected (not open access schemes)
A daily record of the names of the children looked after on the premises, their hours of attendance and the names of the persons who look after them (not open access schemes)	A written procedure to be followed where a parent has a complaint about the service provided by the registered person
A record of accidents occurring on the premises	A statement of the arrangements in place for the protection of children, including arrangements to safeguard the children from abuse or neglect and procedures to be followed in the event of abuse or neglect
A record of any medicinal product administered to any child on the premises, including the date and circumstances of its administration, by whom it was administered, including medicinal products which the child is permitted to administer to himself/herself, together with a record of a parent's consent	
A record of complaints that includes brief details of the complaint, the national standard(s) it relates to, how it was dealt with, the outcome of any investigation including any action(s) taken, and whether and when the parent was notified of the outcome	

If you grade your setting as good you might produce a table similar to Table 10.2 to illustrate your self-assessment and attach evidence to explain why you assess yourselves as 'good'.

> **Reflection point**
> What evidence is there to suggest to an inspector that the outcomes relating to healthy eating and lifestyles are good in your setting? What can be done to improve? Set three key priorities.

Staying safe

The outcome for children 'staying safe' is about children having security, stability and care that protects them from mistreatment and neglect, accidental injury, bullying, discrimination and antisocial behaviour. In discussing your self-evaluation of this area, you would need to think about the most relevant national standards or in the welfare requirements, safeguarding children, as well as health and safety:

Table 10.2 Evidence that children have a wholesome, nutritious and balanced diet

Supporting evidence	Outcomes demonstrated in observed practice
Sample menus, food and drink policy	Meals are freshly prepared using fresh fruit and vegetables, some using organic and even home-grown produce
Sample menus, shopping receipts, food and drink policy	Processed food is not served and children are not given food and drinks with high levels of artificial additives and sugar
Menus on notice board	Menus are produced to give parents information about meal choices. They include dishes from different cultures
Food and drink policy	Drinking water is always available
Records of allergies	The provider is aware of each child's individual dietary needs and ensures these are met
Planning and assessment records Photographs Displays	Children learn about the importance of healthy eating, and are offered healthy choices

- physical environment (Standard 4);
- equipment (Standard 5);
- safety (Standard 6);
- child protection (Standard 13).

You need to question your practice in relation to each of the standards. The next reflection point shows how you could do this in relation to the welfare requirements.

Reflection point
Think about how children are protected from harm or neglect in your setting. Do staff have a good understanding of how to protect children, and recognize that this is their first priority? Are all staff vigilant, aware of the signs and symptoms of possible abuse and do they know the appropriate procedures to follow should they have concerns about a child's well-being? Is there a clear and effective policy and procedure, in line with the LSCB guidance and procedures? Are procedures shared with parents before the child is enrolled? In group day care is there a named person responsible for ensuring that children are safeguarded and concerns are dealt with promptly and appropriately?

This constant self-questioning and review will develop your staff's ability to think about and articulate what they are doing and why they are doing it. Evaluation seeks to find out:

- what you do well;
- what you do less well;
- what you need to do or develop differently.

Self-evaluation gives an overview of the effectiveness of your provision and can be used as a tool to help you and the team prioritize actions and formulate a development plan. It is not sufficient to evaluate subjectively and staff should be gathering evidence to support the grades you enter on your SEF. Self-evaluation is central to the reflective practice cycle of planning and reviewing. It is important to show that your setting has the ability to improve itself and is aware of any shortcomings or areas for development. As a team, you should complete the SEF, systematically, at least quarterly or more often if circumstances change, identifying any areas that need attention. You should keep evidence of improvements such as an improvement diary or monthly log of when things have been changed. This is particularly useful as with three years between inspections some staff may be unaware of the improvements that have taken place.

Staff development

It is essential to ensure that staff knowledge, skills and attitudes are continually developed. With Ofsted inspectors being in the setting for such a short period it is vital that the leader and all the staff are able to articulate what they are doing and why and to show evidence that the *Every Child Matters* outcomes are being promoted and the relevant standards are being met. Hence, knowledge of staff is an all important part of the inspection. The inspectors need to see an ongoing approach where all staff meet welfare requirements such as health and safety. You should encourage all staff to be vigilant in implementing the standards. If staff are familiar with the requirements and all the standards are firmly embedded in practice, only minor improvements are likely to be needed. All staff should also have secure knowledge of the EYFS learning and development standards (see Chapters 6 and 7).

> **Reflection point**
> Do all you staff have knowledge of the learning, development and care standards for children from birth to 5 (DfES 2007)? Are they all familiar with curriculum guidance? Do staff in your setting have knowledge and regard to the SEN *Code of Practice* (DfES 2001b)? Have all staff been involved in developing and implementing the policy and approach to SEN? Have you a trained SENCO? Do you work with other professionals to meet children's individual needs? Have you evidence – for example, IEPs, a written policy, minutes from meetings, contact with the area SENCO?

An inspector calls

When the inspector arrives it is important to try to stay relaxed and continue with your normal day. The team must avoid the temptation to try new things in order to impress and just be themselves. Inspectors are only human, they have a job to do and most conduct the inspections in a professional and unobtrusive manner. The more open and welcoming you can be the more confident and less threatened you will feel. Early on in the inspection you should present your SEF and your essential documents file. The inspector may wish to observe first and look at other paperwork, such as planning and assessment records or staff training records. The inspector will talk to management, some parents and all staff including those with designated responsibilities, such as for safeguarding children. If you and your staff converse with the inspector as you go about your normal routine, this will reduce the necessity for them to ask questions.

During the inspection, inspectors gather evidence of the quality and standards of care by evaluating how well the provider meets the statutory requirements, taking full account of any previous actions or recommendations raised and other information gathered during the visit. If applicable, they collect evidence of the quality and standards of care, learning and development by evaluating how the quality of teaching promotes children's progress. On the day, inspectors will look for information through discussion with children and adults, including parents, direct observation and looking at relevant documents. They will ask questions – for example, relating to planning and assessment, how children's individual needs are supported or how children are safeguarded.

They will be checking the premises and equipment for safety and suitability and examining how effectively the indoor and outdoor environment are used to promote the outcomes. You can be ready for this by ensuring resources are plentiful, appropriate and accessible. You can organize your daily routine, your displays and room layout to reflect the outcomes. Inspectors observe, in particular, what the children are doing, the way in which adults relate to and interact with them, and how well they care for the children and help them learn. For example, are the children following routines? Do they gain awareness of how to keep safe in day-to-day situations such as moving around, road safety, or using equipment safely? How do the children behave and interact with each other?

In addition, the inspector will check the registration procedure and levels of adult supervision at various times of the day to ensure that adult to child ratios are maintained in each age group. You must make sure supervision levels meet the standards all day, every day, including lunchtime and the first and last hour of the day. One survey of 45 day nurseries, conducted by Ofsted in 2005, where inspectors arrived as the nursery opened, and inspected and analysed outcomes for children during the first hour of operation, found that in a fifth of nurseries visited there were not enough staff on duty at the start of the day to offer good care for children (Ofsted 2005c). In a third of the nurseries visited the first hour or more of care lacked sufficient planning and organization to support the needs of all the children attending. For example, babies were strapped in chairs without any toys to play with. The evidence also suggested that security was weak, allowing adults to enter the nursery unchallenged.

Monitoring the quality of leadership and management

Inspectors will make judgements relating to the quality of organization of childcare and the leadership and management in nursery education. It is the designated leader who has overall responsibility for the setting, for the day-to-day management and organization, who has direct responsibility for improvement, for equality of opportunity and for the development of policies and use of resources to meet the aims of the setting. However, as suggested in Chapters 3 and 4, a successful team is one where all the staff are deployed in a way that uses their expertise to best effect. Hence in a well-managed setting, other staff will have clearly defined and effectively delegated leadership and management functions. You could, for example, display a list of staff names and role titles, or key staff groups and rotas. The focus of the inspection is not exclusively on the designated leader but also on the roles and responsibilities of other practitioners. Staff need to be clear about their tasks and responsibilities, and about the limits of their role. One chain of nurseries prepared a list as part of a policy on 'Organisation' (see Figure 10.1).

As well as the more traditional leadership aspects such as self-evaluation, motivating staff, leading by example, teamwork, staff appraisal and development, the inspector will look at organization and administration, for example, recruitment and vetting procedures. The inspector is not judging the style of leadership but looking at how leadership influences the quality of provision. In preparation, it would be useful to ask an external advisory teacher to comment on your leadership and management. In addition, you could investigate the possibility of joining an accredited quality assurance scheme.

> **Reflection point**
> How well does you leadership provide clear direction for the work of the setting? Are teaching and curriculum development monitored and evaluated? Are the setting's policies reflected in practice throughout the setting and known by all staff? Is there a positive ethos which reflects commitment to children's equal opportunities achievement and an effective learning environment? Are statutory requirements met?

Throughout the visit, inspectors will be continually making notes in a notebook or on a laptop. While this can be daunting it is imperative as all the judgements they make must be firmly grounded in evidence from what they have seen or been told. The feedback will normally take place at the end of the inspection. You will not be able to present any fresh evidence in the feedback so, again, it is essential that you have shared as much as possible during the inspection itself.

'You are not alone – We are here with you'

Role name	Overview of key responsibilities	Contact details
Managing director	Registered person, strategic leadership, policy development, liaison with early years development and childcare partnerships, legal and professional issues, e.g. leases, contracts, disciplinary and grievance, publicity, recruitment, governors, management training, Ofsted action plans and correspondence, source of child protection support and advice, responding to written complaints. Company equal opportunities co-ordinator.	
Quality, training and support co-ordinator	Assisting with above, monitoring and improving quality and supporting managers and staff. Staffing, deployment, monitoring and supporting staff development. Staff induction, liaison with managing director, contributing to all aspects of management, notably procedures, and ensuring national standards are met. Keeping up to date. Company wide – health and safety and company SENCO. Makes decisions in absence of managing director.	
Assistant quality co-ordinator/s	Assisting with above, promoting corporate philosophy, staff exchange schemes, IT and fundraising, and quality at Stockingford and Cubbington. Children's Centres, Transformation Fund, staffing cover, ordering resources, general supporting of above on request.	
Graduate leader	Contributing to policy development. Advise and support on EYPS. Promote EYPS standards.	
Branch managers	Day-to-day leadership and management of staff. Managing the provision for all children, ensuring all standards are met and promoting positive relationships with all those involved including parents, other agencies and base schools. Normally designated child protection and health and safety officer.	
Deputies	Supporting managers as above. Normally taking on role of SENCO/equal opportunities.	As above
Administrator	All registration procedures, staff records, wages and receipts, invoices paying and sending to accountant, early education funding, placing of adverts, correspondence and information-sharing, recording staff absences and other relevant admin duties.	
Other staff	Support managers and deputies fulfil role description and contractual obligations. Implement policies and procedures.	

Figure 10.1 Leadership and Management roles and responsibilities

The end of the inspection

At the end of the inspection, inspectors normally thank you for having them and give feedback on their main findings, including the overall judgement on the quality and standards of the care and, where applicable, the nursery education provided. Inspectors share with the provider the inspection report paragraphs on 'information about the setting' and 'previous complaints' for the provider to check for factual accuracy. They should also show you the summary sheet so you know the overall judgement in each of the areas. The inspector will then go through each area giving a few significant examples to support their judgements. They will also spell out clearly any actions or recommendations for improvement. Table 10.3 below provides a comprehensive list of the possibilities.

> **Reflection point**
> Look at the recommendations for each area. Could they apply to you? What can you do to avoid these being suggested in your report?

Inspectors will not usually give advice as it is not in their remit. The report should arrive in approximately 15 working days. It will not contain anything that the inspector did not see on the day. The two extracts below clearly illustrate how the written report reflects the evidence gathered during the visit.

> The childminder gives high priority to ensuring that children's individual needs are provided for, particularly in relation to hygiene. Children are provided with their own beaker, flannel and toothbrush to use at the setting. She encourages children to brush their teeth after eating, is aware of the need to provide shade for children in the sun, and recognizes the importance of hand washing. The childminder also provides individual creams and talc for nappy changing according to parents' wishes for each child.
>
> The childminder has attended a number of training courses related to child protection. In this way she has ensured that her practice is underpinned by a good and up to date knowledge of the possible signs and symptoms of abuse and neglect and also the correct procedure to follow should she have any concerns. Her willingness to make notes on existing injuries and to discuss these with parents ensures that the safety of children in her care is always a priority. She has an excellent written statement about child protection and she makes sure that this is discussed with all parents before their children attend.

Table 10.3 Actions and recommendations for improvement (Ofsted 2005a)

Outcome	Standard	Typical actions and recommendations following inspection
Being healthy	7 Health	• Improve documentation on administration of medication • Improve documentation following accidents • Attend a paediatric first-aid training course • Seek permission from parents for emergency medical treatment, or to administer medication
	8 Food and drink	• Ensure children have access to drinking water at all times • Ensure snacks and meals are healthy and nutritious • Ensure a record is kept of babies' food intake
Staying safe	4 Premises 5 Equipment 6 Safety	• Ensure sufficient provision for children to move freely and for quieter activities • Ensure toys and materials promote equality of opportunity • Make areas safe or inaccessible for children • Ensure emergency evacuation procedures and all required fire safety precautions are in place including fire blanket and smoke detectors • Ensure a clear procedure if a parent fails to collect a child or a child becomes lost • Ensure risks and hazards are identified and reduced effectively both inside and outside, and on outings
	13 Child protection	• Ensure clear procedures for action if you suspect abuse, or if an allegation is made against you
Enjoying and achieving	3 Care, learning and play	• Extend the range of planned activities and experiences for children, appropriate for their stages of development and based on their individual needs • Improve opportunities for children to make independent choices by using a range of resources and responding to their spontaneous interests • Consider ways of recording children's progress to plan the next steps for their development through play

Table 10.3 *(continued)*

Outcome	Standard	Typical actions and recommendations following inspection
Making a contribution	9 Equal opportunities	• Ensure children have access to a broad range of resources and activities which reflect diversity
	10 Special needs	• Ensure that staffing arrangements meet the needs of children with special needs
	11 Behaviour	• Ensure behaviour management methods promote children's welfare, and develop the behaviour policy to include bullying
	12 Working with parents	• Ensure aspects of record-keeping are in place, such as the complaints procedure, and that parental permissions are obtained as appropriate
		• Improve information to parents about their child's experiences and achievements
Organization	1 Suitable person	• Ensure checks are completed for all household members over the age of 16 years (childminders)
		• Complete an appropriate first-aid course that includes training in first aid for infants and young children (childminders)
		• Ensure there are suitable arrangements in place to protect children from persons who are not vetted
		• Ensure that there are effective procedures in place for informing Ofsted of relevant changes
		• Develop and implement an action plan, with timescales, to ensure the person in charge will meet the minimum qualifications requirement and at least half of all childcare staff hold an appropriate Level 2 qualification

Table 10.3 (*continued*)

2 Organization	• Ensure that the record of attendance includes the names of the children looked after on the premises, the names of the persons who look after them and visitors, including arrival and departure times • Demonstrate the arrangements for supervisory cover in the manager's absence by identifying a named deputy • Confirm the named deputy has appropriate qualifications to take charge in the absence of the manager • Ensure that the continuing training needs of staff are met
14 Records	Ensure required records are in place, most often: • A daily record of attendance • A record of accidents occurring on the premises • A record of any medicine administered and parents' consent • Notification of significant changes or events • Update policies in line with the national standards for child protection and for complaints

For quick reference a full report is provided in the Appendix. All reports are available to read on the Ofsted website. Once you receive your report you should share it with staff and parents. You should take note of any actions or recommendations for improvement and draw up a plan to follow-up the inspection. Obviously, no matter what the outcome, congratulate your staff on the positive aspects and encourage them to see any recommendations as helpful for improving provision.

Finally, Ofsted (2005b) suggest various ways you can be ready for your inspection. This will save time on the day and also help build confidence levels.

1   Check that you and your staff are familiar with the relevant documents (e.g. the national standards and associated guidance, the current curriculum guidance or frameworks).
2   Make sure you have put right any areas for improvement identified in the last inspection.
3   Complete the SEF and have the latest version and ideally previous ones ready to share with your inspector.
4   Check you have all the required records.
5   Keep any information you have relating to parental feedback and how you have responded to it.
6   Make sure you have a written record of complaints whether or not they involve Ofsted.
7   Make sure you have notified Ofsted of any significant changes (e.g. a change of person in charge, change of name, premises, opening hours).
8   Make sure you have told Ofsted about significant matters affecting children's welfare.

Key points

- You can prepare positively and thoroughly for your inspection.
- Leaders need to prepare the whole team personally and professionally.
- All the team should self-evaluate systematically, on a regular basis.
- You will need to organize and update policies and essential documentation.
- You can seek advice and support from the local authority.
- Leaders need to update their knowledge of the EYFS.

Practical tasks

1   Arrange a staff meeting to complete your SEF. Prepare a list of discussion prompts for each outcome. Ask staff to work in pairs or groups on one section. Discuss how they would rate it, why and what would they do to improve it? Reach a consensus and complete the SEF systematically.

2   Draw up a checklist of things that need to be done in preparation for Ofsted. This might include self-evaluation, briefing of staff, updating policies and documentation, checking complaints records and/or recording improvements since the last inspection. Develop an action plan in order to be fully prepared for your setting's inspection.

3   Spend a staff meeting reading and discussing reports from the Ofsted website. Compare the practice in the reports with practice in your setting. Make a list of things you need to change, develop or improve.

11 Leadership: where next?

'We cannot wait for great visions from great people, for they are in short supply ... It is up to us to light our own small fires in the darkness.' We encourage you to use your creativity as a leader to light fires of influence and to make a difference in your world.

(Puccio *et al.* 2007: 257 citing Handy 1993)

Introduction

Leaders in early childhood care and education are faced with a mass of legislation, huge but apparently constantly changing responsibilities and expectations, and uncertain financial parameters. But it is not all gloom and doom. They are also faced with the day-to-day reality that what they do with children and families can, and does, change lives.

For example, the director of a children's centre was uncertain whether she would be employed by the end of the week but was moved to tears by the progress made by one of the parents with whom she had been working. Less than two years earlier, the parent in question had been unable to speak to any of the staff – had been unable even to make eye contact with them. This same parent had not only been working towards EYPS but was also able to address a group of prospective students with confidence and flair. A team member involved in training on problem-solving, reasoning and numeracy was suddenly able to take on the importance of asking open-ended questions – a strategy she had previously seemed unable to accept. When a leader noticed a child who had only been in Britain a matter of weeks and was still very new to the English language having a conversation with a member of staff about a new computer program, this breakthrough represented a very special kind of reward.

But such rewards come at a price. The field of early childhood care and education is full of tensions. There are tensions around whether babies should be at home with a parent or other close relative, with a childminder or in a nursery offering day care. There are tensions around whether babies, wherever they are, should be subject to a curriculum framework or simply left to grow and develop. There are innumerable tensions about what should be taught, when and how – as demonstrated in the debate about teaching phonics. Tensions remain (despite the fact that most mothers of young children work) about whether children should just spend half a day in a setting or whether they should have the consistent provision that extended day care can offer. You can undoubtedly add to this list of tensions or issues which you, as a leader in this sector, face daily.

No book can provide answers to these issues – you and your team have to find the answers that work in your context. In this book we have attempted to explore relevant aspects of your work and to provide some strategies and guidance to help you in your journey. In order to do this we have drawn on research and practical experience.

At the beginning of Chapter 2 we highlighted the links between leadership and management and in quoting from Rodd (2006: 21) underlined the fundamental importance of vision, reflection, involvement in pedagogy, positive relationships, effective communication and high expectations. It is these qualities which have to underpin every aspect of the work of leaders in early childhood settings.

Change and development

Change is inevitable in human life. It is natural to resist it since it brings upheaval, but it is equally natural to invite it since it brings stimulation. Society changes; knowledge and understanding of children's learning and development changes; employment opportunities change. In order to help staff cope with the impact of such changes, leaders have a role to play. However, in their role as leaders and people of influence with children and families, team members need to support *them* in dealing with change.

Humans are creative – we have become creative because we have changed our lives and it is creativity that has led us to change our lives. In the past, creativity was often seen as the province of a few people – people of genius perhaps. As time has gone by however we have come to see that creativity is what drives us. This is reflected in curriculum documents and is increasingly understood to be essential to life in the twenty-first century. Puccio *et al.* (2007: xii) suggest that 'creativity is a core leadership competence' and that those who have achieved this core competence 'understand the need for creative thinking in today's complex workplace and therefore seek creativity with intent' (p. xvi).

Gardner (2006: 101) takes this idea further, suggesting that to improve the future: 'Needed today is a generous dollop of creativity in the human sphere – in particular, in the ways in which we human beings relate to one another personally, carry out our work, and fulfil our obligations as citizens.' Nowhere can this need be more true and more far-reaching than in the field of early childhood care and education. The children you lead – for whom you are responsible – are the future and they will need to be what Gardner terms 'ethical and respectful'. This need for enhanced human relationships has many echoes (Miles 1994; Goleman 1996; Gerhardt 2004) and since the roots of social and emotional awareness lie in early childhood we have a responsibility to nurture and develop it at that point.

Vision and influence

Throughout this book we have emphasized the need for vision. Leaders' prime responsibility is to develop a vision which is shared by staff and parents. That vision must have at its heart the well-being of children, but in order to achieve that it must also have concern for the well-being of families and practitioners. It is, however, the role of early childhood leaders to keep children at the centre – since they are the future. Vision means having a view of the future, but it also means holding onto principles and values. Change without values and principles becomes vacuous. With values and principles, leaders and teams are better able to evaluate change and to judge whether or not it is effective and desirable. As we said at the beginning of this book, leadership is only effective if it supports a team in meeting its aims.

Reflection

Reflection is something to be developed at every level of practice. The term *reflective practitioner* may have become something of a cliché but without reflection teams and leaders cannot develop effective practice. In this book, reflective practice has been emphasized as a process through which change is evaluated, problems solved, patterns identified and insights gained. Leaders cannot do without it and practitioners cannot do without it. Moreover, reflection supports professionals in becoming lifelong learners – and provides a mirror on the practitioner's behaviour.

Involvement in pedagogy

Throughout this book we have placed a strong emphasis on the importance of pedagogy. Rodd's (2006) suggestion that leadership and management benefit from involvement in pedagogy is key. We have made the point that the skills developed in professional dealings with children can also have a positive impact on the quality of leadership. The way in which practitioners interact with children can also serve as a model to parents. However, pedagogy should also be influenced by parents' relationships with children. Practitioners have much to learn about individual children from those who know them best. Partnership working between parents and professionals has, as we have discussed, much to contribute to improving children's lives.

We do not wish to overlook other aspects of pedagogy. Leaders ought not to lose sight of their core service or activity. Pedagogy in the sense of teaching and learning strategies can clearly influence all human relationships but particularly those with children. Leaders must not forget that the love and care with which practitioners feed or change a baby has at least as much, if not more, influence on a child's future as the way in which they share a story or support a child in learning to write his or her name. Effective pedagogy requires pedagogues or practitioners to reflect on all that they do with children, and to judge the quality of their relationships, their listening and their caring in a professional and intelligent manner. Nothing relating to the care and education of our youngest children is mundane or merely routine – every interaction moulds learning and development, attitudes and dispositions.

Positive relationships

Young children are highly susceptible to atmosphere. They rely on actions, facial expressions and body language, which adults may be unaware they are exhibiting, in order to make sense of the complex world in which they live. For this reason, if for no other, leaders have a responsibility to maintain positive relationships between team members, with other professionals and with parents. Involvement in pedagogy requires us to help children develop positive relationships with their peers. Some practitioners may need help in this and this will be reflected in the policy you are required to have supporting behaviour.

Interestingly, mainstream leadership literature also places an increasing emphasis on positive relationships. Jo Owen's 3 Ps (2005) – people, being positive and professionalism – are characteristic of this trend. These three qualities were evident in the chapter on working with parents and they remain essential in all your dealings as a leader. A rough, tough approach may work in television programmes but is not one to be emulated in early childhood settings.

Effective communication

Effective communication supports positive relationships, but as we have shown in this book communication is a two-way process. It is important to focus on learning to listen to children and adults. Increasingly leaders need to communicate effectively in writing as well as in face-to-face situations. Communication is about giving (and receiving) information but it is also about influence. As Owen (2005: 12) reminds us, 'the starting point for influencing someone is not your idea or object – it is the other person's needs and wants'. This applies equally to your communications with children, staff, parents, other professionals, community and politicians.

The failure of early childhood specialists to communicate the nature and principles of their field to the general public and to politicians has arguably been the root of the political pressure which practitioners have found themselves under (David 1998). This is in part due to a perceived lack of status which is in turn linked to the low level of training and qualifications across the sector. Practitioners, including leaders, need to develop effective communication in order to:

- inform others about the unique nature of work with young children and their families; and
- influence others to see the importance of enhancing and improving children's care, learning and development.

High expectations

Leaders in early childhood care and education usually have high aspirations for the children with whom they work. As the EPPE project (Sammons *et al.* 2002) demonstrates so effectively, however, what really makes a difference to children's achievement is when parents have high expectations of themselves. This leads them to believe that they can make a difference in their children's lives – and they do.

Leaders in early childhood settings would do well to build on this finding. As leaders and managers take on new qualifications – foundation degrees, honours degrees in early childhood studies and postgraduate qualifications for integrated centre leaders (NPQICL) enhanced self-belief will improve the expectations that team members have of themselves. All too often we hear early childhood practitioners, including leaders, saying things like 'I'm only a playgroup leader' or 'I just work with little children'. This has to change – you undertake a role that has a huge significance for society and for the lives of individuals. You need high expectations for yourself, for children, parents and staff.

What next?

The last ten years have seen rapid and unforeseen changes in early childhood care and education. There have also been vast changes in employment, economies and lifestyles. This makes it very difficult to predict what will or should happen next. But perhaps that is the point. The apparently boundless capacity for creativity and adaptability which humans have needs to be seen as a strength. We need to build children's lives so that they can embrace change while maintaining the quality of relationships which make us human. In order to achieve this, leaders will also need to be creative and resourceful, humane and caring, effective communicators and positive educators – influencing parents, politicians and professionals alike to place children, as our future, at the centre of all we do.

Our society cannot afford to write off any single member of a community. Humans are a valuable resource. Early childhood educators and carers have an awesome responsibility to nurture society's future and you, the leaders of that profession, have an even greater responsibility. You must nurture and develop your teams, the other professionals with whom you work and the parents – since all of them have a role to play in the learning, development and well-being of young children. None of us can undertake this alone. We can only achieve it in harmony.

Appendix: ABC Nursery inspection report

Better education and care

ABC Nursery

Inspection report for early years provision

Unique Reference Number	507737
Inspection date	14 December 2006
Inspector	Hazel Christine White
Setting Address	20 Rochester Road, Coventry, West Midlands, CV5 6AD
Telephone number	02476672660
E-mail	
Registered person	ABC Nurseries (Coventry) Ltd
Type of inspection	Integrated
Type of care	Full day care

ABOUT THIS INSPECTION

The purpose of this inspection is to assure government, parents and the public of the quality of childcare and, if applicable, of nursery education. The inspection was carried out under Part XA Children Act 1989 as introduced by the Care Standards Act 2000 and, where nursery education is provided, under Schedule 26 of the School Standards and Framework Act 1998.

This report details the main strengths and any areas for improvement identified during the inspection. The judgements included in the report are made in relation to the outcomes for children set out in the Children Act 2004; the National Standards for under 8s day care and childminding; and, where nursery education is provided, the *Curriculum guidance for the foundation stage.*

The report includes information on any complaints about the childcare provision which Ofsted has received since the last inspection or registration or 1 April 2004 whichever is the later.

The key inspection judgements and what they mean

Outstanding: this aspect of the provision is of exceptionally high quality
Good: this aspect of the provision is strong
Satisfactory: this aspect of the provision is sound
Inadequate: this aspect of the provision is not good enough

For more information about early years inspections, please see the booklet *Are you ready for your inspection?* which is available from Ofsted's website: *www.ofsted.gov.uk.*

THE QUALITY AND STANDARDS OF THE CARE AND NURSERY EDUCATION

On the basis of the evidence collected on this inspection:

The quality and standards of the care are outstanding. The registered person meets the National Standards for under 8s day care and childminding.

The quality and standards of the nursery education are outstanding.

WHAT SORT OF SETTING IS IT?

ABC Day Nursery has been registered since 1983. It is one of two privately owned nurseries and operates from a converted detached house in the Earlsdon area of Coventry in the West Midlands. There are four play rooms on the ground floor and three on the first floor. Ground floor rooms have direct access to outdoor play areas, with the exception of one. There are local shops, parks and schools within walking distance. The nursery serves the local and surrounding areas.

The nursery is registered to care for a maximum of 55 children under five years of age at any one time. There are currently 68 on roll. Of these, 34 receive funding for nursery education. Children attend a variety of sessions. The nursery is open Monday to Friday, from 08:00 to 17:45 all year round. The provision includes an after school service and pick up for 16 children aged five to 12 years. A play scheme operates during the main school holidays. The setting supports children with special needs and children who speak English as an additional language.

There are 15 staff employed to work directly with the children all of whom hold an appropriate early years qualification. The nursery receives support from the Local Authority Early Years Development and Childcare Partnership.

THE EFFECTIVENESS OF THE PROVISION

Helping children to be healthy

The provision is outstanding.

Children's health is extremely well promoted and they show an excellent understanding and willingness to keep themselves healthy. Children develop a strong understanding of hygiene practices as staff are excellent role models. Children see low level pictures within the bathroom that support their awareness of good hygiene routines. Staff are diligent in following hygiene procedures when preparing snacks and drinks for children. Effective detailed procedures are in place to prevent the spread of infection, including information on notifiable diseases and exclusion periods. Staff respond to accidents well as all have current first aid certificates, with the exception of one. All have an excellent understanding of current first aid practice and have the children's best interest in mind. There is a named person who is responsible for ensuring that first aid boxes are fully stocked and records are kept of when items have been replaced. Children can rest and relax as they need to as staff are extremely sensitive to the needs of the younger children. An additional member of staff is on duty daily to attend to children's intimate care.

Children have nutritious snacks and meals that promote healthy eating. Staff are committed to ensuring that children have a well balanced diet. Managers have enlisted the support of a dietician so that children's meals are of a high standard. The menu ensures that children have a low salt diet and lots of fruit and vegetables which are in season. Children with allergies have their needs well met because staff are very aware of their individual needs as they discuss them with parents and have a list to refer to. Food is attractively presented and plentiful. Snack times are extremely well organised in small groups and good questioning promotes children's understanding of healthy choices effectively. Children pour their drinks and serve fruit. They can independently access drinks from a water dispenser and do so with skill and confidence. Staff encourage detailed discussions with children about healthy eating during activities such as cooking. Children's health and dietary needs are very well met as parents provide comprehensive written information about their child's preferences and specific requirements. The cook is committed to ensuring that children have a balanced diet and uses her imagination to make alternative meals look the same so children are not singled out. The kitchen is well organised and cleaning schedules are effective. Food and temperature records are in place to minimise the risk of cross-infection. All food is probed and covered before it leaves the kitchen.

Children enjoy excellent opportunities to experience physical play and develop their skills because the staff plan an extensive range of activities that enable children to develop their confidence on a wide range of equipment that provides challenge. The outdoor area has been well designed to give children a wealth of experiences. There is a small nature garden, soft area

This inspection was carried out under the provisions of Part XA of the Children Act 1989, as inserted by the Care Standards Act 2000

and pet area. Children are able to climb, ride wheeled toys, play with balls and balance on equipment. The outside area is included in planning to maximise its use. Children have Wellingtons to use in the rain and wrap up in scarf and gloves when it is cold. They have a dance teacher on a weekly basis where they learn to exercise and move to music. Children discuss the changes in their bodies after exercise and how to keep themselves fit and healthy.

Protecting children from harm or neglect and helping them stay safe

The provision is outstanding.

Children's safety is paramount and they are very well cared for in premises which are safe, secure and child centred. They access an extensive range of toys and equipment that enable them to explore and investigate in a safe and vibrant environment. Rigorous routines ensure toys and equipment are checked and cleaned regularly, therefore, children play with safe and suitable resources. Children can move safely and independently in all areas, as risks have been identified and minimised by staff. Pre-school children have a mature attitude and are extremely aware of their own safety. They know for example, that the large red spot on the kitchen door means that they must not go in. Children remind each other of the agreed group safety rules, such as walking carefully through rooms and how to safely use equipment and resources.

The premises and outside areas are exceptionally clean and well maintained. Staff are vigilant when supervising children outdoors and children demonstrate a clear understanding of areas where they need direct supervision, such as when the pond cover is removed so they can observe pond life. Children have a sound awareness of fire safety through discussions and by practising emergency escape routines. This helps children to understand the importance of staying calm in an emergency. Comprehensive risk assessments are in place throughout the nursery. These are updated as and when necessary. Managers are forward thinking and implement individual risk assessments for children as required. For example, when a child was immobilised because of a fractured limb, an additional fire drill was practiced to ensure that he could be safely evacuated in an emergency.

Children are very well protected by staff, who have an excellent understanding of child protection policies and procedures. Managers are fully conversant with reporting procedures and all staff have attended training, giving high priority to children's welfare. Policies are shared with parents to promote a common understanding on safeguarding children.

Helping children achieve well and enjoy what they do

The provision is outstanding.

Children are happy, very confident and enthusiastic in the warm and welcoming environment created by staff. The 'free flow' ethos of the nursery works extremely well, giving children choice and freedom. They are independent and confidently self-select toys and activities from an excellent range of resources. Children thrive and develop well because staff provide exceptionally well balanced routines throughout the session, which helps them feel secure. They have set times during the day when they spend time with their key worker. Children settle quickly into the group and separate confidently and with ease from their parents and carers.

This inspection was carried out under the provisions of Part XA of the Children Act 1989, as inserted by the Care Standards Act 2000

Children make very secure relationships with familiar adults and each other and play exceptionally well together. They confidently initiate conversations, make up their own games and talk about events outside of the group. Children are well supported when trying new activities and have an exemplary range of interesting experiences during a typical week. Staff are skilled and experienced in planning a curriculum using the Birth to three framework. Children have first hand experiences to develop curiosity as learners. They are encouraged and extremely well supported to use appropriate language to communicate their needs. Children communicate their thoughts, ideas and experiences because of excellent questioning by staff to extend their thought process. All children enjoy and share stories, songs and rhymes. Staff listen to and value what children say, talk them and have high expectations of what they can achieve. Staff use every opportunity to extend the children's learning and thinking.

Nursery Education

The quality of teaching and learning for three and four year old children is outstanding. Children make excellent progress in all six areas of learning. Staff have an exceptional knowledge of the foundation stage of learning and plan a strong and effective curriculum to progress children along the stepping stones towards the early learning goals. Observations and assessments for children are used effectively and enable staff to plan for individual learning for all children.

Children confidently engage in a wide range of planned and spontaneous activities. They easily make relationships and demonstrate very good independence skills. Children are settled, keen and motivated to learn. They are self-assured and often take the lead in activities, therefore developing their self-esteem. Children learn right from wrong because staff are good role models. They are extremely sensitive to the children's needs and know them very well. Children show an awareness of their own needs and that of others, and understand that their actions have consequences. They take the initiative and choose activities and access resources for themselves. For example, children put their coats, hats and scarves on to go outside with little or no support. Children persist with difficult tasks such as doing their zips up on their coat and they take care of their personal care such as washing their hands and serving snacks and drinks. Children move with extreme confidence and maturity between outdoor and indoor activities. They are polite, well mannered and are consistently well behaved.

Children are keen to communicate with adults and other children. They listen enthusiastically to stories and have excellent opportunities to look at books independently including reference books. Children notice a wealth of print displayed around the nursery on signs, captions and posters. They recognise their names and more able children write these correctly in well formed letters. Vocabulary is skilfully extended by staff who use good questioning techniques to make children think. They learn to understand how sounds of letters link to words and children have made their own story books. Staff use an 'alphabet resource box' which looks at exciting ways to introduce children to letters. Children have made their own story books and handle them with great care.

Children see connections and relationships in numbers, shapes and measures. They match and sort and are using mathematical language such as more than, one more, one less to help them to solve problems across a wide range of practical activities such as stories, rhymes, games, puzzles and in their imaginative play. All children count beyond 10 and recognise many shapes, colours and numerals. They focus on a different number and colour every week and their understanding of numbers is reinforced as they are used in activities, spontaneous routines and play. Concepts such as more than less than are used frequently. Children develop an awareness of weight and capacity through the use of resources and activities such as sand, water and cooking.

Children learn to make sense of the world around them by investigating and exploring through first hand experiences in an interesting environment. They have opportunities to observe, explore, question and be curious in a broad range of activities. Children notice changes when colours are mixed, washing up liquid and glitter is added to water and when ice melts. They carefully make models from construction toys and recycled tubes and boxes which they glue and stick together. Children frequently go for walks to explore the local community and they see excellent displays of the environment which are linked to topics. They select from a comprehensive range of art and craft materials and create pictures from many forms of media.

Children develop their awareness of customs, cultures and beliefs from celebrations and the many positive resources which they have access to. Children celebrate a wide range of festivals and special days such as Christmas, Diwali, Chinese New Year, Hanukah and Easter. They recently visited the local church and looked at the stain glass windows. Children confidentially and skilfully use the computer to complete simple programmes and show good mouse control. Staff have put a star on the mouse so less able children know where to click and can increase their independence. Children are encouraged to bring in photos of their holidays and tickets from visits to theatres and places of interest so they can be discussed, this increases the children's knowledge of the wider world.

Children enjoy a wide range of physical activities that help them to develop their confidence and skills both when using large and small apparatus, tools and equipment. They have a positive attitude towards physical exercise and a growing awareness of how it can help them to stay healthy. Children are set challenges to develop their physical skills. They balance along tyres and manoeuvre wheeled toys around obstacles. Children confidentially use climbing equipment and need little support to jump and land safely. Children are taught to handle and control small objects, for example, they pick up small beads and handle scissors, pencils, paint brushes and cutlery with good control.

Children are able to be creative, expressing their own ideas and thoughts through art, music, dance, role play and imaginative play. They use their senses and imagination to create their own work and to communicate their feelings. Children use a wide range of materials and tools to help them to express their creativity. They participate enthusiastically in music sessions and tap simple rhythms and use instruments to distinguish between loud and soft sounds. Their use their imagination as they dress up and pretend to be hairdressers, shop owners and travel agents. Children make up their own games and staff support their ideas well. Children have numerous opportunities to freely draw and paint in many different ways. There is an art room which is exceptionally well stocked with paper, paint, glitter, glue, tissue, feathers, dough, clay, sequins, chalk, pencils, crayons, felt pens and junk modelling materials.

This inspection was carried out under the provisions of Part XA of the Children Act 1989, as inserted by the Care Standards Act 2000

Helping children make a positive contribution

The provision is outstanding.

Children develop excellent relationships with adults and other children in an environment where staff work with parents and carers to meet individual children's needs and ensure they are fully included in the life of the setting. Children are able to feel a good sense of belonging, work harmoniously with others and make choices and decisions. These all contribute to the children developing good self-esteem and respect for others. The setting ensure that they know all children extremely well and that they are provided with equality of opportunity. Children are provided with excellent opportunities and activities to learn to appreciate and value each others' similarities and differences. They freely choose from an extensive range of resources, which promote cultural differences and provide positive images of disabilities. For example books, multi-cultural dolls, jigsaws, role play and the celebration of numerous festivals and special days. They can see an excellent range of words written in different languages in books and pictures and posters of children with disabilities taking part in everyday play. This positive approach ensures that children's spiritual, moral, social and cultural development is fostered.

Children with learning and physical disabilities and welcomed, valued and are extremely well supported. Children's needs are met by their individual education plans and one to one support is provided to ensure children fully integrate and have the opportunity to reach their full potential. Staff work very closely with parents and other professionals, for example attending meetings and offering support to ensure that the best care possible is given to each child. The special educational needs co-ordinator has a wealth of experience and expertise to ensure that children are fully integrated into nursery life. They have access to a balanced range of activities and work alongside others. Equipment is loaned or made to ensure they fully participate and have equality of opportunities. The support given to parents is exceptional, they are consulted about any additional services that may be required and are fully included in any decisions made for their child's benefit.

Staff are sensitive and effective in their management of behaviour and because of this children's behaviour is exceptionally good. They are well mannered, polite and very considerate to others. Children learn to manage their own behaviour because of gentle reminders from staff regarding expected behaviour. They demonstrate a very good understanding of sharing and taking turns. Children are consistently praised and thanked for their efforts. They are keen to help and eager to please. For example they tidy away activities without being prompted and proudly tell adults when they have helped others such as how to work the mouse on the computer.

Partnership with parents and carers is outstanding. Exceptional written information is provided for parents to cover both care and education. For example, they receive regular newsletters and daily information on the parents notice board. They are invited to attend sessions before their child commences with a named key worker and have a copy of the prospectus. This includes comprehensive written information about the six areas of learning and the stepping stones for each area. They receive regular written information about the topics and themes and have opportunities to discuss and review their child's progress. Written assessments based on the six areas of learning, clearly identifies children's individual learning needs. Parents are given excellent opportunities to review their child's progress and have frequent opportunities to be actively involved in their learning. For example, volunteer to help in pre-school, contribute resources required for particular themes, join in outings associated with themes and intended learning. Each child has a activity folder based on their current learning and this contains samples of the activities they have take part in and suggestions for parents on how to extend their learning at home. Children talk enthusiastically about taking 'Paddington Bear' home and recording what he did whilst in their care. He has his own bag, disposable camera, book and video. Children recall how he is taken on holiday, library and to parties. The parents forum organises outings, social events, speakers and fund raising events for local charities. It also enables parents to voice their comments and opinions.

Organisation

The organisation is outstanding.

The effective organisation of the setting ensures that children are extremely well cared for by well qualified and suitable staff. Policies and procedures protect children and are effectively implemented to promote all the outcomes for children. Managers are pro-active in ensuring that the practice of all staff contributes positively to children's good health, safety, enjoyment, achievement and ability to take an active part in the setting.

Children are happy, relaxed and cared for in a friendly environment. Rooms are welcoming and resources are stored safely. Activities are varied and familiar daily routines provide children with security and consistency. Children move confidentially between rooms to facilitate different types of play. The vast range of experiences supports children's learning and encourages their independence and freedom of choice. Children have plenty of space to relax and play in comfort and safety.

Children's welfare is exceptionally well promoted by visible and committed management, working alongside a friendly and enthusiastic staff team. Records, policies and procedures which are required for the safe and effective management of the provision are well-maintained. Robust systems are in in place to ensure the continued suitability of staff and there are good procedures for recruitment and induction. Staff are well deployed, ratios exceed minimum requirements at every session to ensure that children receive a good level of interaction and supervision. Additional staff are employed to cover children's personal care and managers are supernumerary. Children are cared for in age related groups and an effective key worker system is in operation. Young children are allocated two key workers each, therefore, they experience security and continuity of care.

High priority is given to keeping staff up to date with current practice. Staff meetings and appraisals are regularly held which enables individuals to identify their own learning goals. Staff demonstrate that they are highly motivated and committed to ongoing training to improve their knowledge, which impacts on children's learning. Children's play and learning experiences are enhanced because all staff are encouraged to develop their existing knowledge and understanding of child care related issues. They attend a wide range of courses and all staff hold early year's qualifications. Staff are encouraged to evaluate and improve their own practice and they contribute ideas within staff meetings.

Leadership and management are outstanding. Nursery education is monitored and developed to ensure that children make excellent progress towards the early learning goals. All children

This inspection was carried out under the provisions of Part XA of the Children Act 1989, as inserted by the Care Standards Act 2000

are supported well to achieve their potential by staff knowing their starting points and working with parents and carers to support this progress. Managers play and active role in providing a secure, vibrant learning environment for children. They attend all training sessions with staff and implement new procedures as they arise. Pre-school staff have a strong knowledge of the foundation stage curriculum and are very capable of planning a programme of activities to enhance the children's learning. They have a wealth of experience and expertise and take on their individual roles and responsibilities with enthusiasm. Managers provide exceptional support for staff and excellent team work is apparent. Managers have a shared vision with the provider of how they want the setting to operate for the children. Weaknesses in the provision are identified by all staff members at team meetings and any strengths are shared as good practise, this includes the early years partnership teacher who has strong links with the provision. The setting is constantly looking to improve practice and is currently updating 'Quality Counts' an accredited quality assurance scheme. Overall, children's needs are met.

Improvements since the last inspection

At the last inspection the provider agreed to continue to review and update staff knowledge of child protection. All staff have attended training and demonstrate an excellent understanding of child protection policies and procedures. Therefore children's welfare is safeguarded.

The provider was asked to consider ways in which to increase parents involvement in their children's learning in relation to nursery education. The setting already provided a prospectus for parents which covered both care and education. Parents receive regular newsletters and daily information on the notice board which includes comprehensive information about the six areas of learning and the stepping stones for each area. Parents have opportunities to discuss and review their child's progress and receive written assessments. The provider has introduced a questionnaire for parents to complete which enables her to evaluate practice and introduce changes. Parents are actively encouraged to become involved in their children's learning. For example by volunteering to help in pre-school, contributing resources required for particular themes and joining in outings. Each child has a activity folder based on the current learning which contains samples of the activities they have take part in and suggestions for parents on how to extend their learning at home. Children take 'Paddington Bear' home and record what he did whilst in their care. He has his own bag, disposable camera, book and video. The parent's forum organises outings, social events, speakers and fund raising events for local charities. It also enables parents to voice their comments and opinions. Therefore, excellent progress have been made in working in partnership with parents and involving them in their child's learning.

Complaints since the last inspection

Since the last inspection there have been no complaints made to Ofsted that required the provider or Ofsted to take any action in order to meet the National Standards. The provider is required to keep a record of complaints made by parents, which they can see on request. The complaints record may contain complaints other than those made to Ofsted.

THE QUALITY AND STANDARDS OF THE CARE AND NURSERY EDUCATION

On the basis of the evidence collected on this inspection:

The quality and standards of the care are outstanding. The registered person meets the National Standards for under 8s day care and childminding.

The quality and standards of the nursery education are outstanding.

WHAT MUST BE DONE TO SECURE FUTURE IMPROVEMENT?

The quality and standards of the care

No recommendations for improvement are made because the quality and standards of care are outstanding.

The quality and standards of the nursery education

No recommendations for improvement are made because the quality and standards of nursery education are outstanding.

Any complaints about the inspection or the report should be made following the procedures set out in the leaflet *Complaints about Ofsted Early Years: concerns or complaints about Ofsted's role in regulating and inspecting childcare and early education (HMI ref no 2599)* which is available from Ofsted's website: *www.ofsted.gov.uk*

This inspection was carried out under the provisions of Part XA of the Children Act 1989, as inserted by the Care Standards Act 2000

References

Abbott, L. and Hevey, D. (2001) Training to work in the early years: developing the climbing frame, in G. Pugh (ed.) *Contemporary Issues in the Early Years*, 3rd edn. London: Paul Chapman Publishing.

Anning, A. (2001) Knowing who I am and what I know: developing new versions of professional knowledge in integrated service settings. Paper presented to the BERA Annual Conference, University of Leeds, 13–15 September.

Arnold, C. (2001) Persistence pays off: working with 'hard to reach' parents, in M. Whalley and the Pen Green Centre, *Involving Parents in their Children's Learning*. London: Paul Chapman Publishing.

Athey, C. (2007) *Extending Thought in Young Children*, 2nd edn. London: Paul Chapman Publishing.

Ball, C. (1994) *Start Right: The Importance of Early Learning*. London: RSA.

Belbin, R. M. (1981) *Management Teams*. London: Heinemann.

Board of Education (1933) *The Hadow Report*. London: HMSO.

Bolton, G. (2005) *Reflective Practice*, 2nd edn. London: Sage.

Brooker, L. (2002) *Starting School – Young Children Learning Cultures*. Buckingham: Open University Press.

Browne, N. (2004) *Gender Equity in the Early Years*. Maidenhead: Open University Press.

Bruce, T. (2005) *Early Childhood Education*, 3rd edition. London: Hodder Arnold.

Bush, T. (2003) *Theories of Educational Leadership and Management*. London: Sage.

Bush, T. and Coleman, M. (2000) *Leadership and Strategic Management in Education*. London: Paul Chapman Publishing.

Carr, M. (1998) *Assessing Children's Learning in Early Childhood Settings*. Wellington: NCER.

Carr, M. (2001) *Assessment in Early Childhood Settings*. London: Paul Chapman Publishing.

Cartwright, P., Scott, K. and Stevens, J. (2002) *A Place to Learn*. Lewisham: LEARN.

Clark, A. and Moss, P. (2001) *Listening to Young Children: The Mosaic Approach*. London: National Children's Bureau/Joseph Rowntree Foundation.

Coles, M.J. and Southworth, G. (eds) (2005) *Developing Leadership – Creating the Schools of Tomorrow*. Maidenhead: Open University Press.

Collins, J., Insley, K. and Soler, J. (2001) *Developing Pedagogy*. London: Paul Chapman Publishing.

Crompton, D. (1997) Community leadership, in S. Kagan and B. Bowman (eds)

Leadership in Early Care and Education. Washington, DC: National Association for the Education of Young Children.

Crow, G. (2005) Developing leadership for schools facing challenging circumstances, in M. Coles and G. Southworth (eds) *Developing Leadership – Creating the Schools of Tomorrow*. Maidenhead: Open University Press.

David, T. (1998) Introduction: researching early childhood education in Europe, in T. David (ed.) *Researching Early Childhood Education*. London: Paul Chapman Publishing.

DeLoache, J. and Gottlieb, A. (2000) *A World of Babies*. Cambridge: Cambridge University Press.

DES (Department of Education and Science) (1990) *The Rumbold Report*. London: DES.

Desforges, C. (2003) *The Impact of Parental Involvement, Parental Support and Family Education on Pupil Achievement and Adjustment*. DfES Research Report No. 433. London: DfES.

Dewey, J. ([1910] 1991) *How we Think* New York: Prometheus.

DfES (Department for Education and Skills) (2001a) *National Standards for Under Eights Daycare and Childminding: Full Daycare*. Nottingham: DfES.

DfES (Department for Education and Skills) (2001b) *Special Educational Needs Code of Practice*. Nottingham: DfES.

DfES (Department for Education and Skills) (2002a) *Birth to Three Matters: A Framework to Support Children in their Earliest Years*. Nottingham: DfES.

DfES (Department for Education and Skills) (2002b) *Developing Management Skills*. Nottingham: DfES.

DfES (Department for Education and Skills) (2003) *Every Child Matters,* Cm 5860. London: The Stationery Office.

DfES (Department for Education and Skills) (2005) *Statutory Guidance on Interagency Co-operation to Improve the Wellbeing of Children: Children's Trusts*. Nottingham: DfES.

DfES (Department for Education and Skills) (2006a) *The Common Assessment Framework for Children and Young People: Manager's Guide*, available at: www.everychild matters.gov.uk/caf/?cidm=booklet, accessed 9 January 2007.

DfES (Department for Education and Skills) (2006b) *Common Assessment Form and Pre-assessment Checklist*, available at: www.everychildmatters.gov.uk/resources, accessed 9 January 2007.

DfES (Department for Education and Skills) (2006c) *Information Sharing: Practitioners Guide*, available at: www.everychildmatters.gov.uk/information, accessed 10 January 2007.

DfES (Department for Education and Skills) (2007) *Statutory Framework for the Early Years Foundation Stage: Setting the Standards for Learning Development and Care for Children from Birth to Five*. Nottingham: DfES.

Doherty, J. and Bailey, R. (2003) *Supporting Physical Development and Physical Education in the Early Years*. Buckingham: Open University Press.

Driscoll, V. and Rudge, C. (2005) Channels for listening to young children and parents, in A. Clark, A. Kjorholt and P. Moss (eds) *Beyond Listening: Children's Perspectives on Early Childhood Services*. Bristol: Policy Press.

Drummond, M-J. (1993) *Assessing Children's Learning*. London: David Fulton.

Drummond, M-J., Lally, M. and Pugh, G. (1989) *Working with Children: Developing a Curriculum for the Early Years*. London: National Children's Bureau.

Edgington, M. (2004) *The Foundation Stage Teacher in Action*, 3rd edn. London: Paul Chapman Publishing.

Eide, B.J. and Winger, N. (2005) From the children's point of view: methodological and ethical challenges, in A. Clark, A.T. Kjorholt and P. Moss (eds) *Beyond Listening*. Bristol: Policy Press.

Elfer, P., Goldschmied, E. and Selleck, D. (2003) *Key Persons in the Nursery*. London: Fontana.

Freire, P. (2005) *Education for Critical Consciousness*. London: Continuum.

Foskett, N. and Lumby, J. (2003) *Leading and Managing Education: International Perspectives*. London: Paul Chapman Publishing.

Furlong, J. (2000) Intuition and the crisis in teacher professionalism, in T. Atkinson and G. Claxton (eds) *The Intuitive Practitioner*. Buckingham: Open University Press.

Gardner, H. (2006) *Five Minds for the Future*. Boston, MA: Harvard Business School Press.

Garrick, R. (2004) *Playing Outdoors in the Early Years*. London: Continuum.

Gerhardt, S. (2004) *Why Love Matters*. Hove: Brunner-Routledge.

Goleman, D. (1996) *Emotional Intelligence*. London: Fontana.

Goleman, D., Boyatzis, R. and McKee, A. (2002) *The New Leaders*. London: Little, Brown.

Gonzalez-Mena, J. (2005) *Diversity in Early Childhood Care and Education*, 4th edn. Maidenhead: McGraw-Hill.

Gronn, P. (2003) *The New Work of Educational Leaders*. London: Sage.

Guidici, C., Rinaldi, C. and Krechevsky, M. (eds) (2001) *Making Learning Visible*. Reggio Emilia: Project Zero/Reggio Children.

Gura, P. (1996) *Resources for Early Learning: Children, Adults and Stuff*. London: Hodder & Stoughton.

Hall, N. and Martello, J. (1996) *Listening to Children Think*. London: Hodder & Stoughton.

Handy, C. (1990) *Inside Organisations*. London: BBC Books.

Handy, C. (1993) *Understanding Organizations*, 3rd edn. London: Penguin.

Handy, C. (1999) *Understanding Organizations*, 4th edn. London: Penguin.

Harms, T. and Clifford, R. (1980) *Early Childhood Environment Rating Scale*. New York: Teachers College Press.

Harpley, A. and Roberts, A (2006) *You Can Survive your Early Years OFSTED inspection*. Leamington Spa: Scholastic.

Harrison R., Mann, G., Murphy. M., Taylor, A. and Thompson, N. (2003) *Partnership*

Made Painless: A Joined Up Guide to Working Together. Dorset: Russell House Publishing.

Hart, B. and Risley, T. (1995) *Meaningful Differences in the Everyday Experience of Young American Children*. London: Brookes Publishing.

HM Government (2006a) *Working Together to Safeguard Children: A Guide to Interagency Working to Safeguard and Promote the Welfare of Children*. London: The Stationery Office.

HM Government (2006b) *What to do if You're Worried a Child is Being Abused*. Nottingham: DfES Publications.

Hobson, P. (2002) *The Cradle of Thought*. London: Macmillan.

Hurless, B. (2004) Early childhood education in France – a personal perspective, *Journal of the National Association for the Education of Young Children*, available at: www.journal.naeyc.org.btj/200409, accessed 30 January 2007.

Hutchin, V. (1999) *Right from the Start – Effective Planning and Assessment in the Early Years*. London: Hodder & Stoughton.

Hutchin, V. (2003) *Observing and Assessing for the Foundation Stage Profile*. London: Hodder & Stoughton.

Isaacs, S. (1929) *The Nursery Years: The Mind of the Child from Birth to Six Years*. London: Routledge & Kegan Paul.

Isles-Buck, E. and Newstead, S. (2003) *Essential Skills for Managers of Child-Centred Settings*. London: David Fulton.

Johns, C. (2004) *Becoming a Reflective Practitioner*, 2nd edn. Malden: Blackwell.

Jones, L., Browne, K., Aitken, S., Keating, I. and Hodson, E. (2005) Working with parents and carers, in L. Jones, R. Homes and J. Powell (eds) *Early Childhood Studies: A Multiprofessional Perspective*. Maidenhead: Open University Press.

Jowett, S. and Baginsky, M. (1991) *Building Bridges: Parental Involvement in Schools*. Windsor: NFER Nelson.

Katz, L. (1997) Pedagogical leadership, in S. Kagan and B. Bowman (eds) *Leadership in Early Care and Education*. Washington, DC: National Association for the Education of Young Children (NAEYC).

Katzenbach, J. and Smith, D. (1993) *The Wisdom of Teams: Creating the High-performance Organization*. Boston, MA: Harvard Business School Press.

Laevers, F. (1997) *A Process-oriented Child Monitoring System for Young Children*. Belgium: Leuven University.

Lancaster, Y.P. (2003) *Promoting Listening to Young Children*. Maidenhead: Open University Press/Coram Family.

Langford, J. and Weissbourd, B. (1997) New directions in parent leadership in a family-support context, in S. Kagan and T. Bowman (eds) *Leadership in Early Care and Education*. Washington, DC: NAEYC.

Lumsden, E. (2005) Joined-up thinking in practice: an exploration of professional collaboration, in T. Waller (ed.) *An Introduction to Early Childhood*. London: Paul Chapman Publishing.

MacNaughton, G. (2003) *Shaping Early Childhood*. Maidenhead: Open University Press.

MacNaughton, G. and Williams, G. (2004) *Teaching Young Children*. Maidenhead: Open University Press.

Malaguzzi, L. (1995) History, ideas and basic philosophy, in C. Edwards, L. Gandini and G. Forman (eds) *The Hundred Languages of Children*. Norwood, NJ: Ablex.

Manning-Morton, J. and Thorp, M. (2001) *KeyTimes: A Framework for Developing High Quality Provision for Children Under Three Years*. London: Camden EYDCP/University of North London.

Manning-Morton, J. and Thorp, M. (2003) *Key Times for Play*. Maidenhead: Open University Press.

Manz, C. and Sims, H. (1991) Super leadership: beyond the myth of heroic leadership, *Organizational Dynamics*, 32: 1.

Martin, P. (1998) *The Sickening Mind*. London: Flamingo.

McCall, C. and Lawlor, H. (2000) *School Leadership: Leadership Examined*. London: The Stationery Office.

McGregor, J. (2003) Collaboration in communities of practice, in N. Bennett and L. Anderson (eds) *Rethinking Educational Leadership*. London: Sage.

Melhuish, E., Sylva, K., Siraj-Blatchford, I. and Taggart, B. (2001) *Technical Paper 7: Social, Behavioural and Cognitive Development at 3–4 Years Relative to Family Background. Report from the Effective Provision of Preschool Education Research*. London: Institute of Education, University of London.

Miles, R. (1994) *The Children we Deserve*. London: Harper Collins.

Ministry of Education (1996) *Te Whariki*. Wellington, NZ: Ministry of Education.

Moss, G. (ed.) (1996) *Effective Management of Special Needs*. Birmingham: Questions Publishing Company Ltd.

Moss, P. (2001) The otherness of Reggio, in L. Abbott and C. Nutbrown (eds) *Experiencing Reggio Emilia: Implications for Pre-school Provision*. Buckingham: Open University Press.

Moss, P. (2004) Getting beyond childcare: future directions for early childhood services in Europe. Paper presented on 22 September at Equal ECO Conference, available at: www.kinderopvangaanhuis.nl/library/Presentation, accessed 30 January 2007.

Moyles, J. (2006) *Effective Leadership and Management in the Early Years*. Maidenhead: Open University Press.

Moyles, J., Adams, S. and Musgrove, A. (2002) *SPEEL: Study of Pedagogical Effectiveness in Early Learning*, research report 363. London: DfES.

Moylett, H. and Holyman, K. (2006) 'Don't you tell me what to do', in L. Abbott and A. Langston (eds) *Parents Matter: Supporting the Birth to Three Matters Framework*. Maidenhead: Open University Press.

Neugebauer, B. and Neugebauer, R. (eds) (1998) *The Art of Leadership: Managing Early Childhood Organisations*, vol. 2. Perth: Child Care Information Exchange.

Nutbrown, C. (2001) *Experiencing Reggio Emilia*. Buckingham: Open University Press.

Nutbrown, C. (2006) *Threads of Thinking*, 3rd edition. London: Paul Chapman Publishing.

O'Sullivan, J. (2003) *Manager's Handbook*. Leamington Spa: Scholastic.

Ofsted (Office for Standards in Education) (2005a) *Firm Foundations*, ref HMI2436, available at: www.ofsted.gov.uk/assets/3111.pdf, accessed 18 September 2007.

Ofsted (Office for Standards in Education) (2005b) *Are You Ready for Your Inspection?* Short version, ref 2447A. Ofsted Publications Centre.

Ofsted (Office for Standards in Education) (2005c) *Early Doors: Experiences for Children in Day Care During the First Hour of the Day*, available at: www.ofsted.gov.uk, accessed 19 September 2007.

Ofsted (Office for Standards in Education) (2006) *Framework for the Regulation of Daycare and Childminding*, available at: www.ofsted.gov.uk/publications/2601, accessed 13 May 2007.

Ofsted (Office for Standards in Education) (2007) *The Foundation Stage: A Survey of 144 Settings*. London: DfES/Ofsted.

Ouvry, M. (2003) *Of Muscles and Minds* London: National Children's Bureau.

Owen, J. (2005) *How to Lead*. Harlow: Pearson Education.

Paley, V.G. (1990) *The Boy Who Would be a Helicopter*. Cambridge, MA: Harvard University Press.

Pascal, C. and Bertram, T. (1997) *Effective Early Learning: Case Studies in Improvement*. London: Paul Chapman Publishing.

Pen Green (2000) *Growing Together*. Corby: Pen Green.

Piaget, J. (1952) *The Origin of Intelligence in the Child*. London: Routledge & Kegan Paul.

Pierce, J. and Newstrom, J. (2006) *Leaders and the Leadership Process*, 4th edn. New York: McGraw-Hill.

Pound, L. (2006) Ocean Mathematics Project: evaluation of foundation stage pilot project 2005–6. Unpublished paper.

Pound, L. (in press) Exploring leadership – the roles and responsibilities of the early years professional, in A. Paige-Smith and A. Craft (eds) *Reflecting on Practice – Exploring Issues in Early Years Education and Care*. Maidenhead: Open University Press.

Powell, J. (2005) Multiprofessional perspectives, in L. Jones, R. Holmes and J. Powell (eds) *Early Childhood Studies: A Multiprofessional Perspective*. Maidenhead: Open University Press.

Puccio, G., Murdock, M. and Mance, M. (2007) *Creative Leadership*. London: Sage.

QCA (1998) *Assessment and Reporting Arrangements for Key Stage 1*. London: QCA.

QCA (2003) *Foundation Stage Profile*. London: QCA/DfES.

QCA/DfES (Qualifications and Curriculum Authority/Department for Education and Skills) (2000) *Curriculum Guidance for the Foundation Stage*. London: QCA/DfES.

Raelin, J. (2003) *Creating Leaderful Organizations*. San Francisco, CA: Berrett-Koehler Publishers Inc.

Read, M. and Rees, M. (2003) Working in teams in early years settings, in J. Devereux and L. Miller (eds) *Working with Children in the Early Years*. London: David Fulton.

Riddell, S. and Tett, L. (2001) Education, social justice and inter-agency working: joined-up or fractured policy? in S. Riddell and L. Tett (eds) (2001) *Education, Social Justice and Inter-agency Working: Joined-up or fractured policy?* London: Routledge.

Rinaldi, C. (2001) The courage of Utopia, in C. Guidici, C. Rinaldi and M. Krechevsky (eds) *Making Learning Visible*. Reggio Emilia: Project Zero/Reggio Children.

Rinaldi, C. (2005) Documentation and assessment: what is the relationship? in A. Clark, A.T. Kjorholt and P. Moss (eds) *Beyond Listening*. Bristol: Policy Press.

Rodd, J. (1998) *Leadership in Early Childhood: The Pathway to Professionalism*, 2nd edn. Buckingham: Open University Press.

Rodd, J. (2006) *Leadership in Early Childhood*, 3rd edn. Maidenhead: Open University Press.

Rogoff, B. (1990) *Apprenticeship in Thinking*. Oxford: Oxford University Press.

Ronco, W. and Ronco, S. (2005) *The Partnering Solution*. Franklin Lakes, NJ: Career Press Inc.

Ross, A. (2001) What is the curriculum? in J. Collins, K. Insley and J. Soler (eds) *Developing Pedagogy*. London: Paul Chapman Publishing.

Sammons, P., Sylva, K., Melhuish, E., Siraj-Blatchford, I., Taggart, B. and Elliot, K. (2002) *Measuring the Impact of Pre-school on Children's Cognitive Progress over the Pre-school Period*. London: The Institute of Education, University of London.

Sanders, B. (2004) Interagency and multidisciplinary working, in T. Maynard and N. Thomas (eds) *An Introduction to Early Childhood Studies*. London: Sage.

Sayeed, Z. and Guerin, E. (2000) *Early Years Play*. London: David Fulton.

SCAA (School Curriculum and Assessment Authority) (1996) *Nursery Education: Desirable Outcomes for Children's Learning on Entering Compulsory Education*. London: SCAA/DfEE.

Scott, W. (2001) Listening and learning, in L. Abbott and C. Nutbrown (eds) *Experiencing Reggio Emilia: Implications for Pre-school Provision* Buckingham: Open University Press.

Siegel, D. (1999) *The Developing Mind*. New York: Guilford Press.

Simmons, K. (1994) Decoding a new message, *British Journal of Special Education*, 21(2): 56–9.

Siraj-Blatchford, I., Sylva, K., Muttock, S., Gilden, R. and Bell, D. (2002) *Researching Effective Pedagogy in the Early Years*, research report 356. London: DfES.

Sloper, P. (2004) Facilitators and barriers for co-ordinated multi-agency services, *Child Care, Health and Development*, 30(6): 571–80.

Smith, A. and Langston, A. (1999) *Managing Staff in Early Years Settings*. London: Routledge.

Spencer, B., Bruce, T. and Dowling, M. (2007) A real achievement, *Nursery World*, 5 July 2007: 10–1.

Stoll, L., Fink, D. and Earl, L. (2003) *It's About Learning (and it's about time)*. London: Routledge/Falmer.

Sylva, K., Melhuish, E., Sammons, P. and Siraj-Blatchford, I. (1999*) Technical Paper 6A: Characteristics of Pre-school Environments. Report from the Effective Provision of Pre-school Education Research*. London: Institute of Education, University of London.

Sylva, K., Siraj-Blatchford, I. and Taggart, B. (2003) *Assessing Quality in the Early Years*. Stoke-on-Trent: Trentham Books.

Tizard, B. and Hughes, M. (1984) *Young Children Learning*. London: Fontana.

TTA (Teacher Training Agency) (1998) *National Standards for Special Educational Needs Co-ordinators*. London: TTA.

TTA (Teacher Training Agency) (2004) *Foundation Stage Audit Materials*. London: TTA.

Vygotsky, L. (1978) *Mind in Society*. Cambridge, MA: Harvard University Press.

Wall, K. (2006) *Special Needs and Early Years*, 2nd edn. London: Paul Chapman Publishing.

WCC (Warwickshire County Council) (2002) *Guidance for Early Education Settings in Warwickshire*. Warwick: Warwickshire Early Years Development and Childcare Partnership.

Weikart, D. (2000) *Early Childhood Education: Needs and Opportunity*. Paris: UNESCO International Institute for Educational Planning.

Whalley, M. (1994) *Learning to be Strong*. Sevenoaks: Hodder and Stoughton.

Whalley, M. (2001) *Involving Parents in their Children's Learning*. London: Paul Chapman Publishing.

Whalley, M. for the National College for School Leadership (NCSL) (2004) *Participants' Guide: Book 6, 'Developing the Practitioner Researcher Research Stages 1–8', National Professional Qualification in Integrated Centre Leadership*. Nottingham: NCSL.

Whalley, M. for the National College for School Leadership (NCSL) (2005) *Programme Leaders' Guide: National Professional Qualification in Integrated Centre Leadership*. Nottingham: NCSL.

Wood, C. and Caulier-Grice, J. (2006) *Fade or Flourish: How Primary Schools can Build on Children's Early Progress*. London: Social Market Foundation.

Yukl, G. (1999) an evaluation of conceptual weaknesses in transformational and charismatic leadership theories, *Leadership Quarterly* 10(2): 285–305.

Index